Software Engineering

Software Engineering

Edited by
Cersei Page

Larsen & Keller
www.larsen-keller.com

Software Engineering
Edited by Cersei Page
ISBN: 978-1-63549-262-0 (Hardback)

≣ Larsen & Keller

Published by Larsen and Keller Education,
5 Penn Plaza,
19th Floor,
New York, NY 10001, USA

Cataloging-in-Publication Data

Software engineering / edited by Cersei Page.
   p. cm.
Includes bibliographical references and index.
ISBN 978-1-63549-262-0
1. Software engineering. 2. Computer programming. 3. Computer networks.
4. Automatic programming (Computer science). I. Page, Cersei.
QA76.758 .S64 2017
005.1--dc23

The publisher's policy is to use permanent paper from mills that operate a sustainable forestry policy. Furthermore, the publisher ensures that the text paper and cover boards used have met acceptable environmental accreditation standards.

Printed and bound in the United States of America.

For more information regarding Larsen and Keller Education and its products, please visit the publisher's website www.larsen-keller.com

Table of Contents

Permissions

Index

Preface

The book aims to shed light on some of the unexplored aspects of software engineering. It elucidates new techniques and their applications in a multidisciplinary approach. Software engineering refers to the development, design, testing, implementation and maintenance of software. Most of the topics introduced in this text cover new techniques and the applications of software engineering. It glances at the various sub-fields of this subject along with technological progress that have future implications. Coherent flow of topics, student-friendly language and extensive use of examples make the text an invaluable source of knowledge. Different approaches, evaluations and production practices relating to software engineering have been included in this book.

To facilitate a deeper understanding of the contents of this book a short introduction of every chapter is written below:

Chapter 1- Software engineering is application of engineering concepts towards the creation of software systems. Software plays a key role in our lives by running electronic devices. Software engineering is an emerging field of study; the following chapter will not only provide an overview, it will also delve deep into the variegated topics related to it.

Chapter 2- The manufacture of software is dependent on the manufacture of hardware and vice-versa. What this implies is that many pieces of hardware are technically competent to implement the same software. Software design and development must keep these existing devices into account while in manufacture. Some of the sub-disciplines of software engineering that are included in this chapter are software testing, engineering management, software design etc.

Chapter 3- Software, like all applications created in the computer, uses code in its design. These codes are basically programming language. Each language has its function that it fulfils and programs now run on multi-paradigm procedures. This chapter is a compilation of the various branches of software engineering that form an integral part of the broader subject matter.

Chapter 4- The digital breakthroughs that have been achieved through software engineering techniques have led to the development of hi-tech gadgets such as heads-up displays (HUD), speech recognition and logic based AI. Some of the categories explored by this chapter include artificial intelligence and augmented reality. The topics discussed in the chapter are of great importance to broaden the existing knowledge on software engineering.

Chapter 5- Computer languages were developed with a view to ensure the system adheres to certain actions and patterns. Computer languages perform a variety of functions. Some popular languages are FORTRAN and COBOL. Software engineering is best understood in confluence with the major topics listed in the following chapter.

Chapter 6- Automatic programming uses artificially created source code that can be further developed by software programmers. It allows for quicker program development and easy optimization of programs. Program architecture becomes easier to visualize and multi-platform code can be created simultaneously. This chapter will provide an integrated understanding of automatic programming.

Chapter 7- Software distribution, usage and development has greatly benefitted from the development of computer networks and the Internet. Programs can be quickly distributed, tested and edited with fast computing and networking technology. This chapter looks at themes such as network topology, network packet and computer network.

Chapter 8- The history of computers has also been a history of software. Software that is produced has to keep up with mechanical developments such as computers, tablets and android phones as well as to cultural products such as the cyberculture and social networking. This chapter discusses the methods of software engineering in a critical manner providing key analysis to the subject matter.

Finally, I would like to thank the entire team involved since the inception of this book for their valuable time and contribution. This book would not have been possible without their efforts. I would also like to thank my friends and family for their constant support.

Editor

Introduction to Software Engineering

Software engineering is application of engineering concepts towards the creation of software systems. Software plays a key role in our lives by running electronic devices. Software engineering is an emerging field of study; the following chapter will not only provide an overview, it will also delve deep into the variegated topics related to it.

Software Engineering

A software engineer programming for the Wikimedia Foundation

Software engineering is the application of engineering to the design, development, implementation, testing and maintenance of software in a systematic method.

Typical formal definitions of software engineering are:

- "research, design, develop, and test operating systems-level software, compilers, and network distribution software for medical, industrial, military, communications, aerospace, business, scientific, and general computing applications."

- "the systematic application of scientific and technological knowledge, methods, and experience to the design, implementation, testing, and documentation of software";

- "the application of a systematic, disciplined, quantifiable approach to the development, operation, and maintenance of software";

- "an engineering discipline that is concerned with all aspects of software production";

- and "the establishment and use of sound engineering principles in order to economically obtain software that is reliable and works efficiently on real machines."

History

When the first digital computers appeared in the early 1940s, the instructions to make them operate were wired into the machine. Practitioners quickly realized that this design was not flexible and came up with the "stored program architecture" or von Neumann architecture. Thus the division between "hardware" and "software" began with abstraction being used to deal with the complexity of computing.

Programming languages started to appear in the 1950s and this was also another major step in abstraction. Major languages such as Fortran, ALGOL, and COBOL were released in the late 1950s to deal with scientific, algorithmic, and business problems respectively. Edsger W. Dijkstra wrote his seminal paper, "Go To Statement Considered Harmful", in 1968 and David Parnas introduced the key concept of modularity and information hiding in 1972 to help programmers deal with the ever increasing complexity of software systems.

The term "software engineering" was coined by Anthony Oettinger and then was used in 1968 as a title for the world's first conference on software engineering, sponsored and facilitated by NATO. The conference was attended by international experts on software who agreed on defining best practices for software grounded in the application of engineering. The result of the conference is a report that defines how software should be developed. The original report is publicly available.

The discipline of software engineering was created to address poor quality of software, get projects exceeding time and budget under control, and ensure that software is built systematically, rigorously, measurably, on time, on budget, and within specification. Engineering already addresses all these issues, hence the same principles used in engineering can be applied to software. The widespread lack of best practices for software at the time was perceived as a "software crisis".

Barry W. Boehm documented several key advances to the field in his 1981 book, 'Software Engineering Economics'. These include his Constructive Cost Model (COCOMO), which relates software development effort for a program, in man-years T, to *source lines of code* (SLOC). $T = k * (SLOC)(1+x)$ The book analyzes sixty-three software projects and concludes the cost of fixing errors escalates as the project moves toward field use. The book also asserts that the key driver of software cost is the capability of the software development team.

In 1984, the Software Engineering Institute (SEI) was established as a federally funded research and development center headquartered on the campus of Carnegie Mellon University in Pittsburgh, Pennsylvania, United States. Watts Humphrey founded the SEI Software Process Program, aimed at understanding and managing the software engineering process. His 1989 book, Managing the Software Process, asserts that the Software Development Process can and should be controlled, measured, and improved. The Process Maturity Levels introduced would become the Capability Maturity Model Integration for Development(CMMi-DEV), which has defined how the US Government evaluates the abilities of a software development team.

Modern, generally accepted best-practices for software engineering have been collected by the ISO/IEC JTC 1/SC 7 subcommittee and published as the Software Engineering Body of Knowledge (SWEBOK).

Subdisciplines

Software engineering can be divided into 15 sub-disciplines. They are:

- Software requirements (or Requirements engineering): The elicitation, analysis, specification, and validation of requirements for software.

- Software design: The process of defining the architecture, components, interfaces, and other characteristics of a system or component. It is also defined as the result of that process.

    o Software design#Design considerations — Compatibility, extensibility, fault-tolerance, maintainability, modularity, reliability, reusability, robustness, security, usability, performance, portability, scalability

- Software construction: The detailed creation of working, meaningful software through a combination of coding,verification, unit testing, integration testing, and debugging.

- Software testing: An empirical, technical investigation conducted to provide stakeholders with information about the quality of the product or service under test.

- Software maintenance: The totality of activities required to provide cost-effective support to software.

- Software configuration management: The identification of the configuration of a system at distinct points in time for the purpose of systematically controlling changes to the configuration, and maintaining the integrity and traceability of the configuration throughout the system life cycle.

- Software engineering management: The application of management activities—planning, coordinating, measuring, monitoring, controlling, and reporting—to ensure that the development and maintenance of software is systematic, disciplined, and quantified.

- Software process: The definition, implementation, assessment, measurement, management, change, and improvement of the software life cycle process itself.

- Software engineering methods and models impose structure on software engineering with the goal of making that activity systematic, repeatable, and ultimately more success-oriented

- Software quality

- Software Engineering Professional Practice is concerned with the knowledge, skills, and attitudes that software engineers must possess to practice software engineering in a professional, responsible, and ethical manner

- Software Engineering Economics is about making decisions related to software engineering in a business context

- Computing Foundations

- Mathematical Foundations

- Engineering Foundations

Education

Knowledge of computer programming is a prerequisite to becoming a software engineer. In 2004 the IEEE Computer Society produced the SWEBOK, which has been published as ISO/IEC Technical Report 1979:2004, describing the body of knowledge that they recommend to be mastered by a graduate software engineer with four years of experience. Many software engineers enter the profession by obtaining a university degree or training at a vocational school. One standard international curriculum for undergraduate software engineering degrees was defined by the CCSE, and updated in 2004. A number of universities have Software Engineering degree programs; as of 2010, there were 244 Campus Bachelor of Software Engineering programs, 70 Online programs, 230 Masters-level programs, 41 Doctorate-level programs, and 69 Certificate-level programs in the United States.

For practitioners who wish to become proficient and recognized as professional software engineers, the IEEE offers two certifications that extend knowledge above level achieved by an academic degree: *Certified Software Development Associate* and *Certified Software Development Professional.*

In addition to university education, many companies sponsor internships for students wishing to pursue careers in information technology. These internships can introduce the student to interesting real-world tasks that typical software engineers encounter every day. Similar experience can be gained through military service in software engineering.

Profession

Legal requirements for the licensing or certification of professional software engineers vary around the world. In the UK, the British Computer Society licenses software engineers and members of the society can also become Chartered Engineers (CEng), while in some areas of Canada, such as Alberta, British Columbia, Ontario, and Quebec, software engineers can hold the Professional Engineer (P.Eng) designation and/or the Information Systems Professional (I.S.P.) designation. In Canada, there is a legal requirement to have P.Eng when one wants to use the title "engineer" or practice "software engineering".

The United States, starting from 2013 offers an *NCEES Professional Engineer* exam for Software Engineering, thereby allowing Software Engineers to be licensed and recognized. Mandatory licensing is currently still largely debated, and perceived as controversial. In some parts of the US such as Texas, the use of the term Engineer is regulated by law and reserved only for use by individuals who have a Professional Engineer license. The IEEE informs the professional engineer license is not required unless the individual would work for public where health of others could be at risk if the engineer was not fully qualified to required standards by the particular state. Professional engineer licenses are specific to the state which has awarded them, and have to be regularly retaken.

The IEEE Computer Society and the ACM, the two main US-based professional organizations of software engineering, publish guides to the profession of software engineering. The IEEE's *Guide to the Software Engineering Body of Knowledge - 2004 Version*, or SWEBOK, defines the field and describes the knowledge the IEEE expects a practicing software engineer to have. The most current SWEBOK v3 is an updated version and was released in 2014. The IEEE also promulgates a "Software Engineering Code of Ethics".

Employment

In 2004, the U. S. Bureau of Labor Statistics counted 760,840 software engineers holding jobs in the U.S.; in the same time period there were some 1.4 million practitioners employed in the U.S. in all other engineering disciplines combined. Due to its relative newness as a field of study, formal education in software engineering is often taught as part of a computer science curriculum, and many software engineers hold computer science degrees and have no engineering background whatsoever.

Many software engineers work as employees or contractors. Software engineers work with businesses, government agencies (civilian or military), and non-profit organizations. Some software engineers work for themselves as freelancers. Some organizations have specialists to perform each of the tasks in the software development process. Other organizations require software engineers to do many or all of them. In large projects, people may specialize in only one role. In small projects, people may fill several or all roles at the same time. Specializations include: in industry (analysts, architects, developers, testers, technical support, middleware analysts, managers) and in academia (educators, researchers).

Most software engineers and programmers work 40 hours a week, but about 15 percent of software engineers and 11 percent of programmers worked more than 50 hours a week in 2008. Injuries in these occupations are rare. However, like other workers who spend long periods in front of a computer terminal typing at a keyboard, engineers and programmers are susceptible to eyestrain, back discomfort, and hand and wrist problems such as carpal tunnel syndrome.

The field's future looks bright according to Money Magazine and Salary.com, which rated Software Engineer as the best job in the United States in 2006. In 2012, software engineering was again ranked as the best job in the United States, this time by CareerCast.com.

Certification

The Software Engineering Institute offers certifications on specific topics like security, process improvement and software architecture. Apple, IBM, Microsoft and other companies also sponsor their own certification examinations. Many IT certification programs are oriented toward specific technologies, and managed by the vendors of these technologies. These certification programs are tailored to the institutions that would employ people who use these technologies.

Broader certification of general software engineering skills is available through various professional societies. As of 2006, the IEEE had certified over 575 software professionals as a Certified Software Development Professional (CSDP). In 2008 they added an entry-level certification known as the Certified Software Development Associate (CSDA). The ACM had a professional certification program in the early 1980s, which was discontinued due to lack of interest. The ACM examined the possibility of professional certification of software engineers in the late 1990s, but eventually decided that such certification was inappropriate for the professional industrial practice of software engineering.

In the U.K. the British Computer Society has developed a legally recognized professional certification called *Chartered IT Professional (CITP)*, available to fully qualified members (*MBCS*). Software engineers may be eligible for membership of the Institution of Engineering and Technology and so qualify for Chartered Engineer status. In Canada the Canadian Information Processing Society has developed a legally recognized professional certification called *Information Systems Professional (ISP)*. In Ontario, Canada, Software Engineers who graduate from a *Canadian Engineering Accreditation Board (CEAB)* accredited program, successfully complete PEO's (*Professional Engineers Ontario*) Professional Practice Examination (PPE) and have at least 48 months of acceptable engineering experience are eligible to be licensed through the *Professional Engineers Ontario* and can become Professional Engineers P.Eng. The PEO does not recognize any online or distance education however; and does not consider Computer Science programs to be equivalent to software engineering programs despite the tremendous overlap between the two. This has sparked controversy and a certification war. It has also held the number of P.Eng holders for the profession exceptionally low. The vast majority of working professionals in the field hold a degree in CS, not SE. Given the difficult certification path for holders of non-SE degrees, most never bother to pursue the license.

Impact of Globalization

The initial impact of outsourcing, and the relatively lower cost of international human resources in developing third world countries led to a massive migration of software development activities from corporations in North America and Europe to India and later: China, Russia, and other developing countries. This approach had some flaws, mainly the distance / timezone difference that prevented human interaction between clients and developers and the massive job transfer. This had a negative impact on many aspects of the software engineering profession. For example, some students in the developed world avoid education related to software engineering because of the fear of offshore outsourcing (importing software products or services from other countries) and of being displaced by foreign visa workers. Although statistics do not currently show a threat to software engineering itself; a related career, computer programming does appear to have been affected. Nevertheless, the ability to smartly leverage offshore and near-shore resources via the follow-the-sun workflow has improved the overall operational capability of many organizations. When North Americans are leaving work, Asians are just arriving to work. When Asians are leaving work, Europeans are arriving to work. This provides a continuous ability to have human oversight on business-critical processes 24 hours per day, without paying overtime compensation or disrupting a key human resource, sleep patterns.

While global outsourcing has several advantages, global - and generally distributed - development can run into serious difficulties resulting from the distance between developers. This is due to the key elements of this type of distance which have been identified as geographical, temporal, cultural and communication (which includes the use of different languages and dialects of English in different locations). Research has been carried out in the area of global software development over the last 15 years and an extensive body of relevant work published which highlights the benefits and problems associated with the complex activity. As with other aspects of software engineering research is ongoing in this and related areas.

Related Fields

Software engineering is a direct sub-field of engineering and has an overlap with computer science and management science. It is also considered a part of overall systems engineering.

Controversy

Over Definition

Typical formal definitions of software engineering are:

- "the application of a systematic, disciplined, quantifiable approach to the development, operation, and maintenance of software".

- "an engineering discipline that is concerned with all aspects of software production"

- "the establishment and use of sound engineering principles in order to economically obtain software that is reliable and works efficiently on real machines"

The term has been used less formally:

- as the informal contemporary term for the broad range of activities that were formerly called computer programming and systems analysis;

- as the broad term for all aspects of the *practice* of computer programming, as opposed to the *theory* of computer programming, which is called computer science;

- as the term embodying the *advocacy* of a specific approach to computer programming, one that urges that it be treated as an engineering discipline rather than an art or a craft, and advocates the codification of recommended practices.

Criticism

Software Engineering sees its practitioners as individuals who follow well-defined engineering approaches to problem-solving. These approaches are specified in various software engineering books and research papers, always with the connotations of predictability, precision, mitigated risk and professionalism. This perspective has led to calls for licensing, certification and codified bodies of knowledge as mechanisms for spreading the engineering knowledge and maturing the field.

Software Craftsmanship has been proposed by a body of software developers as an alternative that emphasizes the coding skills and accountability of the software developers themselves without professionalism or any prescribed curriculum leading to ad-hoc problem-solving (craftmanship) without engineering (lack of predictability, precision, missing risk mitigation, methods are informal and poorly defined). The Software Craftsmanship Manifesto extends the Agile Software Manifesto and draws a metaphor between modern software development and the apprenticeship model of medieval Europe.

Software engineering extends engineering and draws on the engineering model, i.e. engineering process, engineering project management, engineering requirements, engineering design, engineering construction, and engineering validation. The concept is so new that it is rarely understood, and it is widely misinterpreted, including in software engineering textbooks, papers, and among the communities of programmers and crafters.

One of the core issues in software engineering is that its approaches are not empirical enough because a real-world validation of approaches is usually absent, or very limited and hence software engineering is often misinterpreted as feasible only in a "theoretical environment."

Dijkstra who developed computer languages in the last century refuted the concepts of "software engineering" which was prevalent thirty years ago in the 1980s, arguing that those terms were poor analogies for what he called the "radical novelty" of computer science:

A number of these phenomena have been bundled under the name "Software Engineering". As economics is known as "The Miserable Science", software engineering should be known as "The Doomed Discipline", doomed because it cannot even approach its goal since its goal is self-contradictory. Software engineering, of course, presents itself as another worthy cause, but that is eyewash: if you carefully read its literature and analyse what its devotees actually do, you will discover that software engineering has accepted as its charter "How to program if you cannot."

Software Archaeology

Software archaeology or software archeology is the study of poorly documented or undocumented legacy software implementations, as part of software maintenance. Software archaeology, named by analogy with archaeology, includes the reverse engineering of software modules, and the application of a variety of tools and processes for extracting and understanding program structure and recovering design information. Software archaeology may reveal dysfunctional team processes which have produced poorly designed or even unused software modules. The term has been in use for decades, and reflects a fairly natural metaphor: a programmer reading legacy code may feel that he or she is in the same situation as an archaeologist exploring the rubble of an ancient civilization.

Techniques

A workshop on Software Archaeology at the 2001 OOPSLA (Object-Oriented Programming, Systems, Languages & Applications) conference identified the following software archaeology techniques, some of which are specific to object-oriented programming:

- Scripting languages to build static reports and for filtering diagnostic output

- Ongoing documentation in HTML pages or Wikis

- Synoptic signature analysis, statistical analysis, and software visualization tools

- Reverse-engineering tools

- Operating-system-level tracing via truss or strace

- Search engines and tools to search for keywords in source files

- IDE file browsing

- Unit testing frameworks such as JUnit and CppUnit

- API documentation generation using tools such as Javadoc and doxygen

- Debuggers

More generally, Andy Hunt and Dave Thomas note the importance of version control, dependency management, text indexing tools such as GLIMPSE and SWISH-E, and "[drawing] a map as you begin exploring."

Like true archaeology, software archaeology involves investigative work to understand the thought processes of one's predecessors. At the OOPSLA workshop, Ward Cunningham suggested a synoptic signature analysis technique which gave an overall "feel" for a program by showing only punctuation, such as semicolons and curly braces. In the same vein, Cunningham has suggested viewing programs in 2 point font in order to understand the overall structure. Another technique identified at the workshop was the use of aspect-oriented programming tools such as AspectJ to systematically introduce tracing code without directly editing the legacy program.

Network and temporal analysis techniques can reveal the patterns of collaborative activity by the developers of legacy software, which in turn may shed light on the strengths and weaknesses of the software artifacts produced.

Michael Rozlog of Embarcadero Technologies has described software archaeology as a six-step process which enables programmers to answer questions such as "What have I just inherited?" and "Where are the scary sections of the code?" These steps, similar to those identified by the OOPSLA workshop, include using visualization to obtain a visual representation of the program's design, using software metrics to look for design and style violations, using unit testing and profiling to look for bugs and performance bottlenecks, and assembling design information recovered by the process. Software archaeology can also be a service provided to programmers by external consultants.

Mitch Rosenberg of InfoVentions.net, Inc. claims that the first law of software archaeology (he calls it code or data archaeology) is:

Everything that is there is there for a reason, and there are 3 possible reasons:

1. *It used to need to be there but no longer does*

2. *It never needed to be there and the person that wrote the code had no clue*

3. *It STILL needs to be there and YOU have no clue*

The corollary to this "law" is that, until you know which was the reason, you should NOT modify the code (or data).

Software archaeology has continued to be a topic of discussion at more recent software engineering conferences.

References

- Richard Hopkins and Kevin Jenkins, Eating the IT Elephant: Moving from greenfield development to brownfield, Addison-Wesley, 2008, ISBN 0-13-713012-0, p. 93.

- Abran, Alain; Moore, James W.; Bourque, Pierre; Dupuis, Robert; Tripp, Leonard L. (2004). Guide to the Software Engineering Body of Knowledge. IEEE. ISBN 0-7695-2330-7.

- Sommerville, Ian (2008). Software Engineering (7 ed.). Pearson Education. ISBN 978-81-7758-530-8. Retrieved 10 January 2013.

Sub-disciplines of Software Engineering

The manufacture of software is dependent on the manufacture of hardware and vice-versa. What this implies is that many pieces of hardware are technically competent to implement the same software. Software design and development must keep these existing devices into account while in manufacture. Some of the sub-disciplines of software engineering that are included in this chapter are software testing, engineering management, software design etc.

Software Requirements

Software Requirements is a field within software engineering that deals with establishing the needs of stakeholders that are to be solved by software. The IEEE Standard Glossary of Software Engineering Terminology defines a requirement as:

1. A condition or capability needed by a user to solve a problem or achieve an objective.

2. A condition or capability that must be met or possessed by a system or system component to satisfy a contract, standard, specification, or other formally imposed document.

3. A documented representation of a condition or capability as in 1 or 2.

The activities related to working with software requirements can broadly be broken up into Elicitation, Analysis, Specification, and Management.

Elicitation

Elicitation is the gathering and discovery of requirements from stakeholders and other sources. A variety of techniques can be used such as joint application design (JAD) sessions, interviews, document analysis, focus groups, etc. Elicitation is the first step of requirements development.

Analysis

Analysis is the logical breakdown that proceeds from elicitation. Analysis involves reaching a richer and more precise understanding of each requirement and representing sets of requirements in multiple, complementary ways.

Specification

Specification involves representing and storing the collected requirements knowledge in a persistent and well-organized fashion that facilitates effective communication and change management. Use cases, user stories, functional requirements, and visual analysis models are popular choices for requirements specification.

Validation

Validation involves techniques to confirm that the correct set of requirements has been specified to build a solution that satisfies the project's business objectives.

Management

Requirements change during projects and there are often many of them. Management of this change becomes paramount to ensuring that the correct software is built for the stakeholders.

Tool Support for Requirements Engineering

Specialized commercial tools for requirements engineering are 3SL Cradle, IRise, Gatherspace, Rational RequisitePro, Doors, CaliberRM or QFDCapture, but also free tools like FreeMind, Req-checker together with MS Office, Concordion can be used. Issue trackers implementing the Volere requirements template have been used successfully in distributed environments.

Software Design

Software design is the process by which an agent creates a specification of a software artifact, intended to accomplish goals, using a set of primitive components and subject to constraints. Software design may refer to either "all the activity involved in conceptualizing, framing, implementing, commissioning, and ultimately modifying complex systems" or "the activity following requirements specification and before programming, as … [in] a stylized software engineering process."

Software design usually involves problem solving and planning a software solution. This includes both a low-level component and algorithm design and a high-level, architecture design.

Overview

Software design is the process of implementing software solutions to one or more sets of problems. One of the main components of software design is the software requirements analysis (SRA). SRA is a part of the software development process that lists specifications used in software engineering. If the software is "semi-automated" or user centered, software design may involve user experience design yielding a storyboard to help determine those specifications. If the software is completely automated (meaning no user or user interface), a software design may be as simple as a flow chart or text describing a planned sequence of events. There are also semi-standard methods like Unified Modeling Language and Fundamental modeling concepts. In either case, some documentation of the plan is usually the product of the design. Furthermore, a software design may be platform-independent or platform-specific, depending upon the availability of the technology used for the design.

The main difference between software analysis and design is that the output of a software analysis consists of smaller problems to solve. Additionally, the analysis should not be designed very differently across different team members or groups. In contrast, the design focuses on capabilities, and thus multiple designs for the same problem can and will exist. Depending on the environment, the design often varies, whether it is created from reliable frameworks or implemented with suitable design patterns. Design examples include operation systems, webpages, mobile devices or even the new cloud computing paradigm.

Software design is both a process and a model. The design process is a sequence of steps that enables the designer to describe all aspects of the software for building. Creative skill, past experience, a sense of what makes "good" software, and an overall commitment to quality are examples of critical success factors for a competent design. It is important to note, however, that the design process is not always a straightforward procedure; the design model can be compared to an architect's plans for a house. It begins by representing the totality of the thing that is to be built (e.g., a three-dimensional rendering of the house); slowly, the thing is refined to provide guidance for constructing each detail (e.g., the plumbing layout). Similarly, the design model that is created for software provides a variety of different views of the computer software. Basic design principles enable the software engineer to navigate the design process. Davis [DAV95] suggests a set of principles for software design, which have been adapted and extended in the following list:

- The design process should not suffer from "tunnel vision." A good designer should consider alternative approaches, judging each based on the requirements of the problem, the resources available to do the job.

- The design should be traceable to the analysis model. Because a single element of the design model can often be traced back to multiple requirements, it is necessary to have a means for tracking how requirements have been satisfied by the design model.

- The design should not reinvent the wheel. Systems are constructed using a set of design patterns, many of which have likely been encountered before. These patterns should always be chosen as an alternative to reinvention. Time is short and resources are limited; design time should be invested in representing truly new ideas and integrating patterns that already exist when applicable.

- The design should "minimize the intellectual distance" between the software and the problem as it exists in the real world. That is, the structure of the software design should, whenever possible, mimic the structure of the problem domain.

- The design should exhibit uniformity and integration. A design is uniform if it appears fully coherent. In order to achieve this outcome, rules of style and format should be defined for a design team before design work begins. A design is integrated if care is taken in defining interfaces between design components.

- The design should be structured to accommodate change. The design concepts discussed in the next section enable a design to achieve this principle.

- The design should be structured to degrade gently, even when aberrant data, events, or operating conditions are encountered. Well- designed software should never "bomb"; it should be designed to accommodate unusual circumstances, and if it must terminate processing, it should do so in a graceful manner.

- Design is not coding, coding is not design. Even when detailed procedural designs are created for program components, the level of abstraction of the design model is higher than the source code. The only design decisions made at the coding level should address the small implementation details that enable the procedural design to be coded.

- The design should be assessed for quality as it is being created, not after the fact. A variety of design concepts and design measures are available to assist the designer in assessing quality throughout the development process.

- The design should be reviewed to minimize conceptual (semantic) errors. There is sometimes a tendency to focus on minutiae when the design is reviewed, missing the forest for the trees. A design team should ensure that major conceptual elements of the design (omissions, ambiguity, inconsistency) have been addressed before worrying about the syntax of the design model.

Design Concepts

The design concepts provide the software designer with a foundation from which more sophisticated methods can be applied. A set of fundamental design concepts has evolved. They are as follows:

1. Abstraction - Abstraction is the process or result of generalization by reducing the information content of a concept or an observable phenomenon, typically in order to retain only information which is relevant for a particular purpose.

2. Refinement - It is the process of elaboration. A hierarchy is developed by decomposing a macroscopic statement of function in a step-wise fashion until programming language statements are reached. In each step, one or several instructions of a given program are decomposed into more detailed instructions. Abstraction and Refinement are complementary concepts.

3. Modularity - Software architecture is divided into components called modules.

4. Software Architecture - It refers to the overall structure of the software and the ways in which that structure provides conceptual integrity for a system. Good software architecture will yield a good return on investment with respect to the desired outcome of the project, e.g. in terms of performance, quality, schedule and cost.

5. Control Hierarchy - A program structure that represents the organization of a program component and implies a hierarchy of control.

6. Structural Partitioning - The program structure can be divided both horizontally and vertically. Horizontal partitions define separate branches of modular hierarchy for each major program function. Vertical partitioning suggests that control and work should be distributed top down in the program structure.

7. Data Structure - It is a representation of the logical relationship among individual elements of data.

8. Software Procedure - It focuses on the processing of each module individually.

9. Information Hiding - Modules should be specified and designed so that information contained within a module is inaccessible to other modules that have no need for such information.

In his object model, Grady Booch mentions Abstraction, Encapsulation, Modularisation, and Hierarchy as fundamental design principles. The acronym PHAME (Principles of Hierarchy, Abstraction, Modularisation, and Encapsulation) is sometimes used to refer to these four fundamental principles.

Design Considerations

There are many aspects to consider in the design of a piece of software. The importance of each consideration should reflect the goals and expectations that the software is being created to meet. Some of these aspects are:

- Compatibility - The software is able to operate with other products that are designed for interoperability with another product. For example, a piece of software may be backward-compatible with an older version of itself.

- Extensibility - New capabilities can be added to the software without major changes to the underlying architecture.

- Modularity - the resulting software comprises well defined, independent components which leads to better maintainability. The components could be then implemented and tested in isolation before being integrated to form a desired software system. This allows division of work in a software development project.

- Fault-tolerance - The software is resistant to and able to recover from component failure.

- Maintainability - A measure of how easily bug fixes or functional modifications can be accomplished. High maintainability can be the product of modularity and extensibility.

- Reliability (Software durability) - The software is able to perform a required function under stated conditions for a specified period of time.

- Reusability - The ability to use some or all of the aspects of the preexisting software in other projects with little to no modification.

- Robustness - The software is able to operate under stress or tolerate unpredictable or invalid input. For example, it can be designed with a resilience to low memory conditions.

- Security - The software is able to withstand and resist hostile acts and influences.

- Usability - The software user interface must be usable for its target user/audience. Default values for the parameters must be chosen so that they are a good choice for the majority of the users.

- Performance - The software performs its tasks within a time-frame that is acceptable for the user, and does not require too much memory.

- Portability - The software should be usable across a number of different conditions and environments.

- Scalability - The software adapts well to increasing data or number of users.

Modeling Language

A modeling language is any artificial language that can be used to express information, knowledge or systems in a structure that is defined by a consistent set of rules. These rules are used for interpretation of the components within the structure. A modeling language can be graphical or textual. Examples of graphical modeling languages for software design are:

- Architecture description language (ADL) is a language used to describe and represent the software architecture of a software system.

- Business Process Modeling Notation (BPMN) is an example of a Process Modeling language.

- EXPRESS and EXPRESS-G (ISO 10303-11) is an international standard general-purpose data modeling language.

- Extended Enterprise Modeling Language (EEML) is commonly used for business process modeling across a number of layers.

- Flowchart is a schematic representation of an algorithm or step-wise process.

- Fundamental Modeling Concepts (FMC) is modeling language for software-intensive systems.

- IDEF is a family of modeling languages, the most notable of which include IDEF0 for functional modeling, IDEF1X for information modeling, and IDEF5 for modeling ontologies.

- Jackson Structured Programming (JSP) is a method for structured programming based on correspondences between data stream structure and program structure.

- LePUS3 is an object-oriented visual Design Description Language and a formal specification language that is suitable primarily for modeling large object-oriented (Java, C++, C#) programs and design patterns.

- Unified Modeling Language (UML) is a general modeling language to describe software both structurally and behaviorally. It has a graphical notation and allows for extension with a Profile (UML).

- Alloy (specification language) is a general purpose specification language for expressing complex structural constraints and behavior in a software system. It provides a concise language base on first-order relational logic.

- Systems Modeling Language (SysML) is a new general-purpose modeling language for systems engineering.

- Service-oriented modeling framework (SOMF)

Design Patterns

A software designer or architect may identify a design problem which has been visited and perhaps even solved by others in the past. A template or pattern describing a solution to a common problem is known as a design pattern. The reuse of such patterns can help speed up the software development process.

Technique

The difficulty of using the term "design" in relation to software is that in some senses, the source code of a program *is* the design for the program that it produces. To the extent that this is true, "software design" refers to the design of the design. Edsger W. Dijkstra referred to this layering of semantic levels as the "radical novelty" of computer programming, and Donald Knuth used his experience writing TeX to describe the futility of attempting to design a program prior to implementing it:

TEX would have been a complete failure if I had merely specified it and not participated fully in its initial implementation. The process of implementation constantly led me to unanticipated questions and to new insights about how the original specifications could be improved.

Usage

Software design documentation may be reviewed or presented to allow constraints, specifications and even requirements to be adjusted prior to computer programming. Redesign may occur after review of a programmed simulation or prototype. It is possible to design software in the process of programming, without a plan or requirement analysis, but for more complex projects this would not be considered feasible. A separate design prior to programming allows for multidisciplinary designers and Subject Matter Experts (SMEs) to collaborate with highly skilled programmers for software that is both useful and technically sound.

Software Construction

Software construction is a software engineering discipline. It is the detailed creation of working meaningful software through a combination of coding, verification, unit testing, integration testing, and debugging. It is linked to all the other software engineering disciplines, most strongly to software design and software testing.

Software Construction Fundamentals

Minimizing Complexity

The need to reduce complexity is mainly driven by limited ability of most people to hold complex structures and information in their working memories. Reduced complexity is achieved through emphasizing the creation of code that is simple and readable rather than clever. Minimizing complexity is accomplished through making use of standards, and through numerous specific techniques in coding. It is also supported by the construction-focused quality techniques.

Anticipating Change

Anticipating change helps software engineers build extensible software, which means they can enhance a software product without disrupting the underlying structure. Research over 25 years showed that the cost of rework can be 10 to 100 times (5 to 10 times for smaller projects) more expensive than getting the requirements right the first time. Given that 25% of the requirements change during development on average project, the need to reduce the cost of rework elucidates the need for anticipating change.

Constructing for Verification

Constructing for verification means building software in such a way that faults can be ferreted out readily by the software engineers writing the software, as well as during independent testing and operational activities. Specific techniques that support constructing for verification include following coding standards to support code reviews, unit testing, organizing code to support automated testing, and restricted use of complex or hard-to-understand language structures, among others.

Reuse

Systematic reuse can enable significant software productivity, quality, and cost improvements. Reuse has two closely related facets:

- Construction for reuse: Create reusable software assets.

- Construction with reuse: Reuse software assets in the construction of a new solution.

Standards in Construction

Standards, whether external (created by international organizations) or internal (created at the corporate level), that directly affect construction issues include:

- Communication methods: Such as standards for document formats and contents.
- Programming languages
- Coding standards
- Platforms
- Tools: Such as diagrammatic standards for notations like UML.

Managing Construction

Construction Models

Numerous models have been created to develop software, some of which emphasize construction more than others. Some models are more linear from the construction point of view, such as the waterfall and staged-delivery life cycle models. These models treat construction as an activity which occurs only after significant prerequisite work has been completed—including detailed requirements work, extensive design work, and detailed planning. Other models are more iterative, such as evolutionary prototyping, Extreme Programming, and Scrum. These approaches tend to treat construction as an activity that occurs concurrently with other software development activities, including requirements, design, and planning, or overlaps them.

Construction Planning

The choice of construction method is a key aspect of the construction planning activity. The choice of construction method affects the extent to which construction prerequisites (e.g. Requirements analysis, Software design, .. etc) are performed, the order in which they are performed, and the degree to which they are expected to be completed before construction work begins. Construction planning also defines the order in which components are created and integrated, the software quality management processes, the allocation of task assignments to specific software engineers, and the other tasks, according to the chosen method.

Construction Measurement

Numerous construction activities and artifacts can be measured, including code developed, code modified, code reused, code destroyed, code complexity, code inspection statistics, fault-fix and fault-find rates, effort, and scheduling. These measurements can be useful for purposes of managing construction, ensuring quality during construction, improving the construction process, as well as for other reasons.

Practical Considerations

Software construction is driven by many practical considerations:

Construction Design

In order to account for the unanticipated gaps in the software design, during software construction some design modifications must be made on a smaller or larger scale to flesh out details of the software design.

Low Fan-out is one of the design characteristics found to be be beneficial by researchers. Information hiding proved to be a useful design technique in large programs that made them easier to modify by a factor of 4.

Construction Languages

Construction languages include all forms of communication by which a human can specify an executable problem solution to a computer. They include configuration languages, toolkit languages, and programming languages:

- Configuration languages are languages in which software engineers choose from a limited set of predefined options to create new or custom software installations.

- Toolkit languages are used to build applications out of toolkits and are more complex than configuration languages.

- Scripting languages are kinds of application programming languages that supports scripts which are often interpreted rather than compiled.

- Programming languages are the most flexible type of construction languages which use three general kinds of notation:

    o Linguistic notations which are distinguished in particular by the use of word-like strings of text to represent complex software constructions, and the combination of such word-like strings into patterns that have a sentence-like syntax.

    o Formal notations which rely less on intuitive, everyday meanings of words and text strings and more on definitions backed up by precise, unambiguous, and formal (or mathematical) definitions.

    o Visual notations which rely much less on the text-oriented notations of both linguistic and formal construction, and instead rely on direct visual interpretation and placement of visual entities that represent the underlying software.

Programmers working in a language they have used for three years or more are about 30 percent more productive than programmers with equivalent experience who are new to a language. High-level languages such as C++, Java, Smalltalk, and Visual Basic yield 5 to 15 times better productivity, reliability, simplicity, and comprehensibility than low-level languages such as assembly and C. Equivalent code has been shown to need less lines to be implemented in high level languages than lower level languages.

Coding

The following considerations apply to the software construction coding activity:

- Techniques for creating understandable source code, including naming and source code layout

- Use of classes, enumerated types, variables, named constants, and other similar entities. A study done by NASA showed that the putting the code into well-factored classes can double the code reusability compared to the code developed using functional design.

- Use of control structures

- Handling of error conditions—both planned errors and exceptions (input of bad data, for example)

- Prevention of code-level security breaches (buffer overruns or array index overflows, for example)

- Resource usage via use of exclusion mechanisms and discipline in accessing serially reusable resources (including threads or database locks)

- Source code organization (into statements and routines). When considering routine cohesion, highly cohesive routines proved to be less error prone than routines with lower cohesion. A study of 450 routines found that 50 percent of the highly cohesive routines were fault free compared to only 18 percent of routines with low cohesion. Another study of a different 450 routines found that routines with the highest coupling-to-cohesion ratios had 7 times as many errors as those with the lowest coupling-to-cohesion ratios and were 20 times as costly to fix. Although studies showed inconclusive results regarding the correlation between routine sizes and the rate of errors in them, but one study found that routines with less than 143 lines of code were 2.4 times less expensive to fix than larger routines. Another study showed that the code needed to be changed least when routines averaged 100 to 150 lines of code. Another study found that structural complexity and amount of data in a routine were correlated with errors regardless of its size.

- Source code organization (into classes, packages, or other structures). When considering containment, the maximum number of data members in a class shouldn't exceed 7±2. Research has shown that this number is the number of discrete items a person can remember while performing other tasks. When considering inheritance, the number of levels in the inheritance tree should be limited. Deep inheritance trees have been found to be significantly associated with increased fault rates. When considering the number of routines in a class, it should be kept as small as possible. A study on C++ programs has found an association between the number of routines and the number of faults.

- Code documentation

- Code tuning

Construction Testing

The purpose of construction testing is to reduce the gap between the time at which faults are inserted into the code and the time those faults are detected. In some cases, construction testing is performed after code has been written. In test-first programming, test cases are created before code is written. Construction involves two forms of testing, which are often performed by the software engineer who wrote the code:

- Unit testing

- Integration testing

Reuse

Implementing software reuse entails more than creating and using libraries of assets. It requires formalizing the practice of reuse by integrating reuse processes and activities into the software life cycle. The tasks related to reuse in software construction during coding and testing are:

- The selection of the reusable units, databases, test procedures, or test data.

- The evaluation of code or test re-usability.

- The reporting of reuse information on new code, test procedures, or test data.

Construction Quality

The primary techniques used to ensure the quality of code as it is constructed include:

- Unit testing and integration testing

- Test-first development

- Code stepping

- Use of assertions

- Debugging

- Technical reviews

- Static analysis (IEEE1028)

Integration

A key activity during construction is the integration of separately constructed routines, classes, components, and subsystems. In addition, a particular software system may need to be integrated with other software or hardware systems. Concerns related to construction integration include planning the sequence in which components will be integrated, creating scaffolding to support interim versions of the software, determining the degree of testing and quality work performed on components before they are integrated, and determining points in the project at which interim versions of the software are tested.

Construction Technologies

Object-oriented Runtime Issues

Object-oriented languages support a series of runtime mechanisms that increase the flexibility and adaptability of the programs like data abstraction, encapsulation, modularity, inheritance, polymorphism, and reflection.

Data abstraction is the process by which data and programs are defined with a representation similar in form to its meaning, while hiding away the implementation details. Academic research showed that data abstraction makes programs about 30% easier to understand than functional programs.

Software Testing

Software testing is an investigation conducted to provide stakeholders with information about the quality of the product or service under test. Software testing can also provide an objective, independent view of the software to allow the business to appreciate and understand the risks of software implementation. Test techniques include the process of executing a program or application with the intent of finding software bugs (errors or other defects).

Software testing involves the execution of a software component or system component to evaluate one or more properties of interest. In general, these properties indicate the extent to which the component or system under test:

- meets the requirements that guided its design and development,

- responds correctly to all kinds of inputs,

- performs its functions within an acceptable time,

- is sufficiently usable,

- can be installed and run in its intended environments, and

- achieves the general result its stakeholders desire.

As the number of possible tests for even simple software components is practically infinite, all software testing uses some strategy to select tests that are feasible for the available time and resources. As a result, software testing typically (but not exclusively) attempts to execute a program or application with the intent of finding software bugs (errors or other defects). The job of testing is an iterative process as when one bug is fixed, it can illuminate other, deeper bugs, or can even create new ones.

Software testing can provide objective, independent information about the quality of software and risk of its failure to users and/or sponsors.

Software testing can be conducted as soon as executable software (even if partially complete) exists. The overall approach to software development often determines when and how testing is conducted. For example, in a phased process, most testing occurs after system requirements have been defined and then implemented in testable programs. In contrast, under an Agile approach, requirements, programming, and testing are often done concurrently.

Overview

Although testing can determine the correctness of software under the assumption of some specific hypotheses, testing cannot identify all the defects within software. Instead, it furnishes a *criticism* or *comparison* that compares the state and behavior of the product against oracles— principles or mechanisms by which someone might recognize a problem. These oracles may include (but are not limited to) specifications, contracts, comparable products, past versions of the same product, inferences about intended or expected purpose, user or customer expectations, relevant standards, applicable laws, or other criteria.

A primary purpose of testing is to detect software failures so that defects may be discovered and corrected. Testing cannot establish that a product functions properly under all conditions but can only establish that it does not function properly under specific conditions. The scope of software testing often includes examination of code as well as execution of that code in various environments and conditions as well as examining the aspects of code: does it do what it is supposed to do and do what it needs to do. In the current culture of software development, a testing organization may be separate from the development team. There are various roles for testing team members. Information derived from software testing may be used to correct the process by which software is developed.

Every software product has a target audience. For example, the audience for video game software is completely different from banking software. Therefore, when an organization develops or otherwise invests in a software product, it can assess whether the software product will be acceptable to its end users, its target audience, its purchasers and other stakeholders. Software testing is the process of attempting to make this assessment.

Defects and Failures

Not all software defects are caused by coding errors. One common source of expensive defects is requirement gaps, e.g., unrecognized requirements which result in errors of omission by the program designer. Requirement gaps can often be non-functional requirements such as testability, scalability, maintainability, usability, performance, and security.

Software faults occur through the following processes. A programmer makes an error (mistake), which results in a defect (fault, bug) in the software source code. If this defect is executed, in certain situations the system will produce wrong results, causing a failure. Not all defects will necessarily result in failures. For example, defects in dead code will never result in failures. A defect can turn into a failure when the environment is changed. Examples of these changes in environment include the software being run on a new computer hardware platform, alterations in source data, or interacting with different software. A single defect may result in a wide range of failure symptoms.

Input Combinations and Preconditions

A fundamental problem with software testing is that testing under *all* combinations of inputs and preconditions (initial state) is not feasible, even with a simple product. This means that the number of defects in a software product can be very large and defects that occur infrequently are difficult to find in testing. More significantly, non-functional dimensions of quality (how it is supposed to *be* versus what it is supposed to *do*)—usability, scalability, performance, compatibility, reliability—can be highly subjective; something that constitutes sufficient value to one person may be intolerable to another.

Software developers can't test everything, but they can use combinatorial test design to identify the minimum number of tests needed to get the coverage they want. Combinatorial test design enables users to get greater test coverage with fewer tests. Whether they are looking for speed or test depth, they can use combinatorial test design methods to build structured variation into their test cases. Note that "coverage", as used here, is referring to combinatorial coverage, not requirements coverage.

Economics

A study conducted by NIST in 2002 reports that software bugs cost the U.S. economy $59.5 billion annually. More than a third of this cost could be avoided if better software testing was performed.

It is commonly believed that the earlier a defect is found, the cheaper it is to fix it. The following table shows the cost of fixing the defect depending on the stage it was found. For example, if a problem in the requirements is found only post-release, then it would cost 10–100 times more to fix than if it had already been found by the requirements review. With the advent of modern continuous deployment practices and cloud-based services, the cost of re-deployment and maintenance may lessen over time.

Cost to fix a defect Requirements		Time detected				
		Architecture	Construc-tion	System test	Post-re-lease	
Time introduced	Requirements	1×	3×	5–10×	10×	10–100×
	Architecture	–	1×	10×	15×	25–100×
	Construction	–	–	1×	10×	10–25×

The data from which this table is extrapolated is scant. Laurent Bossavit says in his analysis:

The "smaller projects" curve turns out to be from only two teams of first-year students, a sample size so small that extrapolating to "smaller projects in general" is totally indefensible. The GTE study does not explain its data, other than to say it came from two projects, one large and one small. The paper cited for the Bell Labs "Safeguard" project specifically disclaims having collected the fine-grained data that Boehm's data points suggest. The IBM study (Fagan's paper) contains claims which seem to contradict Boehm's graph, and no numerical results which clearly correspond to his data points.

Boehm doesn't even cite a paper for the TRW data, except when writing for "Making Software" in 2010, and there he cited the original 1976 article. There exists a large study conducted at TRW at the right time for Boehm to cite it, but that paper doesn't contain the sort of data that would support Boehm's claims.

Roles

Software testing can be done by software testers. Until the 1980s, the term "software tester" was used generally, but later it was also seen as a separate profession. Regarding the periods and the different goals in software testing, different roles have been established: *manager, test lead, test analyst, test designer, tester, automation developer*, and *test administrator*.

History

The separation of debugging from testing was initially introduced by Glenford J. Myers in 1979. Although his attention was on breakage testing ("a successful test is one that finds a bug") it illustrated the desire of the software engineering community to separate fundamental development activities, such as debugging, from that of verification. Dave Gelperin and William C. Hetzel classified in 1988 the phases and goals in software testing in the following stages:

- Until 1956 – Debugging oriented
- 1957–1978 – Demonstration oriented
- 1979–1982 – Destruction oriented
- 1983–1987 – Evaluation oriented
- 1988–2000 – Prevention oriented

Testing Methods

Static vs. Dynamic Testing

There are many approaches available in software testing. Reviews, walkthroughs, or inspections are referred to as static testing, whereas actually executing programmed code with a given set of test cases is referred to as dynamic testing. Static testing is often implicit, as proofreading, plus when programming tools/text editors check source code structure or compilers (pre-compilers) check syntax and data flow as static program analysis. Dynamic testing takes place when the program itself is run. Dynamic testing may begin before the program is 100% complete in order to test particular sections of code and are applied to discrete functions or modules. Typical techniques for this are either using stubs/drivers or execution from a debugger environment.

Static testing involves verification, whereas dynamic testing involves validation. Together they help improve software quality. Among the techniques for static analysis, mutation testing can be used to ensure the test cases will detect errors which are introduced by mutating the source code.

The Box Approach

Software testing methods are traditionally divided into white- and black-box testing. These two approaches are used to describe the point of view that a test engineer takes when designing test cases.

White-box Testing

White-box testing (also known as]]'clear box testing, glass box testing, transparent box testing and structural testing, by seeing the source code) tests internal structures or workings of a program, as opposed to the functionality exposed to the end-user. In white-box testing an internal perspective of the system, as well as programming skills, are used to design test cases. The tester chooses inputs to exercise paths through the code and determine the appropriate outputs. This is analogous to testing nodes in a circuit, e.g. in-circuit testing (ICT).

While white-box testing can be applied at the unit, integration and system levels of the software testing process, it is usually done at the unit level. It can test paths within a unit, paths between units during integration, and between subsystems during a system–level test. Though this method of test design can uncover many errors or problems, it might not detect unimplemented parts of the specification or missing requirements.

Techniques used in white-box testing include:

- API testing – testing of the application using public and private APIs (application programming interfaces)

- Code coverage – creating tests to satisfy some criteria of code coverage (e.g., the test designer can create tests to cause all statements in the program to be executed at least once)

- Fault injection methods –[]] intentionally introducing faults to gauge the efficacy of testing strategies

- Mutation testing methods

- Static testing methods

Code coverage tools can evaluate the completeness of a test suite that was created with any method, including black-box testing. This allows the software team to examine parts of a system that are rarely tested and ensures that the most important function points have been tested. Code coverage as a software metric can be reported as a percentage for:

- *Function coverage*, which reports on functions executed

- *Statement coverage*, which reports on the number of lines executed to complete the test

- *Decision coverage*, which reports on whether both the True and the False branch of a given test has been executed

100% statement coverage ensures that all code paths or branches (in terms of control flow) are executed at least once. This is helpful in ensuring correct functionality, but not sufficient since the same code may process different inputs correctly or incorrectly.

Black-box Testing

Black box diagram

Black-box testing treats the software as a "black box", examining functionality without any knowledge of internal implementation, without seeing the source code. The testers are only aware of what the software is supposed to do, not how it does it. Black-box testing methods include: equivalence partitioning, boundary value analysis, all-pairs testing, state transition tables, decision table testing, fuzz testing, model-based testing, use case testing, exploratory testing and specification-based testing.

Specification-based testing aims to test the functionality of software according to the applicable requirements. This level of testing usually requires thorough test cases to be provided to the tester, who then can simply verify that for a given input, the output value (or behavior), either "is" or "is not" the same as the expected value specified in the test case. Test cases are built around specifications and requirements, i.e., what the application is supposed to do. It uses external descriptions of the software, including specifications, requirements, and designs to derive test cases. These tests can be functional or non-functional, though usually functional.

Specification-based testing may be necessary to assure correct functionality, but it is insufficient to guard against complex or high-risk situations.

One advantage of the black box technique is that no programming knowledge is required. Whatever biases the programmers may have had, the tester likely has a different set and may emphasize different areas of functionality. On the other hand, black-box testing has been said to be "like a walk in a dark labyrinth without a flashlight." Because they do not examine the source code, there are situations when a tester writes many test cases to check something that could have been tested by only one test case, or leaves some parts of the program untested.

This method of test can be applied to all levels of software testing: unit, integration, system and acceptance. It typically comprises most if not all testing at higher levels, but can also dominate unit testing as well.

Visual Testing

The aim of visual testing is to provide developers with the ability to examine what was happening at the point of software failure by presenting the data in such a way that the developer can easily find the information she or he requires, and the information is expressed clearly.

At the core of visual testing is the idea that showing someone a problem (or a test failure), rather than just describing it, greatly increases clarity and understanding. Visual testing therefore requires the recording of the entire test process – capturing everything that occurs on the test system in video format. Output videos are supplemented by real-time tester input via picture-in-a-picture webcam and audio commentary from microphones.

Visual testing provides a number of advantages. The quality of communication is increased drastically because testers can show the problem (and the events leading up to it) to the developer as opposed to just describing it and the need to replicate test failures will cease to exist in many cases. The developer will have all the evidence he or she requires of a test failure and can instead focus on the cause of the fault and how it should be fixed.

Visual testing is particularly well-suited for environments that deploy agile methods in their development of software, since agile methods require greater communication between testers and developers and collaboration within small teams.

Ad hoc testing and exploratory testing are important methodologies for checking software integrity, because they require less preparation time to implement, while the important bugs can be found quickly. In ad hoc testing, where testing takes place in an improvised, impromptu way, the ability of a test tool to visually record everything that occurs on a system becomes very important in order to document the steps taken to uncover the bug.

Visual testing is gathering recognition in customer acceptance and usability testing, because the test can be used by many individuals involved in the development process. For the customer, it becomes easy to provide detailed bug reports and feedback, and for program users, visual testing can record user actions on screen, as well as their voice and image, to provide a complete picture at the time of software failure for the developers.

Grey-box Testing

Grey-box testing (American spelling: gray-box testing) involves having knowledge of internal data structures and algorithms for purposes of designing tests, while executing those tests at the user, or black-box level. The tester is not required to have full access to the software's source code. Manipulating input data and formatting output do not qualify as grey-box, because the input and output are clearly outside of the "black box" that we are calling the system under test. This distinction is particularly important when conducting integration testing between two modules of code written by two different developers, where only the interfaces are exposed for test.

However, tests that require modifying a back-end data repository such as a database or a log file does qualify as grey-box, as the user would not normally be able to change the data repository in normal production operations. Grey-box testing may also include reverse engineering to determine, for instance, boundary values or error messages.

By knowing the underlying concepts of how the software works, the tester makes better-informed testing choices while testing the software from outside. Typically, a grey-box tester will be permitted to set up an isolated testing environment with activities such as seeding a database. The tester can observe the state of the product being tested after performing certain actions such as executing SQL statements against the database and then executing queries to ensure that the expected changes have been reflected. Grey-box testing implements intelligent test scenarios, based on limited information. This will particularly apply to data type handling, exception handling, and so on.

Testing Levels

There are generally four recognized levels of tests: unit testing, integration testing, component interface testing, and system testing. Tests are frequently grouped by where they are added in the software development process, or by the level of specificity of the test. The main levels during the development process as defined by the SWEBOK guide are unit-, integration-, and system testing that are distinguished by the test target without implying a specific process model. Other test levels are classified by the testing objective.

There are two different levels of tests from the perspective of customers: low-level testing (LLT) and high-level testing (HLT). LLT is a group of tests for different level components of software application or product. HLT is a group of tests for the whole software application or product.

Unit Testing

Unit testing, also known as component testing, refers to tests that verify the functionality of a specific section of code, usually at the function level. In an object-oriented environment, this is usually at the class level, and the minimal unit tests include the constructors and destructors.

These types of tests are usually written by developers as they work on code (white-box style), to ensure that the specific function is working as expected. One function might have multiple tests, to catch corner cases or other branches in the code. Unit testing alone cannot verify the functionality of a piece of software, but rather is used to ensure that the building blocks of the software work independently from each other.

Unit testing is a software development process that involves synchronized application of a broad spectrum of defect prevention and detection strategies in order to reduce software development risks, time, and costs. It is performed by the software developer or engineer during the construction phase of the software development lifecycle. Rather than replace traditional QA focuses, it augments it. Unit testing aims to eliminate construction errors before code is promoted to QA; this strategy is intended to increase the quality of the resulting software as well as the efficiency of the overall development and QA process.

Depending on the organization's expectations for software development, unit testing might include static code analysis, data-flow analysis, metrics analysis, peer code reviews, code coverage analysis and other software verification practices.

Integration Testing

Integration testing is any type of software testing that seeks to verify the interfaces between components against a software design. Software components may be integrated in an iterative way or all together ("big bang"). Normally the former is considered a better practice since it allows interface issues to be located more quickly and fixed.

Integration testing works to expose defects in the interfaces and interaction between integrated components (modules). Progressively larger groups of tested software components corresponding to elements of the architectural design are integrated and tested until the software works as a system.

Component Interface Testing

The practice of component interface testing can be used to check the handling of data passed between various units, or subsystem components, beyond full integration testing between those units. The data being passed can be considered as "message packets" and the range or data types can be checked, for data generated from one unit, and tested for validity before being passed into another unit. One option for interface testing is to keep a separate log file of data items being passed, often with a timestamp logged to allow analysis of thousands of cases of data passed between units for days or weeks. Tests can include checking the handling of some extreme data values while other interface variables are passed as normal values. Unusual data values in an interface can help explain unexpected performance in the next unit. Component interface testing is a variation of black-box testing, with the focus on the data values beyond just the related actions of a subsystem component.

System Testing

System testing, or end-to-end testing, tests a completely integrated system to verify that the system meets its requirements. For example, a system test might involve testing a logon interface, then creating and editing an entry, plus sending or printing results, followed by summary processing or deletion (or archiving) of entries, then logoff.

Operational Acceptance Testing

Operational Acceptance is used to conduct operational readiness (pre-release) of a product, service or system as part of a quality management system. OAT is a common type of non-functional software testing, used mainly in software development and software maintenance projects. This type of testing focuses on the operational readiness of the system to be supported, and/or to become part of the production environment. Hence, it is also known as operational readiness testing

(ORT) or Operations readiness and assurance (OR&A) testing. Functional testing within OAT is limited to those tests which are required to verify the *non-functional* aspects of the system.

In addition, the software testing should ensure that the portability of the system, as well as working as expected, does not also damage or partially corrupt its operating environment or cause other processes within that environment to become inoperative.

Testing Types

Installation Testing

An installation test assures that the system is installed correctly and working at actual customer's hardware.

Compatibility Testing

A common cause of software failure (real or perceived) is a lack of its compatibility with other application software, operating systems (or operating system versions, old or new), or target environments that differ greatly from the original (such as a terminal or GUI application intended to be run on the desktop now being required to become a web application, which must render in a web browser). For example, in the case of a lack of backward compatibility, this can occur because the programmers develop and test software only on the latest version of the target environment, which not all users may be running. This results in the unintended consequence that the latest work may not function on earlier versions of the target environment, or on older hardware that earlier versions of the target environment was capable of using. Sometimes such issues can be fixed by proactively abstracting operating system functionality into a separate program module or library.

Smoke and Sanity Testing

Sanity testing determines whether it is reasonable to proceed with further testing.

Smoke testing consists of minimal attempts to operate the software, designed to determine whether there are any basic problems that will prevent it from working at all. Such tests can be used as build verification test.

Regression Testing

Regression testing focuses on finding defects after a major code change has occurred. Specifically, it seeks to uncover software regressions, as degraded or lost features, including old bugs that have come back. Such regressions occur whenever software functionality that was previously working correctly, stops working as intended. Typically, regressions occur as an unintended consequence of program changes, when the newly developed part of the software collides with the previously existing code. Common methods of regression testing include re-running previous sets of test cases and checking whether previously fixed faults have re-emerged. The depth of testing depends on the phase in the release process and the risk of the added features. They can either be complete, for changes added late in the release or deemed to be risky, or be very shallow, consisting of positive tests on each feature, if the changes are early in the release or deemed to be of low risk. Regression testing is typically the largest test effort in commercial software development, due to checking numerous details in prior software features, and even new software can be developed while using some old test cases to test parts of the new design to ensure prior functionality is still supported.

Acceptance Testing

Acceptance testing can mean one of two things:

1. A smoke test is used as an acceptance test prior to introducing a new build to the main testing process, i.e., before integration or regression.

2. Acceptance testing performed by the customer, often in their lab environment on their own hardware, is known as user acceptance testing (UAT). Acceptance testing may be performed as part of the hand-off process between any two phases of development.

Alpha Testing

Alpha testing is simulated or actual operational testing by potential users/customers or an independent test team at the developers' site. Alpha testing is often employed for off-the-shelf software as a form of internal acceptance testing, before the software goes to beta testing.

Beta Testing

Beta testing comes after alpha testing and can be considered a form of external user acceptance testing. Versions of the software, known as beta versions, are released to a limited audience outside of the programming team known as beta testers. The software is released to groups of people so that further testing can ensure the product has few faults or bugs. Beta versions can be made available to the open public to increase the feedback field to a maximal number of future users and to deliver value earlier, for an extended or even indefinite period of time (perpetual beta).

Functional vs non-functional Testing

Functional testing refers to activities that verify a specific action or function of the code. These are usually found in the code requirements documentation, although some development methodologies work from use cases or user stories. Functional tests tend to answer the question of "can the user do this" or "does this particular feature work."

Non-functional testing refers to aspects of the software that may not be related to a specific function or user action, such as scalability or other performance, behavior under certain constraints, or security. Testing will determine the breaking point, the point at which extremes of scalability or performance leads to unstable execution. Non-functional requirements tend to be those that reflect the quality of the product, particularly in the context of the suitability perspective of its users.

Continuous Testing

Continuous testing is the process of executing automated tests as part of the software delivery pipeline to obtain immediate feedback on the business risks associated with a software release candidate. Continuous testing includes the validation of both functional requirements and non-functional requirements; the scope of testing extends from validating bottom-up requirements or user stories to assessing the system requirements associated with overarching business goals.

Destructive Testing

Destructive testing attempts to cause the software or a sub-system to fail. It verifies that the software functions properly even when it receives invalid or unexpected inputs, thereby establishing the robustness of input validation and error-management routines. Software fault injection, in the form of fuzzing, is an example of failure testing. Various commercial non-functional testing tools are linked from the software fault injection page; there are also numerous open-source and free software tools available that perform destructive testing.

Software Performance Testing

Performance testing is generally executed to determine how a system or sub-system performs in terms of responsiveness and stability under a particular workload. It can also serve to investigate, measure, validate or verify other quality attributes of the system, such as scalability, reliability and resource usage.

Load testing is primarily concerned with testing that the system can continue to operate under a specific load, whether that be large quantities of data or a large number of users. This is generally referred to as software scalability. The related load testing activity of when performed as a non-functional activity is often referred to as *endurance testing*. *Volume testing* is a way to test software functions even when certain components (for example a file or database) increase radically in size. *Stress testing* is a way to test reliability under unexpected or rare workloads. *Stability testing* (often referred to as load or endurance testing) checks to see if the software can continuously function well in or above an acceptable period.

There is little agreement on what the specific goals of performance testing are. The terms load testing, performance testing, scalability testing, and volume testing, are often used interchangeably.

Real-time software systems have strict timing constraints. To test if timing constraints are met, real-time testing is used.

Usability Testing

Usability testing is to check if the user interface is easy to use and understand. It is concerned mainly with the use of the application.

Accessibility Testing

Accessibility testing may include compliance with standards such as:

- Americans with Disabilities Act of 1990
- Section 508 Amendment to the Rehabilitation Act of 1973
- Web Accessibility Initiative (WAI) of the World Wide Web Consortium (W3C)

Security Testing

Security testing is essential for software that processes confidential data to prevent system intrusion by hackers.

The International Organization for Standardization (ISO) defines this as a "type of testing conducted to evaluate the degree to which a test item, and associated data and information, are protected to that unauthorised persons or systems cannot use, read or modify them, and authorized persons or systems are not denied access to them."

Internationalization and Localization

The general ability of software to be internationalized and localized can be automatically tested without actual translation, by using pseudolocalization. It will verify that the application still works, even after it has been translated into a new language or adapted for a new culture (such as different currencies or time zones).

Actual translation to human languages must be tested, too. Possible localization failures include:

- Software is often localized by translating a list of strings out of context, and the translator may choose the wrong translation for an ambiguous source string.

- Technical terminology may become inconsistent if the project is translated by several people without proper coordination or if the translator is imprudent.

- Literal word-for-word translations may sound inappropriate, artificial or too technical in the target language.

- Untranslated messages in the original language may be left hard coded in the source code.

- Some messages may be created automatically at run time and the resulting string may be ungrammatical, functionally incorrect, misleading or confusing.

- Software may use a keyboard shortcut which has no function on the source language's keyboard layout, but is used for typing characters in the layout of the target language.

- Software may lack support for the character encoding of the target language.

- Fonts and font sizes which are appropriate in the source language may be inappropriate in the target language; for example, CJK characters may become unreadable if the font is too small.

- A string in the target language may be longer than the software can handle. This may make the string partly invisible to the user or cause the software to crash or malfunction.

- Software may lack proper support for reading or writing bi-directional text.

- Software may display images with text that was not localized.

- Localized operating systems may have differently named system configuration files and environment variables and different formats for date and currency.

Development Testing

Development Testing is a software development process that involves synchronized application of a broad spectrum of defect prevention and detection strategies in order to reduce software development risks, time, and costs. It is performed by the software developer or engineer during the construction phase of the software development lifecycle. Rather than replace traditional QA focuses, it augments it. Development Testing aims to eliminate construction errors before code is promoted to QA; this strategy is intended to increase the quality of the resulting software as well as the efficiency of the overall development and QA process.

Depending on the organization's expectations for software development, Development Testing might include static code analysis, data flow analysis, metrics analysis, peer code reviews, unit testing, code coverage analysis, traceability, and other software verification practices.

A/B Testing

A/B testing is basically a comparison of two outputs, generally when only one variable has changed: run a test, change one thing, run the test again, compare the results. This is more useful with more small-scale situations, but very useful in fine-tuning any program. With more complex projects, multivariant testing can be done.

Concurrent Testing

In concurrent testing, the focus is on the performance while continuously running with normal input and under normal operational conditions, as opposed to stress testing, or fuzz testing. Memory leak, as well as basic faults are easier to find with this method.

Conformance Testing or Type Testing

In software testing, conformance testing verifies that a product performs according to its specified standards. Compilers, for instance, are extensively tested to determine whether they meet the recognized standard for that language.

Testing Process

Traditional Waterfall Development Model

A common practice of software testing is that testing is performed by an independent group of testers after the functionality is developed, before it is shipped to the customer. This practice often results in the testing phase being used as a project buffer to compensate for project delays, thereby compromising the time devoted to testing.

Another practice is to start software testing at the same moment the project starts and it is a continuous process until the project finishes.

Agile or Extreme Development Model

In contrast, some emerging software disciplines such as extreme programming and the agile software development movement, adhere to a "test-driven software development" model. In this process, unit tests are written first, by the software engineers (often with pair programming in the extreme programming methodology). Of course these tests fail initially; as they are expected to. Then as code is written it passes incrementally larger portions of the test suites. The test suites are continuously updated as new failure conditions and corner cases are discovered, and they are integrated with any regression tests that are developed. Unit tests are maintained along with the rest of the software source code and generally integrated into the build process (with inherently interactive tests being relegated to a partially manual build acceptance process). The ultimate goal of this test process is to achieve continuous integration where software updates can be published to the public frequently.

This methodology increases the testing effort done by development, before reaching any formal testing team. In some other development models, most of the test execution occurs after the requirements have been defined and the coding process has been completed.

Top-down and Bottom-up

Bottom Up Testing is an approach to integrated testing where the lowest level components (modules, procedures, and functions) are tested first, then integrated and used to facilitate the testing of higher level components. After the integration testing of lower level integrated modules, the next level of modules will be formed and can be used for integration testing. The process is repeated until the components at the top of the hierarchy are tested. This approach is helpful only when all or most of the modules of the same development level are ready. This method also helps to determine the levels of software developed and makes it easier to report testing progress in the form of a percentage.

Top Down Testing is an approach to integrated testing where the top integrated modules are tested and the branch of the module is tested step by step until the end of the related module.

In both, method stubs and drivers are used to stand-in for missing components and are replaced as the levels are completed.

A Sample Testing Cycle

Although variations exist between organizations, there is a typical cycle for testing. The sample below is common among organizations employing the Waterfall development model. The same practices are commonly found in other development models, but might not be as clear or explicit.

- Requirements analysis: Testing should begin in the requirements phase of the software development life cycle. During the design phase, testers work to determine what aspects of a design are testable and with what parameters those tests work.

- Test planning: Test strategy, test plan, testbed creation. Since many activities will be carried out during testing, a plan is needed.

- Test development: Test procedures, test scenarios, test cases, test datasets, test scripts to use in testing software.

- Test execution: Testers execute the software based on the plans and test documents then report any errors found to the development team.

- Test reporting: Once testing is completed, testers generate metrics and make final reports on their test effort and whether or not the software tested is ready for release.

- Test result analysis: Or Defect Analysis, is done by the development team usually along with the client, in order to decide what defects should be assigned, fixed, rejected (i.e. found software working properly) or deferred to be dealt with later.

- Defect Retesting: Once a defect has been dealt with by the development team, it is retested by the testing team. AKA Resolution testing.

- Regression testing: It is common to have a small test program built of a subset of tests, for each integration of new, modified, or fixed software, in order to ensure that the latest delivery has not ruined anything, and that the software product as a whole is still working correctly.

- Test Closure: Once the test meets the exit criteria, the activities such as capturing the key outputs, lessons learned, results, logs, documents related to the project are archived and used as a reference for future projects.

Automated Testing

Many programming groups are relying more and more on automated testing, especially groups that use test-driven development. There are many frameworks to write tests in, and continuous integration software will run tests automatically every time code is checked into a version control system.

While automation cannot reproduce everything that a human can do (and all the ways they think of doing it), it can be very useful for regression testing. However, it does require a well-developed test suite of testing scripts in order to be truly useful.

Testing Tools

Program testing and fault detection can be aided significantly by testing tools and debuggers. Testing/debug tools include features such as:

- Program monitors, permitting full or partial monitoring of program code including:

  o Instruction set simulator, permitting complete instruction level monitoring and trace facilities

  o Hypervisor, permitting complete control of the execution of program code including:-

  o Program animation, permitting step-by-step execution and conditional breakpoint at source level or in machine code

  o Code coverage reports

- Formatted dump or symbolic debugging, tools allowing inspection of program variables on error or at chosen points

- Automated functional GUI testing tools are used to repeat system-level tests through the GUI

- Benchmarks, allowing run-time performance comparisons to be made

- Performance analysis (or profiling tools) that can help to highlight hot spots and resource usage

Some of these features may be incorporated into a single composite tool or an Integrated Development Environment (IDE).

Measurement in Software Testing

Usually, quality is constrained to such topics as correctness, completeness, security, but can also include more technical requirements as described under the ISO standard ISO/IEC 9126, such as capability, reliability, efficiency, portability, maintainability, compatibility, and usability.

There are a number of frequently used software metrics, or measures, which are used to assist in determining the state of the software or the adequacy of the testing.

Hierarchy of Testing Difficulty

Based on the amount of test cases required to construct a complete test suite in each context (i.e. a test suite such that, if it is applied to the implementation under test, then we collect enough information to precisely determine whether the system is correct or incorrect according to some specification), a hierarchy of testing difficulty has been proposed. It includes the following testability classes:

- Class I: there exists a finite complete test suite.

- Class II: any partial distinguishing rate (i.e., any incomplete capability to distinguish correct systems from incorrect systems) can be reached with a finite test suite.

- Class III: there exists a countable complete test suite.

- Class IV: there exists a complete test suite.

- Class V: all cases.

It has been proved that each class is strictly included into the next. For instance, testing when we assume that the behavior of the implementation under test can be denoted by a deterministic finite-state machine for some known finite sets of inputs and outputs and with some known number of states belongs to Class I (and all subsequent classes). However, if the number of states is not known, then it only belongs to all classes from Class II on. If the implementation under test must be a deterministic finite-state machine failing the specification for a single trace (and its continuations), and its number of states is unknown, then it only belongs to classes from Class III on. Testing temporal machines where transitions are triggered if inputs are produced within some real-bounded interval only belongs to classes from Class IV on, whereas testing many non-deterministic systems only belongs to Class V (but not all, and some even belong to Class I). The inclusion into Class I does not require the simplicity of the assumed computation model, as some testing cases involving implementations written in any programming language, and testing implementations defined as machines depending on continuous magnitudes, have been proved to be in Class I. Other elaborated cases, such as the testing framework by Matthew Hennessy under must semantics, and temporal machines with rational timeouts, belong to Class II.

Testing Artifacts

The software testing process can produce several artifacts.

Test plan

> A test plan is a document detailing the objectives, target market, internal beta team, and processes for a specific beta test. The developers are well aware what test plans will be executed and this information is made available to management and the developers. The idea is to make them more cautious when developing their code or making additional changes. Some companies have a higher-level document called a test strategy.

Traceability matrix

> A traceability matrix is a table that correlates requirements or design documents to test documents. It is used to change tests when related source documents are changed, to select test cases for execution when planning for regression tests by considering requirement coverage.

Test case

> A test case normally consists of a unique identifier, requirement references from a design specification, preconditions, events, a series of steps (also known as actions) to follow, input, output, expected result, and actual result. Clinically defined, a test case is an input and an expected result. This can be as terse as 'for condition x your derived result is y', although normally test cases describe in more detail the input scenario and what results might be expected. It can occasionally be a series of steps (but often steps are contained in a separate test procedure that can be exercised against multiple test cases, as a matter of economy) but with one expected result or expected outcome. The optional fields are a test case ID, test step, or order of execution number, related requirement(s), depth, test category, author, and check boxes for whether the test is automatable and has been automated. Larger test cases may also contain prerequisite states or steps, and descriptions. A test case should also contain a place for the actual result. These steps can be stored in a word processor document, spreadsheet, database, or other common repository. In a database system, you may also be able to see past test results, who generated the results, and what system configuration was used to generate those results. These past results would usually be stored in a separate table.

Test script

> A test script is a procedure, or programing code that replicates user actions. Initially the

term was derived from the product of work created by automated regression test tools. Test case will be a baseline to create test scripts using a tool or a program.

Test suite

The most common term for a collection of test cases is a test suite. The test suite often also contains more detailed instructions or goals for each collection of test cases. It definitely contains a section where the tester identifies the system configuration used during testing. A group of test cases may also contain prerequisite states or steps, and descriptions of the following tests.

Test fixture or test data

In most cases, multiple sets of values or data are used to test the same functionality of a particular feature. All the test values and changeable environmental components are collected in separate files and stored as test data. It is also useful to provide this data to the client and with the product or a project.

Test harness

The software, tools, samples of data input and output, and configurations are all referred to collectively as a test harness.

Certifications

Several certification programs exist to support the professional aspirations of software testers and quality assurance specialists. No certification now offered actually requires the applicant to show their ability to test software. No certification is based on a widely accepted body of knowledge. This has led some to declare that the testing field is not ready for certification. Certification itself cannot measure an individual's productivity, their skill, or practical knowledge, and cannot guarantee their competence, or professionalism as a tester.

Software testing certification types

Exam-based: Formalized exams, which need to be passed; can also be learned by self-study [e.g., for ISTQB or QAI]

Education-based: Instructor-led sessions, where each course has to be passed [e.g., International Institute for Software Testing (IIST)]

Testing certifications

ISEB offered by the Information Systems Examinations Board

ISTQB Certified Tester, Foundation Level (CTFL) offered by the International Software Testing Qualification Board

ISTQB Certified Tester, Advanced Level (CTAL) offered by the International Software Testing Qualification Board iSQI Certified Agile Tester (CAT) offered by the International Software Quality Institute

Quality assurance certifications

CSQE offered by the American Society for Quality (ASQ)

CQIA offered by the American Society for Quality (ASQ)

Controversy

Some of the major software testing controversies include:

What constitutes responsible software testing?

Members of the "context-driven" school of testing believe that there are no "best practices" of testing, but rather that testing is a set of skills that allow the tester to select or invent testing practices to suit each unique situation.

Agile vs. traditional

Should testers learn to work under conditions of uncertainty and constant change or should they aim at process "maturity"? The agile testing movement has received growing popularity since 2006 mainly in commercial circles, whereas government and military software providers use this methodology but also the traditional test-last models (e.g., in the Waterfall model).

Exploratory test vs. scripted

Should tests be designed at the same time as they are executed or should they be designed beforehand?

Manual testing vs. automated

Some writers believe that test automation is so expensive relative to its value that it should be used sparingly. More in particular, test-driven development states that developers should write unit-tests, as those of XUnit, before coding the functionality. The tests then can be considered as a way to capture and implement the requirements. As a general rule, the larger the system and the greater the complexity, the greater the ROI in test automation. Also, the investment in tools and expertise can be amortized over multiple projects with the right level of knowledge sharing within an organization.

Software design vs. software implementation

Should testing be carried out only at the end or throughout the whole process?

Who watches the watchmen?

The idea is that any form of observation is also an interaction — the act of testing can also affect that which is being tested.

Is the existence of the ISO 29119 software testing standard justified?

Significant opposition has formed out of the ranks of the context-driven school of software testing about the ISO 29119 standard. Professional testing associations, such as The International Society for Software Testing, are driving the efforts to have the standard withdrawn.

Related Processes

Software Verification and Validation

Software testing is used in association with verification and validation:

- Verification: Have we built the software right? (i.e., does it implement the requirements).

- Validation: Have we built the right software? (i.e., do the deliverables satisfy the customer).

The terms verification and validation are commonly used interchangeably in the industry; it is also common to see these two terms incorrectly defined. According to the IEEE Standard Glossary of Software Engineering Terminology:

> Verification is the process of evaluating a system or component to determine whether the products of a given development phase satisfy the conditions imposed at the start of that phase.

> Validation is the process of evaluating a system or component during or at the end of the development process to determine whether it satisfies specified requirements.

According to the ISO 9000 standard:

> Verification is confirmation by examination and through provision of objective evidence that specified requirements have been fulfilled.

> Validation is confirmation by examination and through provision of objective evidence that the requirements for a specific intended use or application have been fulfilled.

Software Quality Assurance (SQA)

Software testing is a part of the software quality assurance (SQA) process. In SQA, software process specialists and auditors are concerned for the software development process rather than just the artifacts such as documentation, code and systems. They examine and change the software engineering process itself to reduce the number of faults that end up in the delivered software: the so-called "defect rate". What constitutes an "acceptable defect rate" depends on the nature of the software; A flight simulator video game would have much higher defect tolerance than software for an actual airplane. Although there are close links with SQA, testing departments often exist independently, and there may be no SQA function in some companies.

Software testing is a task intended to detect defects in software by contrasting a computer program's expected results with its actual results for a given set of inputs. By contrast, QA (quality assurance) is the implementation of policies and procedures intended to prevent defects from occurring in the first place.

Software Maintenance

Software maintenance in software engineering is the modification of a software product after delivery to correct faults, to improve performance or other attributes.

A common perception of maintenance is that it merely involves fixing defects. However, one study indicated that over 80% of maintenance effort is used for non-corrective actions. This perception is perpetuated by users submitting problem reports that in reality are functionality enhancements to the system. More recent studies put the bug-fixing proportion closer to 21%.

History

Software maintenance and evolution of systems was first addressed by Meir M. Lehman in 1969. Over a period of twenty years, his research led to the formulation of Lehman's Laws (Lehman 1997). Key findings of his research include that maintenance is really evolutionary development and that maintenance decisions are aided by understanding what happens to systems (and software) over time. Lehman demonstrated that systems continue to evolve over time. As they evolve, they grow more complex unless some action such as code refactoring is taken to reduce the complexity.

In the late 1970s, a famous and widely cited survey study by Lientz and Swanson, exposed the very high fraction of life-cycle costs that were being expended on maintenance. They categorized maintenance activities into four classes:

- Adaptive – modifying the system to cope with changes in the software environment (DBMS, OS)

- Perfective – implementing new or changed user requirements which concern functional enhancements to the software

- Corrective – diagnosing and fixing errors, possibly ones found by users

- Preventive – increasing software maintainability or reliability to prevent problems in the future

The survey showed that around 75% of the maintenance effort was on the first two types, and error correction consumed about 21%. Many subsequent studies suggest a similar magnitude of the problem. Studies show that contribution of end user is crucial during the new requirement data gathering and analysis. And this is the main cause of any problem during software evolution and maintenance. So software maintenance is important because it consumes a large part of the overall lifecycle costs and also the inability to change software quickly and reliably means that business opportunities are lost.

Importance of Software Maintenance

The key software maintenance issues are both managerial and technical. Key management issues are: alignment with customer priorities, staffing, which organization does maintenance, estimating costs. Key technical issues are: limited understanding, impact analysis, testing, maintainability measurement.

Software maintenance is a very broad activity that includes error correction, enhancements of capabilities, deletion of obsolete capabilities, and optimization. Because change is inevitable, mechanisms must be developed for evaluation, controlling and making modifications.

So any work done to change the software after it is in operation is considered to be maintenance work. The purpose is to preserve the value of software over the time. The value can be enhanced by expanding the customer base, meeting additional requirements, becoming easier to use, more efficient and employing newer technology. Maintenance may span for 20 years, whereas development may be 1-2 years.

Software Maintenance Planning

An integral part of software is the maintenance one, which requires an accurate maintenance plan to be prepared during the software development. It should specify how users will request modifications or report problems. The budget should include resource and cost estimates. A new decision should be addressed for the developing of every new system feature and its quality objectives. The software maintenance, which can last for 5–6 years (or even decades) after the development process, calls for an effective plan which can address the scope of software maintenance, the tailoring of the post delivery/deployment process, the designation of who will provide maintenance, and an estimate of the life-cycle costs. The selection of proper enforcement of standards is the challenging task right from early stage of software engineering which has not got definite importance by the concerned stakeholders.

Software Maintenance Processes

This section describes the six software maintenance processes as:

1. The implementation process contains software preparation and transition activities, such as the conception and creation of the maintenance plan; the preparation for handling problems identified during development; and the follow-up on product configuration management.

2. The problem and modification analysis process, which is executed once the application has become the responsibility of the maintenance group. The maintenance programmer must analyze each request, confirm it (by reproducing the situation) and check its validity, investigate it and propose a solution, document the request and the solution proposal, and finally, obtain all the required authorizations to apply the modifications.

3. The process considering the implementation of the modification itself.

4. The process acceptance of the modification, by confirming the modified work with the individual who submitted the request in order to make sure the modification provided a solution.

5. The migration process (platform migration, for example) is exceptional, and is not part of daily maintenance tasks. If the software must be ported to another platform without any change in functionality, this process will be used and a maintenance project team is likely to be assigned to this task.

6. Finally, the last maintenance process, also an event which does not occur on a daily basis, is the retirement of a piece of software.

There are a number of processes, activities and practices that are unique to maintainers, for example:

- Transition: a controlled and coordinated sequence of activities during which a system is transferred progressively from the developer to the maintainer;

- Service Level Agreements (SLAs) and specialized (domain-specific) maintenance contracts negotiated by maintainers;

- Modification Request and Problem Report Help Desk: a problem-handling process used by maintainers to prioritize, documents and route the requests they receive;

Categories of Maintenance in ISO/IEC 14764

E.B. Swanson initially identified three categories of maintenance: corrective, adaptive, and perfective. These have since been updated and ISO/IEC 14764 presents:

- Corrective maintenance: Reactive modification of a software product performed after delivery to correct discovered problems.

- Adaptive maintenance: Modification of a software product performed after delivery to keep a software product usable in a changed or changing environment.

- Perfective maintenance: Modification of a software product after delivery to improve performance or maintainability.

- Preventive maintenance: Modification of a software product after delivery to detect and correct latent faults in the software product before they become effective faults.

There is also a notion of pre-delivery/pre-release maintenance which is all the good things you do to lower the total cost of ownership of the software. Things like compliance with coding standards that includes software maintainability goals. The management of coupling and cohesion of the software. The attainment of software supportability goals (SAE JA1004, JA1005 and JA1006 for example). Note also that some academic institutions[who?] are carrying out research to quantify the cost to ongoing software maintenance due to the lack of resources such as design documents and system/software comprehension training and resources (multiply costs by approx. 1.5-2.0 where there is no design data available).

Maintenance Factors

Impact of key adjustment factors on maintenance (sorted in order of maximum positive impact)

Maintenance Factors	Plus Range
Maintenance specialists	35%
High staff experience	34%
Table-driven variables and data	33%
Low complexity of base code	32%

Y2K and special search engines	30%
Code restructuring tools	29%
Re-engineering tools	27%
High level programming languages	25%
Reverse engineering tools	23%
Complexity analysis tools	20%
Defect tracking tools	20%
Y2K "mass update" specialists	20%
Automated change control tools	18%
Unpaid overtime	18%
Quality measurements	16%
Formal base code inspections	15%
Regression test libraries	15%
Excellent response time	12%
Annual training of > 10 days	12%
High management experience	12%
HELP desk automation	12%
No error prone modules	10%
On-line defect reporting	10%
Productivity measurements	8%
Excellent ease of use	7%
User satisfaction measurements	5%
High team morale	5%
Sum	**503%**

Not only are error-prone modules troublesome, but many other factors can degrade performance too. For example, very complex "spaghetti code" is quite difficult to maintain safely. A very common situation which often degrades performance is lack of suitable maintenance tools, such as defect tracking software, change management software, and test library software. Below describe some of the factors and the range of impact on software maintenance.

Impact of key adjustment factors on maintenance (sorted in order of maximum negative impact)

Maintenance Factors	**Minus Range**
Error prone modules	-50%
Embedded variables and data	-45%
Staff inexperience	-40%
High code complexity	-30%
No Y2K of special search engines	-28%
Manual change control methods	-27%
Low level programming languages	-25%
No defect tracking tools	-24%
No Y2K "mass update" specialists	-22%
Poor ease of use	-18%

No quality measurements	-18%
No maintenance specialists	-18%
Poor response time	-16%
No code inspections	-15%
No regression test libraries	-15%
No help desk automation	-15%
No on-line defect reporting	-12%
Management inexperience	-15%
No code restructuring tools	-10%
No annual training	-10%
No reengineering tools	-10%
No reverse-engineering tools	-10%
No complexity analysis tools	-10%
No productivity measurements	-7%
Poor team morale	-6%
No user satisfaction measurements	-4%
No unpaid overtime	0%
Sum	**-500%**

Software Configuration Management

In software engineering, software configuration management (SCM or S/W CM) is the task of tracking and controlling changes in the software, part of the larger cross-disciplinary field of configuration management. SCM practices include revision control and the establishment of baselines. If something goes wrong, SCM can determine what was changed and who changed it. If a configuration is working well, SCM can determine how to replicate it across many hosts.

The acronym "SCM" is also expanded as source configuration management process and software change and configuration management. However, "configuration" is generally understood to cover changes typically made by a system administrator.

Purposes

The goals of SCM are generally:

- Configuration identification - Identifying configurations, configuration items and baselines.

- Configuration control - Implementing a controlled change process. This is usually achieved by setting up a change control board whose primary function is to approve or reject all change requests that are sent against any baseline.

- Configuration status accounting - Recording and reporting all the necessary information on the status of the development process.

- Configuration auditing - Ensuring that configurations contain all their intended parts and are sound with respect to their specifying documents, including requirements, architectural specifications and user manuals.

- Build management - Managing the process and tools used for builds.

- Process management - Ensuring adherence to the organization's development process.

- Environment management - Managing the software and hardware that host the system.

- Teamwork - Facilitate team interactions related to the process.

- Defect tracking - Making sure every defect has traceability back to the source.

With the introduction of cloud computing the purposes of SCM tools have become merged in some cases. The SCM tools themselves have become virtual appliances that can be instantiated as virtual machines and saved with state and version. The tools can model and manage cloud-based virtual resources, including virtual appliances, storage units, and software bundles. The roles and responsibilities of the actors have become merged as well with developers now being able to dynamically instantiate virtual servers and related resources.

History

The history of software configuration management (SCM) in computing can be traced back as early as the 1950s, when CM (for Configuration Management), originally for hardware development and production control, was being applied to software development. Early software had a physical footprint, such as cards, tapes, and other media. The first software configuration management was a manual operation. With the advances in language and complexity, software engineering, involving configuration management and other methods, became a major concern due to issues like schedule, budget, and quality. Practical lessons, over the years, had led to the definition, and establishment, of procedures and tools. Eventually, the tools became systems to manage software changes. Industry-wide practices were offered as solutions, either in an open or proprietary manner (such as Revision Control System). With the growing use of computers, systems emerged that handled a broader scope, including requirements management, design alternatives, quality control, and more; later tools followed the guidelines of organizations, such as the Capability Maturity Model of the Software Engineering Institute.

Engineering Management

Engineering management is a specialized form of management that is concerned with the application of engineering principles to business practice. Engineering management is a career that brings together the technological problem-solving savvy of engineering and the organizational, administrative, and planning abilities of management in order to oversee complex enterprises from conception to completion. A Master of Science in Engineering Management (MSEM, or MS in Engineering Management) is sometimes compared to a Master of Business Administration (MBA) for professionals seeking a graduate degree as a qualifying credential for a career in engineering management.

Ron Diftler (left), NASA Robonaut manager assisting in a Robonaut familiarization training session in the Space Environment Simulation Laboratory at NASA's Johnson Space Center.

Engineering management is considered to be a subdiscipline of industrial engineering/systems engineering. Successful engineering managers typically require training and experience in business and engineering. Technically inept managers tend to be deprived of support by their technical team, and non-commercial managers tend to lack commercial acumen to deliver in a market economy. Largely, engineering managers manage engineers who are driven by non-entrepreneurial thinking, and thus require the necessary people skills to coach, mentor and motivate technical professionals. Engineering professionals joining manufacturing companies sometimes become engineering managers by default after a period of time. They are required to learn how to manage once they are on the job, though this is usually an ineffective way to develop managerial abilities.

History

Stevens Institute of Technology is believed to have the oldest Engineering management department, established as the School of Business Engineering in 1908. This was later called the Bachelor of Engineering in Engineering Management (BEEM) program and moved into the School of Systems and Enterprises. Drexel University established the first graduate engineering management degree in the U.S., which was first offered in 1959. In 1967 the first university department titled "Engineering Management" was founded at the Missouri University of Science and Technology (Missouri S&T, formerly the University of Missouri-Rolla, formerly Missouri School of Mines).

Outside the USA, in Germany the first department concentrating on Engineering Management was established 1927 in Berlin. In Turkey the Istanbul Technical University has a Management Engineering Department established in 1982, offering a number of graduate and undergraduate programs in Management Engineering. In UK the University of Warwick has a specialised department WMG (previously known as Warwick Manufacturing Group) established in 1980, which offers a graduate programme in MSc Engineering Business Management .

More recently in the United Kingdom, Teesside University's School of Science and Engineering introduced an MSc Engineering Management alongside its engineering-focused MSc Project Management.

Michigan Technological University began an Engineering Management program in the School of Business & Economics in the Fall of 2012.

In Canada, Memorial University of Newfoundland has started a complete master's degree Program in Engineering Management Master of Engineering Management.

In Denmark, the Technical University of Denmark offers a MSc program in Engineering Management (in English). MSc in Engineering Management.

In Pakistan, NED University of Engineering & Technology, Karachi has been running a Master of Engineering in Engineering Management program since 2005. A variant of this program is within Quality Management. COMSATS (CIIT) offers a MSc Project Management program to Local and Overseas Pakistanis as an on-campus/off-campus student.

Areas

Operations Research and Supply Chain Management

Operations research deals with quantitative models of complex operations and uses these models to support decision-making in any sector of industry or public services. Supply chain management is the process of planning, implementing and managing the flow of goods, services and related information from the point of origin to the point of consumption.

Information Technologies

The "information technologies" theme focuses on how technology is designed and managed to support effective decision-making. Topics deal with technical applications in software design and development, data mining and telecommunication as well as the organizational and social issues associated with the use of information technologies.

Decision Engineering

Decision engineering seeks to use engineering principles in the creation of a decision, which it views as an engineering artifact in its own right. From this point of view, the creation of a decision includes agreeing to objectives, developing a detailed specification, and then creating a decision model, which captures the key cause-and-effect elements of the decision environment (a systems thinking approach) with a focus on the particular decision, instead of the entire system (which can be otherwise intractable). Like other engineered artifacts, a decision model can be subject to Quality assurance review, and-since it is documented-is amenable to Process improvement over time. Decision engineering models draw from the information technologies described above for data supporting the decision, but are distinguished from IT in that they model the decision, not just the data supporting it.

Management of Technology

The Management of Technology (MOT) theme builds on the foundation of management topics in accounting, finance, economics, organizational behavior and organizational design. Courses in this theme deal with operational and organizational issues related to managing innovation and technological change.

Education

Engineering Management programs typically include instruction in accounting, economics, finance, project management, systems engineering, mathematical modeling and optimization, management information systems, quality control & six sigma, operations research, human resources management, industrial psychology, safety and health.

There are many options for entering into engineering management, albeit that the foundation requirement is an engineering degree (or other computer science, mathematics or science degree) and a business degree.

Undergraduate Degrees

Although most engineering management programs are geared for graduate studies, there are a few elite institutions that teach EM at the undergraduate level. Some of the ones that are accredited and/or recognized by ASEM include: West Point (United States Military Academy), Norwich University, New York Institute of Technology, Stevens Institute of Technology, Illinois Institute of Technology, Rensselaer Polytechnic Institute, George Washington University, Arizona State University, Missouri University of Science and Technology. Graduates of these programs regularly command nearly $65,000 their first year out of school.

Outside the USA, Istanbul Technical University Management Engineering Department offers an elite undergraduate degree in Management Engineering, attracting top students. The University of Waterloo offers a 4-year undergraduate degree (5 years including co-op education) in the field of Management Engineering. This is the first program of its kind in Canada. In Peru, Pacifico University offers a 5-year undergraduate degree in this field, the first program in this country.

Graduate Degrees

Many universities offer Master of Engineering Management degrees. Missouri S&T is credited with awarding the first Ph.D. in Engineering Management in 1984. The National Institute of Industrial Engineering based in Mumbai has been awarding degrees in the field of Post Graduate Diploma in Industrial Engineering since 1973 and the Fellowship (Doctoral) degrees have been awarded since 2008. Massachusetts Institute of Technology offers a Master in System Design and Management, which is a member of the Consortium of Engineering Management.

Students in the University of Kansas' Engineering Management Program are practicing professionals employed by over 100 businesses, manufacturing, government or consulting firms. There are over 200 actively enrolled students in the program and approximately 500 alumni.

Istanbul Technical University Management Engineering Department offers a graduate degree, and a Ph.D. degree in Management Engineering.

According to the American Society for Engineering Education (ASEE) PRISM Magazine (March 2008) the largest Master's of Engineering Management (MEM) programs (in terms of degrees awarded for 2005 -2006) are shown in the following chart.

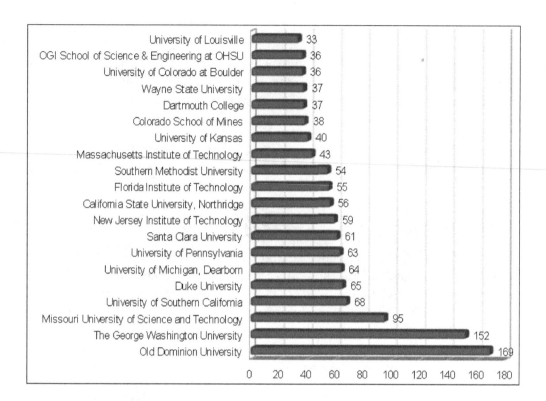

Engineering Management Consulting

As engineering firms are usually small partnerships, they cannot afford in-house management, therefore giving rise to the need for engineering management consultancy. It involves providing management consulting advice that is specific to engineering. Indifferent from the traditional focus of the, A T Kearney, Boston Consulting Group and McKinsey, science and engineering requires a particularly holistic approach involving art and science. There are many branches of engineering management consultancy (commerce), including law, accounting, human resources, marketing, politics, economics, finance, public affairs, and communication. Commonly, engineering management consultants are also used when firms require special technical knowledge, though many prefer to use engineering educational consultants for such a task, to upgrade organizational knowledge and in able to keep the intellectual property confidential. Though many firms opt to use traditional management consulting firms, many lack the know-how to tailor the traditional theories to accommodate professional engineers and other technical workers.

Engineering management consulting is concerned with the development, improvement, implementation and evaluation of integrated systems of people, money, knowledge, information, equipment, energy, materials and/or processes. Consultants strive to improve upon existing processes, products or systems. Engineering management consulting draws upon the principles and methods of engineering analysis and synthesis, as well as the mathematical, physical and social sciences together with the principles and methods of engineering design to specify, predict, and evaluate the results to be obtained from such systems or processes. Engineering management consulting puts a focus on the social impact of the product, process or system that is being analyzed.

Examples of where engineering management consulting might be used include designing new product development process, or an assembly workstation, strategizing for various operational logistics, consulting as an efficiency expert, developing a new financial algorithm or loan system for a bank, streamlining operation and emergency room location or usage in a hospital, planning complex distribution schemes for materials or products (referred to as Supply Chain Management), and shortening lines (or queues) at a bank, hospital, or a theme park. Management engineering consultants typically use computer simulation (especially discrete event simulation), along with extensive mathematical tools and modeling and computational methods for system analysis, evaluation, and optimization.

Professional Organizations

There are a number of societies and organizations dedicated to the field of engineering management. One of the largest societies is a division of IEEE, the Engineering Management Society, which regularly publishes a trade magazine. Another prominent professional organization in the field is the American Society for Engineering Management (ASEM), which was founded in 1979 by a group of 20 engineering managers from industry. ASEM currently certifies engineering managers (two levels) via the Associate Engineering Manager (AEM) or Professional Engineering Manager (PEM) certification exam. The Master of Engineering Management Programs Consortium is a newly formed consortium of prominent universities intended to raise the value and visibility of the MEM degree. Also, engineering management university programs have the possibility of being accredited by ABET, ATMAE, or ASEM. In Canada, the Canadian Society for Engineering Management (CSEM) is a constituent society of the Engineering Institute of Canada (EIC), Canada's oldest learned engineering society.

Software Development Process

In software engineering, a software development methodology (also known as a system development methodology, software development life cycle, software development process, software process) is a splitting of software development work into distinct phases (or stages) containing activities with the intent of better planning and management. It is often considered a subset of the systems development life cycle. The methodology may include the pre-definition of specific deliverables and artifacts that are created and completed by a project team to develop or maintain an application.

Common methodologies include waterfall, prototyping, iterative and incremental development, spiral development, rapid application development, extreme programming and various types of agile methodology. Some people consider a life-cycle "model" a more general term for a category of methodologies and a software development "process" a more specific term to refer to a specific process chosen by a specific organization. For example, there are many specific software development processes that fit the spiral life-cycle model.

In Practice

A variety of such frameworks have evolved over the years, each with its own recognized strengths and weaknesses. One software development methodology framework is not necessarily suitable for use by all projects. Each of the available methodology frameworks are best suited to specific kinds of projects, based on various technical, organizational, project and team considerations.

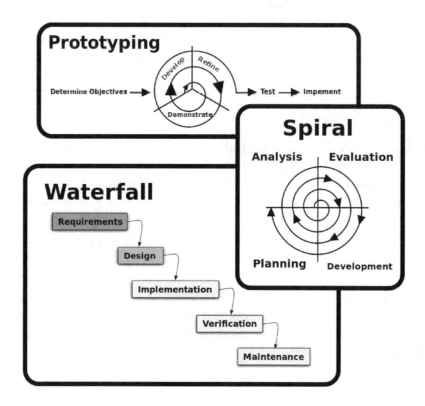

The three basic approaches applied to software development methodology frameworks.

Software development organizations implement process methodologies to ease the process of development. Sometimes, contractors may require methodologies employed, an example is the U.S. defense industry, which requires a rating based on process models to obtain contracts. The international standard for describing the method of selecting, implementing and monitoring the life cycle for software is ISO/IEC 12207.

A decades-long goal has been to find repeatable, predictable processes that improve productivity and quality. Some try to systematize or formalize the seemingly unruly task of designing software. Others apply project management techniques to designing software. Large numbers of software projects do not meet their expectations in terms of functionality, cost, or delivery schedule.

Organizations may create a Software Engineering Process Group (SEPG), which is the focal point for process improvement. Composed of line practitioners who have varied skills, the group is at the center of the collaborative effort of everyone in the organization who is involved with software engineering process improvement.

A particular development team may also agree to programming environment details, such as which integrated development environment is used, and one or more dominant programming paradigms, programming style rules, or choice of specific software libraries or software frameworks. These details are generally not dictated by the choice of model or general methodology.

History

The software development methodology (also known as SDM) framework didn't emerge until the 1960s. According to Elliott (2004) the systems development life cycle (SDLC) can be considered to be the oldest formalized methodology framework for building information systems. The main idea of the SDLC has been "to pursue the development of information systems in a very deliberate, structured and methodical way, requiring each stage of the life cycle––from inception of the idea to delivery of the final system––to be carried out rigidly and sequentially" within the context of the framework being applied. The main target of this methodology framework in the 1960s was "to develop large scale functional business systems in an age of large scale business conglomerates. Information systems activities revolved around heavy data processing and number crunching routines".

Methodologies, processes, and frameworks range from specific proscriptive steps that can be used directly by an organization in day-to-day work, to flexible frameworks that an organization uses to generate a custom set of steps tailored to the needs of a specific project or group. In some cases a "sponsor" or "maintenance" organization distributes an official set of documents that describe the process. Specific examples include:

1970s

- Structured programming since 1969

- Cap Gemini SDM, originally from PANDATA, the first English translation was published in 1974. SDM stands for System Development Methodology

1980s

- Structured systems analysis and design method (SSADM) from 1980 onwards

- Information Requirement Analysis/Soft systems methodology

1990s

- Object-oriented programming (OOP) developed in the early 1960s, and became a dominant programming approach during the mid-1990s
- Rapid application development (RAD), since 1991
- Dynamic systems development method (DSDM), since 1994
- Scrum, since 1995
- Team software process, since 1998
- Rational Unified Process (RUP), maintained by IBM since 1998
- Extreme programming, since 1999

2000s

- Agile Unified Process (AUP) maintained since 2005 by Scott Ambler

- Disciplined agile delivery (DAD) Supersedes AUP

It is notable that since DSDM in 1994, 22 years ago, all of the methodologies on the above list except RUP have been agile methodologies - yet many organisations, especially governments, still struggle on with pre-agile processes (often waterfall or similar).

Approaches

Several software development approaches have been used since the origin of information technology, in two main categories. Typically an approach or a combination of approaches is chosen by management or a development team.

"Traditional" methodologies such as waterfall that have distinct phases are sometimes known as software development life cycle (SDLC) methodologies, though this term could also be used more generally to refer to any methodology. A "life cycle" approach with distinct phases is in contrast to Agile approaches which define a process of iteration, but where design, construction, and deployment of different pieces can occur simultaneously.

Waterfall Development

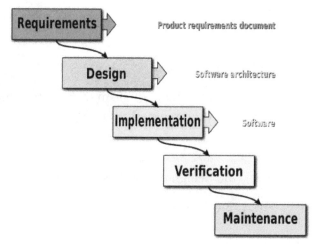

The activities of the software development process represented in the waterfall model. There are several other models to represent this process.

The waterfall model is a sequential development approach, in which development is seen as flowing steadily downwards (like a waterfall) through several phases, typically:

- Requirements analysis resulting in a software requirements specification

- Software design

- Implementation

- Testing

- Integration, if there are multiple subsystems

- Deployment (or Installation)

- Maintenance

The first formal description of the method is often cited as an article published by Winston W. Royce in 1970 although Royce did not use the term "waterfall" in this article. The basic principles are:

- Project is divided into sequential phases, with some overlap and splashback acceptable between phases.

- Emphasis is on planning, time schedules, target dates, budgets and implementation of an entire system at one time.

- Tight control is maintained over the life of the project via extensive written documentation, formal reviews, and approval/signoff by the user and information technology management occurring at the end of most phases before beginning the next phase. Written documentation is an explicit deliverable of each phase.

The waterfall model is a traditional engineering approach applied to software engineering. A strict waterfall approach discourages revisiting and revising any prior phase once it is complete. This "inflexibility" in a pure waterfall model has been a source of criticism by supporters of other more "flexible" models. It has been widely blamed for several large-scale government projects running over budget, over time and sometimes failing to deliver on requirements due to the Big Design Up Front approach. Except when contractually required, the waterfall model has been largely superseded by more flexible and versatile methodologies developed specifically for software development.

The waterfall model is sometimes taught with the mnemonic A Dance In The Dark Every Monday, representing Analysis, Design, Implementation, Testing, Documentation and Execution, and Maintenance.

Prototyping

Software prototyping is about creating prototypes, i.e., incomplete versions of the software program being developed.

The basic principles are:

- Prototyping is not a standalone, complete development methodology, but rather an approach to try out particular features in the context of a full methodology (such as incremental, spiral, or rapid application development (RAD)).

- Attempts to reduce inherent project risk by breaking a project into smaller segments and providing more ease-of-change during the development process.

- The user is involved throughout the development process, which increases the likelihood of user acceptance of the final implementation.

- While some prototypes are developed with the expectation that they will be discarded, it is possible in some cases to evolve from prototype to working system.

A basic understanding of the fundamental business problem is necessary to avoid solving the wrong problems, but this is true for all software methodologies.

Incremental Development

Various methods are acceptable for combining linear and iterative systems development methodologies, with the primary objective of each being to reduce inherent project risk by breaking a project into smaller segments and providing more ease-of-change during the development process.

There are three main variants of incremental development:

1. A series of mini-Waterfalls are performed, where all phases of the Waterfall are completed for a small part of a system, before proceeding to the next increment, or

2. Overall requirements are defined before proceeding to evolutionary, mini-Waterfall development of individual increments of a system, or

3. The initial software concept, requirements analysis, and design of architecture and system core are defined via Waterfall, followed by incremental implementation, which culminates in installing the final version, a working system.

Iterative and Incremental Development

Iterative development prescribes the construction of initially small but ever-larger portions of a software project to help all those involved to uncover important issues early before problems or faulty assumptions can lead to disaster.

Spiral Development

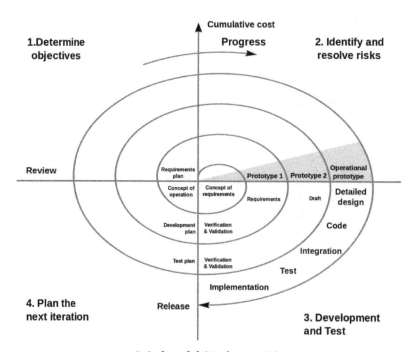

Spiral model (Boehm, 1988)

In 1988, Barry Boehm published a formal software system development "spiral model," which combines some key aspect of the waterfall model and rapid prototyping methodologies, in an effort to combine advantages of top-down and bottom-up concepts. It provided emphasis in a key area many felt had been neglected by other methodologies: deliberate iterative risk analysis, particularly suited to large-scale complex systems.

The basic principles are:

- Focus is on risk assessment and on minimizing project risk by breaking a project into smaller segments and providing more ease-of-change during the development process, as well as providing the opportunity to evaluate risks and weigh consideration of project continuation throughout the life cycle.

- "Each cycle involves a progression through the same sequence of steps, for each part of the product and for each of its levels of elaboration, from an overall concept-of-operation document down to the coding of each individual program."

- Each trip around the spiral traverses four basic quadrants: (1) determine objectives, alternatives, and constraints of the iteration; (2) evaluate alternatives; Identify and resolve risks; (3) develop and verify deliverables from the iteration; and (4) plan the next iteration.

- Begin each cycle with an identification of stakeholders and their "win conditions", and end each cycle with review and commitment.

Rapid Application Development

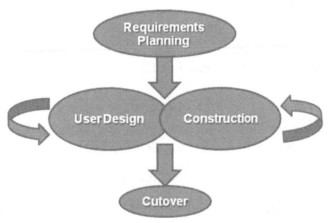

Rapid Application Development (RAD) Model

Rapid application development (RAD) is a software development methodology, which favors iterative development and the rapid construction of prototypes instead of large amounts of up-front planning. The "planning" of software developed using RAD is interleaved with writing the software itself. The lack of extensive pre-planning generally allows software to be written much faster, and makes it easier to change requirements.

The rapid development process starts with the development of preliminary data models and business process models using structured techniques. In the next stage, requirements are verified using prototyping, eventually to refine the data and process models. These stages are repeated iteratively; further development results in "a combined business requirements and technical design statement to be used for constructing new systems".

The term was first used to describe a software development process introduced by James Martin in 1991. According to Whitten (2003), it is a merger of various structured techniques, especially data-driven Information Engineering, with prototyping techniques to accelerate software systems development.

The basic principles of rapid application development are:

- Key objective is for fast development and delivery of a high quality system at a relatively low investment cost.

- Attempts to reduce inherent project risk by breaking a project into smaller segments and providing more ease-of-change during the development process.

- Aims to produce high quality systems quickly, primarily via iterative Prototyping (at any stage of development), active user involvement, and computerized development tools. These tools may include Graphical User Interface (GUI) builders, Computer Aided Software Engineering (CASE) tools, Database Management Systems (DBMS), fourth-generation programming languages, code generators, and object-oriented techniques.

- Key emphasis is on fulfilling the business need, while technological or engineering excellence is of lesser importance.

- Project control involves prioritizing development and defining delivery deadlines or "timeboxes". If the project starts to slip, emphasis is on reducing requirements to fit the timebox, not in increasing the deadline.

- Generally includes joint application design (JAD), where users are intensely involved in system design, via consensus building in either structured workshops, or electronically facilitated interaction.

- Active user involvement is imperative.

- Iteratively produces production software, as opposed to a throwaway prototype.

- Produces documentation necessary to facilitate future development and maintenance.

- Standard systems analysis and design methods can be fitted into this framework.

Agile Development

"Agile software development" refers to a group of software development methodologies based on iterative development, where requirements and solutions evolve via collaboration between self-organizing cross-functional teams. The term was coined in the year 2001 when the Agile Manifesto was formulated.

Agile software development uses iterative development as a basis but advocates a lighter and more people-centric viewpoint than traditional approaches. Agile processes fundamentally incorporate iteration and the continuous feedback that it provides to successively refine and deliver a software system.

There are many agile methodologies, including:

- Dynamic systems development method (DSDM)

- Kanban

- Scrum

Lightweight Methodologies

A lightweight methodology has a small number of rules. Some of these methodologies are also considered "agile".

- Adaptive Software Development by Jim Highsmith, described in his 1999 book *Adaptive Software Development*

- Crystal Clear family of methodologies with Alistair Cockburn,

- Extreme Programming (XP), promoted by people such as Kent Beck and Martin Fowler. In extreme programming, the phases are carried out in extremely small (or "continuous") steps compared to the older, "batch" processes. The (intentionally incomplete) first pass through the steps might take a day or a week, rather than the months or years of each complete step in the Waterfall model. First, one writes automated tests, to provide concrete goals for development. Next is coding (by programmers working in pairs, a technique known as "pair programming"), which is complete when all the tests pass, and the programmers can't think of any more tests that are needed. Design and architecture emerge from refactoring, and come after coding. The same people who do the coding do design. (Only the last feature — merging design and code — is common to *all* the other agile processes.) The incomplete but functional system is deployed or demonstrated for (some subset of) the users (at least one of which is on the development team). At this point, the practitioners start again on writing tests for the next most important part of the system.

- Feature Driven Development (FDD) developed (1999) by Jeff De Luca and Peter Coad

- ICONIX - UML-based object modeling with use cases, a lightweight precursor to the Rational Unified Process

Other

Other high-level software project methodologies include:

- Chaos model - The main rule is always resolve the most important issue first.

- Incremental funding methodology - an iterative approach

- Structured systems analysis and design method - a specific version of waterfall

- Slow programming, as part of the larger Slow Movement, emphasizes careful and gradual work without (or minimal) time pressures. Slow programming aims to avoid bugs and overly quick release schedules.

- V-Model (software development) - an extension of the waterfall model

- Unified Process (UP) is an iterative software development methodology framework, based on Unified Modeling Language (UML). UP organizes the development of software into four phases, each consisting of one or more executable iterations of the software at that stage of development: inception, elaboration, construction, and guidelines. Many tools and products exist to facilitate UP implementation. One of the more popular versions of UP is the Rational Unified Process (RUP).

Code and Fix

"Code and fix" is an anti-pattern. Development is not done through a deliberate strategy or methodology. It is often the result of schedule pressure on the software development team. Without much of a design in the way, programmers immediately begin producing code. At some point, testing begins (often late in the development cycle), and the unavoidable bugs must then be fixed - or at least, the most important ones must be fixed - before the product can be shipped.

Process Meta-models

Some "process models" are abstract descriptions for evaluating, comparing, and improving the specific process adopted by an organization.

- ISO/IEC 12207 is the international standard describing the method to select, implement, and monitor the life cycle for software.

- The Capability Maturity Model Integration (CMMI) is one of the leading models and based on best practice. Independent assessments grade organizations on how well they follow their defined processes, not on the quality of those processes or the software produced. CMMI has replaced CMM.

- ISO 9000 describes standards for a formally organized process to manufacture a product and the methods of managing and monitoring progress. Although the standard was originally created for the manufacturing sector, ISO 9000 standards have been applied to software development as well. Like CMMI, certification with ISO 9000 does not guarantee the quality of the end result, only that formalized business processes have been followed.

- ISO/IEC 15504 *Information technology — Process assessment* also known as Software Process Improvement Capability Determination (SPICE), is a "framework for the assessment of software processes". This standard is aimed at setting out a clear model for process comparison. SPICE is used much like CMMI. It models processes to manage, control, guide and monitor software development. This model is then used to measure what a development organization or project team actually does during software development. This information is analyzed to identify weaknesses and drive improvement. It also identifies strengths that can be continued or integrated into common practice for that organization or team.

- Soft systems methodology - a general method for improving management processes

- Method engineering - a general method for improving information system processes

Formal Methods

Formal methods are mathematical approaches to solving software (and hardware) problems at the requirements, specification, and design levels. Formal methods are most likely to be applied to safety-critical or security-critical software and systems, such as avionics software. Software safety assurance standards, such as DO-178B, DO-178C, and Common Criteria demand formal methods at the highest levels of categorization.

For sequential software, examples of formal methods include the B-Method, the specification languages used in automated theorem proving, RAISE, and the Z notation.

In functional programming, property-based testing has allowed the mathematical specification and testing (if not exhaustive testing) of the expected behaviour of individual functions.

Research and Emerging Technologies

The Object Constraint Language (and specializations such as Java Modeling Language) has allowed object-oriented systems to be formally specified, if not necessarily formally verified.

For concurrent software and systems, Petri nets, process algebra, and finite state machines (which are based on automata theory) allow executable software specification and can be used to build up and validate application behavior.

Another approach to formal methods in software development is to write a specification in some form of logic—usually a variation of first-order logic (FOL)—and then to directly execute the logic as though it were a program. The OWL language, based on Description Logic (DL), is an example. There is also work on mapping some version of English (or another natural language) automatically to and from logic, and executing the logic directly. Examples are Attempto Controlled English, and Internet Business Logic, which do not seek to control the vocabulary or syntax. A feature of systems that support bidirectional English-logic mapping and direct execution of the logic is that they can be made to explain their results, in English, at the business or scientific level.

Software Quality

In the context of software engineering, software quality refers to two related but distinct notions that exist wherever quality is defined in a business context:

- Software functional quality reflects how well it complies with or conforms to a given design, based on functional requirements or specifications. That attribute can also be described as the fitness for purpose of a piece of software or how it compares to competitors in the marketplace as a worthwhile product;

- Software structural quality refers to how it meets non-functional requirements that support the delivery of the functional requirements, such as robustness or maintainability, the degree to which the software was produced correctly.

Structural quality is evaluated through the analysis of the software inner structure, its source code, at the unit level, the technology level and the system level, which is in effect how its architecture adheres to sound principles of software architecture outlined in a paper on the topic by OMG. In contrast, functional quality is typically enforced and measured through software testing.

Historically, the structure, classification and terminology of attributes and metrics applicable to software quality management have been derived or extracted from the ISO 9126-3 and the subsequent ISO 25000:2005 quality model, also known as SQuaRE. Based on these models, the Consortium for IT Software Quality (CISQ) has defined five major desirable structural characteristics needed for a piece of software to provide business value: Reliability, Efficiency, Security, Maintainability and (adequate) Size.

Software quality measurement quantifies to what extent a software or system rates along each of these five dimensions. An aggregated measure of software quality can be computed through a qualitative or a quantitative scoring scheme or a mix of both and then a weighting system reflecting the priorities. This view of software quality being positioned on a linear continuum is supplemented by the analysis of "critical programming errors" that under specific circumstances can lead to catastrophic outages or performance degradations that make a given system unsuitable for use regardless of rating based on aggregated measurements. Such programming errors found at the system level represent up to 90% of production issues, whilst at the unit-level, even if far more numerous, programming errors account for less than 10% of production issues. As a consequence, code quality without the context of the whole system, as W. Edwards Deming described it, has limited value.

To view, explore, analyze, and communicate software quality measurements, concepts and techniques of information visualization provide visual, interactive means useful, in particular, if several software quality measures have to be related to each other or to components of a software or system. For example, software maps represent a specialized approach that "can express and combine information about software development, software quality, and system dynamics".

Motivation

"A science is as mature as its measurement tools," (Louis Pasteur in Ebert Dumke, p. 91). Measuring software quality is motivated by at least two reasons:

- Risk Management: Software failure has caused more than inconvenience. Software errors have caused human fatalities. The causes have ranged from poorly designed user interfaces to direct programming errors. An example of a programming error that led to multiple deaths is discussed in Dr. Leveson's paper. This resulted in requirements for the development of some types of software, particularly and historically for software embedded in medical and other devices that regulate critical infrastructures: "[Engineers who write embedded software] see Java programs stalling for one third of a second to perform garbage collection and update the user interface, and they envision airplanes falling out of the sky.". In the United States, within the Federal Aviation Administration (FAA), the FAA Aircraft Certification Service provides software programs, policy, guidance and training, focus on software and Complex Electronic Hardware that has an effect on the airborne product (a "product" is an aircraft, an engine, or a propeller).

- Cost Management: As in any other fields of engineering, an application with good structural software quality costs less to maintain and is easier to understand and change in response to pressing business needs. Industry data demonstrate that poor application structural quality in core business applications (such as enterprise resource planning (ERP), customer relationship management (CRM) or large transaction processing systems in financial services) results in cost and schedule overruns and creates waste in the form of rework (up to 45% of development time in some organizations). Moreover, poor structural quality is strongly correlated with high-impact business disruptions due to corrupted data, application outages, security breaches, and performance problems.

However, the distinction between measuring and improving software quality in an embedded system (with emphasis on risk management) and software quality in business software (with emphasis on cost and maintainability management) is becoming somewhat irrelevant. Embedded systems now often include a user interface and their designers are as much concerned with issues affecting usability and user productivity as their counterparts who focus on business applications. The latter are in turn looking at ERP or CRM system as a corporate nervous system whose uptime and performance are vital to the well-being of the enterprise. This convergence is most visible in mobile computing: a user who accesses an ERP application on their smartphone is depending on the quality of software across all types of software layers.

Both types of software now use multi-layered technology stacks and complex architecture so software quality analysis and measurement have to be managed in a comprehensive and consistent manner, decoupled from the software's ultimate purpose or use. In both cases, engineers and management need to be able to make rational decisions based on measurement and fact-based analysis in adherence to the precept *"In God (we) trust. All others bring data"*. ((mis-)attributed to W. Edwards Deming and others).

Definitions

There are many different definitions of quality. For some it is the "capability of a software product to conform to requirements." (ISO/IEC 9001, commented by) while for others it can be synonymous with "customer value" (Highsmith, 2002) or even defect level.

The first definition of quality History remembers is from Shewhart in the beginning of 20th century: *There are two common aspects of quality: one of them has to do with the consideration of the quality of a thing as an objective reality independent of the existence of man. The other has to do with what we think, feel or sense as a result of the objective reality. In other words, there is a subjective side of quality.* (Shewhart)

Kitchenham, Pfleeger, and Garvin's Five Perspectives on Quality

Kitchenham and Pfleeger, further reporting the teachings of David Garvin, identify five different perspectives on quality:

- The transcendental perspective deals with the metaphysical aspect of quality. In this view of quality, it is "something toward which we strive as an ideal, but may never implement completely". It can hardly be defined, but is similar to what a federal judge once commented about obscenity: "I know it when I see it".

- The user perspective is concerned with the appropriateness of the product for a given context of use. Whereas the transcendental view is ethereal, the user view is more concrete, grounded in the product characteristics that meet user's needs.

- The manufacturing perspective represents quality as conformance to requirements. This aspect of quality is stressed by standards such as ISO 9001, which defines quality as "the degree to which a set of inherent characteristics fulfills requirements" (ISO/IEC 9001).

- The product perspective implies that quality can be appreciated by measuring the inherent characteristics of the product.

- The final perspective of quality is value-based. This perspective recognises that the different perspectives of quality may have different importance, or value, to various stakeholders.

Software Quality According to Deming

"The problem inherent in attempts to define the quality of a product, almost any product, were stated by the master Walter A. Shewhart. The difficulty in defining quality is to translate future needs of the user into measurable characteristics, so that a product can be designed and turned out to give satisfaction at a price that the user will pay. This is not easy, and as soon as one feels fairly successful in the endeavor, he finds that the needs of the consumer have changed, competitors have moved in, etc."

Software Quality According to Feigenbaum

"Quality is a customer determination, not an engineer's determination, not a marketing determination, nor a general management determination. It is based on the customer's actual experience with the product or service, measured against his or her requirements -- stated or unstated, conscious or merely sensed, technically operational or entirely subjective -- and always representing a moving target in a competitive market".

Software Quality According to Juran

"The word quality has multiple meanings. Two of these meanings dominate the use of the word: 1. Quality consists of those product features which meet the need of customers and thereby provide product satisfaction. 2. Quality consists of freedom from deficiencies. Nevertheless, in a handbook such as this it is convenient to standardize on a short definition of the word quality as "fitness for use"."

CISQ's Quality Model

Even though "quality is a perceptual, conditional and somewhat subjective attribute and may be understood differently by different people" (as noted in the article on quality in business), software structural quality characteristics have been clearly defined by the Consortium for IT Software Quality (CISQ). Under the guidance of Bill Curtis, co-author of the Capability Maturity Model framework and CISQ's first Director; and Capers Jones, CISQ's Distinguished Advisor, CISQ has defined five major desirable characteristics of a piece of software needed to provide business value. In the House of Quality model, these are "Whats" that need to be achieved:

- Reliability: An attribute of resiliency and structural solidity. Reliability measures the level of risk and the likelihood of potential application failures. It also measures the defects injected due to modifications made to the software (its "stability" as termed by ISO). The goal for checking and monitoring Reliability is to reduce and prevent application downtime, application outages and errors that directly affect users, and enhance the image of IT and its impact on a company's business performance.

- Efficiency: The source code and software architecture attributes are the elements that ensure high performance once the application is in run-time mode. Efficiency is especially important for applications in high execution speed environments such as algorithmic or transactional processing where performance and scalability are paramount. An analysis of source code efficiency and scalability provides a clear picture of the latent business risks and the harm they can cause to customer satisfaction due to response-time degradation.

- Security: A measure of the likelihood of potential security breaches due to poor coding practices and architecture. This quantifies the risk of encountering critical vulnerabilities that damage the business.

- Maintainability: Maintainability includes the notion of adaptability, portability and transferability (from one development team to another). Measuring and monitoring maintainability is a must for mission-critical applications where change is driven by tight time-to-market schedules and where it is important for IT to remain responsive to business-driven changes. It is also essential to keep maintenance costs under control.

- Size: While not a quality attribute per se, the sizing of source code is a software characteristic that obviously impacts maintainability. Combined with the above quality characteristics, software size can be used to assess the amount of work produced and to be done by teams, as well as their productivity through correlation with time-sheet data, and other SDLC-related metrics.

Software functional quality is defined as conformance to explicitly stated functional requirements, identified for example using Voice of the Customer analysis (part of the Design for Six Sigma toolkit and/or documented through use cases) and the level of satisfaction experienced by end-users. The latter is referred as to as usability and is concerned with how intuitive and responsive the user interface is, how easily simple and complex operations can be performed, and how useful error messages are. Typically, software testing practices and tools ensure that a piece of software behaves in compliance with the original design, planned user experience and desired testability, i.e. a piece of software's disposition to support acceptance criteria.

The dual structural/functional dimension of software quality is consistent with the model proposed in Steve McConnell's Code Complete which divides software characteristics into two pieces: internal and external quality characteristics. External quality characteristics are those parts of a product that face its users, where internal quality characteristics are those that do not.

Alternative Approaches

One of the challenges in defining quality is that "everyone feels they understand it" and other definitions of software quality could be based on extending the various descriptions of the concept of quality used in business.

Dr. Tom DeMarco has proposed that "a product's quality is a function of how much it changes the world for the better." This can be interpreted as meaning that functional quality and user satisfaction are more important than structural quality in determining software quality.

Another definition, coined by Gerald Weinberg in Quality Software Management: Systems Thinking, is "Quality is value to some person." This definition stresses that quality is inherently subjective—different people will experience the quality of the same software differently. One strength of this definition is the questions it invites software teams to consider, such as "Who are the people we want to value our software?" and "What will be valuable to them?".

Measurement

Although the concepts presented in this section are applicable to both structural and functional software quality, measurement of the latter is essentially performed through testing.

Introduction

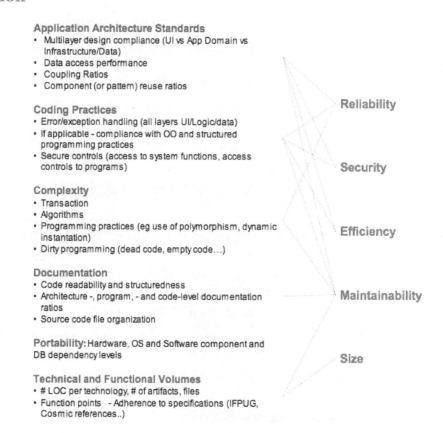

Application Architecture Standards
- Multilayer design compliance (UI vs App Domain vs Infrastructure/Data)
- Data access performance
- Coupling Ratios
- Component (or pattern) reuse ratios

Coding Practices
- Error/exception handling (all layers UI/Logic/data)
- If applicable - compliance with OO and structured programming practices
- Secure controls (access to system functions, access controls to programs)

Complexity
- Transaction
- Algorithms
- Programming practices (eg use of polymorphism, dynamic instantation)
- Dirty programming (dead code, empty code…)

Documentation
- Code readability and structuredness
- Architecture -, program, - and code-level documentation ratios
- Source code file organization

Portability: Hardware, OS and Software component and DB dependency levels

Technical and Functional Volumes
- # LOC per technology, # of artifacts, files
- Function points   - Adherence to specifications (IFPUG, Cosmic references..)

Reliability

Security

Efficiency

Maintainability

Size

Relationship between software desirable characteristics (right) and measurable attributes (left).

Software quality measurement is about quantifying to what extent a system or software possesses desirable characteristics. This can be performed through qualitative or quantitative means or a mix of both. In both cases, for each desirable characteristic, there are a set of measurable attributes the existence of which in a piece of software or system tend to be correlated and associated with this characteristic. For example, an attribute associated with portability is the number of target-dependent statements in a program. More precisely, using the Quality Function Deployment approach, these measurable attributes are the "hows" that need to be enforced to enable the "whats" in the Software Quality definition above.

The structure, classification and terminology of attributes and metrics applicable to software quality management have been derived or extracted from the ISO 9126-3 and the subsequent ISO/IEC 25000:2005 quality model. The main focus is on internal structural quality. Subcategories have been created to handle specific areas like business application architecture and technical characteristics such as data access and manipulation or the notion of transactions.

The dependence tree between software quality characteristics and their measurable attributes is represented in the diagram on the right, where each of the 5 characteristics that matter for the user (right) or owner of the business system depends on measurable attributes (left):

- Application Architecture Practices

- Coding Practices

- Application Complexity

- Documentation

- Portability

- Technical and Functional Volume

Correlations between programming errors and production defects unveil that basic code errors account for 92% of the total errors in the source code. These numerous code-level issues eventually count for only 10% of the defects in production. Bad software engineering practices at the architecture levels account for only 8% of total defects, but consume over half the effort spent on fixing problems, and lead to 90% of the serious reliability, security, and efficiency issues in production.

Code-based Analysis

Many of the existing software measures count structural elements of the application that result from parsing the source code for such individual instructions (Park, 1992), tokens (Halstead, 1977), control structures (McCabe, 1976), and objects (Chidamber & Kemerer, 1994).

Software quality measurement is about quantifying to what extent a system or software rates along these dimensions. The analysis can be performed using a qualitative or quantitative approach or a mix of both to provide an aggregate view [using for example weighted average(s) that reflect relative importance between the factors being measured].

This view of software quality on a linear continuum has to be supplemented by the identification of discrete Critical Programming Errors. These vulnerabilities may not fail a test case, but they are the result of bad practices that under specific circumstances can lead to catastrophic outages, performance degradations, security breaches, corrupted data, and myriad other problems (Nygard, 2007) that make a given system de facto unsuitable for use regardless of its rating based on aggregated measurements. A well-known example of vulnerability is the Common Weakness Enumeration, a repository of vulnerabilities in the source code that make applications exposed to security breaches.

The measurement of critical application characteristics involves measuring structural attributes of the application's architecture, coding, and in-line documentation, as displayed in the picture above. Thus, each characteristic is affected by attributes at numerous levels of abstraction in the application and all of which must be included calculating the characteristic's measure if it is to be a valuable predictor of quality outcomes that affect the business. The layered approach to calculating characteristic measures displayed in the figure above was first proposed by Boehm and his colleagues at TRW (Boehm, 1978) and is the approach taken in the ISO 9126 and 25000 series standards. These attributes can be measured from the parsed results of a static analysis of the application source code. Even dynamic characteristics of applications such as reliability and performance efficiency have their causal roots in the static structure of the application.

Structural quality analysis and measurement is performed through the analysis of the source code, the architecture, software framework, database schema in relationship to principles and standards that together define the conceptual and logical architecture of a system. This is distinct from the basic, local, component-level code analysis typically performed by development tools which are mostly concerned with implementation considerations and are crucial during debugging and testing activities.

Reliability

The root causes of poor reliability are found in a combination of non-compliance with good architectural and coding practices. This non-compliance can be detected by measuring the static quality attributes of an application. Assessing the static attributes underlying an application's reliability provides an estimate of the level of business risk and the likelihood of potential application failures and defects the application will experience when placed in operation.

Assessing reliability requires checks of at least the following software engineering best practices and technical attributes:

- Application Architecture Practices

- Coding Practices

- Complexity of algorithms

- Complexity of programming practices

- Compliance with Object-Oriented and Structured Programming best practices (when applicable)

- Component or pattern re-use ratio

- Dirty programming

- Error & Exception handling (for all layers - GUI, Logic & Data)

- Multi-layer design compliance

- Resource bounds management

- Software avoids patterns that will lead to unexpected behaviors

- Software manages data integrity and consistency

- Transaction complexity level

Depending on the application architecture and the third-party components used (such as external libraries or frameworks), custom checks should be defined along the lines drawn by the above list of best practices to ensure a better assessment of the reliability of the delivered software.

Efficiency

As with Reliability, the causes of performance inefficiency are often found in violations of good architectural and coding practice which can be detected by measuring the static quality attributes of an application. These static attributes predict potential operational performance bottlenecks and future scalability problems, especially for applications requiring high execution speed for handling complex algorithms or huge volumes of data.

Assessing performance efficiency requires checking at least the following software engineering best practices and technical attributes:

- Application Architecture Practices

- Appropriate interactions with expensive and/or remote resources

- Data access performance and data management

- Memory, network and disk space management

- Coding Practices

- Compliance with Object-Oriented and Structured Programming best practices (as appropriate)

- Compliance with SQL programming best practices

Security

Most security vulnerabilities result from poor coding and architectural practices such as SQL injection or cross-site scripting. These are well documented in lists maintained by CWE, and the SEI/Computer Emergency Center (CERT) at Carnegie Mellon University.

Assessing security requires at least checking the following software engineering best practices and technical attributes:

- Application Architecture Practices
- Multi-layer design compliance
- Security best practices (Input Validation, SQL Injection, Cross-Site Scripting, etc.)
- Programming Practices (code level)
- Error & Exception handling
- Security best practices (system functions access, access control to programs)

Maintainability

Maintainability includes concepts of modularity, understandability, changeability, testability, re-usability, and transferability from one development team to another. These do not take the form of critical issues at the code level. Rather, poor maintainability is typically the result of thousands of minor violations with best practices in documentation, complexity avoidance strategy, and basic programming practices that make the difference between clean and easy-to-read code vs. unorganized and difficult-to-read code.

Assessing maintainability requires checking the following software engineering best practices and technical attributes:

- Application Architecture Practices
- Architecture, Programs and Code documentation embedded in source code
- Code readability
- Complexity level of transactions
- Complexity of algorithms
- Complexity of programming practices
- Compliance with Object-Oriented and Structured Programming best practices (when applicable)
- Component or pattern re-use ratio
- Controlled level of dynamic coding
- Coupling ratio
- Dirty programming
- Documentation
- Hardware, OS, middleware, software components and database independence
- Multi-layer design compliance

- Portability

- Programming Practices (code level)

- Reduced duplicate code and functions

- Source code file organization cleanliness

Maintainability is closely related to Ward Cunningham's concept of technical debt, which is an expression of the costs resulting of a lack of maintainability. Reasons for why maintainability is low can be classified as reckless vs. prudent and deliberate vs. inadvertent, and often have their origin in developers' inability, lack of time and goals, their carelessness and discrepancies in the creation cost of and benefits from documentation and, in particular, maintainable source code.

Size

Measuring software size requires that the whole source code be correctly gathered, including database structure scripts, data manipulation source code, component headers, configuration files etc. There are essentially two types of software sizes to be measured, the technical size (footprint) and the functional size:

- There are several software technical sizing methods that have been widely described. The most common technical sizing method is number of Lines of Code (#LOC) per technology, number of files, functions, classes, tables, etc., from which backfiring Function Points can be computed;

- The most common for measuring functional size is function point analysis. Function point analysis measures the size of the software deliverable from a user's perspective. Function point sizing is done based on user requirements and provides an accurate representation of both size for the developer/estimator and value (functionality to be delivered) and reflects the business functionality being delivered to the customer. The method includes the identification and weighting of user recognizable inputs, outputs and data stores. The size value is then available for use in conjunction with numerous measures to quantify and to evaluate software delivery and performance (development cost per function point; delivered defects per function point; function points per staff month.).

The function point analysis sizing standard is supported by the International Function Point Users Group (IFPUG). It can be applied early in the software development life-cycle and it is not dependent on lines of code like the somewhat inaccurate Backfiring method. The method is technology agnostic and can be used for comparative analysis across organizations and across industries.

Since the inception of Function Point Analysis, several variations have evolved and the family of functional sizing techniques has broadened to include such sizing measures as COSMIC, NESMA, Use Case Points, FP Lite, Early and Quick FPs, and most recently Story Points. However, Function Points has a history of statistical accuracy, and has been used as a common unit of work measurement in numerous application development management (ADM) or outsourcing engagements, serving as the "currency" by which services are delivered and performance is measured.

One common limitation to the Function Point methodology is that it is a manual process and therefore it can be labor-intensive and costly in large scale initiatives such as application development or outsourcing engagements. This negative aspect of applying the methodology may be what motivated industry IT leaders to form the Consortium for IT Software Quality focused on introducing a computable metrics standard for automating the measuring of software size while the IFPUG keep promoting a manual approach as most of its activity rely on FP counters certifications.

CISQ announced the availability of its first metric standard, Automated Function Points, to the CISQ membership, in CISQ Technical. These recommendations have been developed in OMG's Request for Comment format and submitted to OMG's process for standardization.

Identifying Critical Programming Errors

Critical Programming Errors are specific architectural and/or coding bad practices that result in the highest, immediate or long term, business disruption risk.

These are quite often technology-related and depend heavily on the context, business objectives and risks. Some may consider respect for naming conventions while others – those preparing the ground for a knowledge transfer for example – will consider it as absolutely critical.

Critical Programming Errors can also be classified per CISQ Characteristics. Basic example below:

- Reliability

    o Avoid software patterns that will lead to unexpected behavior (Uninitialized variable, null pointers, etc.)

    o Methods, procedures and functions doing Insert, Update, Delete, Create Table or Select must include error management

    o Multi-thread functions should be made thread safe, for instance servlets or struts action classes must not have instance/non-final static fields

- Efficiency

    o Ensure centralization of client requests (incoming and data) to reduce network traffic

    o Avoid SQL queries that don't use an index against large tables in a loop

- Security

    o Avoid fields in servlet classes that are not final static

    o Avoid data access without including error management

    o Check control return codes and implement error handling mechanisms

    o Ensure input validation to avoid cross-site scripting flaws or SQL injections flaws

- Maintainability

    o Deep inheritance trees and nesting should be avoided to improve comprehensibility

- o Modules should be loosely coupled (fanout, intermediaries,) to avoid propagation of modifications

- o Enforce homogeneous naming conventions

Operationalized Quality Models

Newer proposals for quality models such as Squale and Quamoco propagate a direct integration of the definition of quality attributes and measurement. By breaking down quality attributes or even defining additional layers, the complex, abstract quality attributes (such as reliability or maintainability) become more manageable and measurable. Those quality models have been applied in industrial contexts but have not received widespread adoption.

References

- Booch, Grady; et al. (2004). Object-Oriented Analysis and Design with Applications (3rd ed.). MA, USA: Addison Wesley. ISBN 0-201-89551-X. Retrieved 30 January 2015.

- Suryanarayana, Girish (November 2014). Refactoring for Software Design Smells. Morgan Kaufmann. p. 258. ISBN 978-0128013977. Retrieved 31 January 2015.

- Carroll, ed., John (1995). Scenario-Based Design: Envisioning Work and Technology in System Development. New York: John Wiley & Sons. ISBN 0471076597.

- Bell, Michael (2008). "Introduction to Service-Oriented Modeling". Service-Oriented Modeling: Service Analysis, Design, and Architecture. Wiley & Sons. ISBN 978-0-470-14111-3.

- Kaner, Cem; Falk, Jack; Nguyen, Hung Quoc (1999). Testing Computer Software, 2nd Ed. New York, et al: John Wiley and Sons, Inc. p. 480. ISBN 0-471-35846-0.

- Kolawa, Adam; Huizinga, Dorota (2007). Automated Defect Prevention: Best Practices in Software Management. Wiley-IEEE Computer Society Press. pp. 41–43. ISBN 0-470-04212-5.

- Kolawa, Adam; Huizinga, Dorota (2007). Automated Defect Prevention: Best Practices in Software Management. Wiley-IEEE Computer Society Press. p. 426. ISBN 0-470-04212-5.

- Binder, Robert V. (1999). Testing Object-Oriented Systems: Objects, Patterns, and Tools. Addison-Wesley Professional. p. 45. ISBN 0-201-80938-9.

- IEEE (1990). IEEE Standard Computer Dictionary: A Compilation of IEEE Standard Computer Glossaries. New York: IEEE. ISBN 1-55937-079-3.

- Black, Rex (December 2008). Advanced Software Testing- Vol. 2: Guide to the ISTQB Advanced Certification as an Advanced Test Manager. Santa Barbara: Rocky Nook Publisher. ISBN 1-933952-36-9.

- Pierre Bourque, Richard E. (Dick) Fairley, eds. (2014). "Chapter 3: Software Construction". Guide to the Software Engineering Body of Knowledge Version 3.0. IEEE Computer Society. ISBN 978-0-7695-5166-1.

- Prause, Christian; Durdik, Zoya (June 3, 2012). "Architectural design and documentation: Waste in agile development?". IEEE Computer Society. Retrieved February 4, 2013.

- Prause, Christian; et al. (2008). "Managing the Iterative Requirements Process in a Multi-National Project using an Issue Tracker" (PDF). IEEE Computer Society. Retrieved February 5, 2013.

- EtestingHub-Online Free Software Testing Tutorial. "e)Testing Phase in Software Testing:". Etestinghub.com. Retrieved 2012-01-13.

Fundamentals of Software Engineering

Software, like all applications created in the computer, uses code in its design. These codes are basically programming language. Each language has its function that it fulfils and programs now run on multi-paradigm procedures. This chapter is a compilation of the various branches of software engineering that form an integral part of the broader subject matter.

Computer Programming

Computer programming (often shortened to programming) is a process that leads from an original formulation of a computing problem to executable computer programs. Programming involves activities such as analysis, developing understanding, generating algorithms, verification of requirements of algorithms including their correctness and resources consumption, and implementation (commonly referred to as coding) of algorithms in a target programming language. Source code is written in one or more programming languages. The purpose of programming is to find a sequence of instructions that will automate performing a specific task or solving a given problem. The process of programming thus often requires expertise in many different subjects, including knowledge of the application domain, specialized algorithms and formal logic.

Related tasks include testing, debugging, and maintaining the source code, implementation of the build system, and management of derived artifacts such as machine code of computer programs. These might be considered part of the programming process, but often the term *software development* is used for this larger process with the term *programming*, *implementation*, or *coding* reserved for the actual writing of source code. Software engineering combines engineering techniques with software development practices.

Overview

Within software engineering, programming (the *implementation*) is regarded as one phase in a software development process.

There is an ongoing debate on the extent to which the writing of programs is an art form, a craft, or an engineering discipline. In general, good programming is considered to be the measured application of all three, with the goal of producing an efficient and evolvable software solution (the criteria for "efficient" and "evolvable" vary considerably). The discipline differs from many other technical professions in that programmers, in general, do not need to be licensed or pass any standardized (or governmentally regulated) certification tests in order to call themselves "programmers" or even "software engineers." Because the discipline covers many areas, which may or may not include critical applications, it is debatable whether licensing is required for the profession as a whole. In most cases, the discipline is self-governed by the entities which require the programming, and sometimes very strict environments are defined (e.g. United States Air Force use of AdaCore and security clearance). However, representing oneself as a "professional software engineer" without a license from an accredited institution is illegal in many parts of the world.

Another ongoing debate is the extent to which the programming language used in writing computer programs affects the form that the final program takes. This debate is analogous to that surrounding the Sapir–Whorf hypothesis in linguistics and cognitive science, which postulates that a particular spoken language's nature influences the habitual thought of its speakers. Different language patterns yield different patterns of thought. This idea challenges the possibility of representing the world perfectly with language, because it acknowledges that the mechanisms of any language condition the thoughts of its speaker community.

History

Ada Lovelace commenting on the work of Luigi Menabrea, created the first algorithm designed for processing by an Analytical Engine and is often recognized as history's first computer programmer.

Ancient cultures seemed to have no conception of computing beyond arithmetic, algebra, and geometry, occasionally devising computational systems with elements of calculus (e.g. the method of exhaustion). The only mechanical device that existed for numerical computation at the beginning of human history was the abacus, invented in Sumeria circa 2500 BC. Later, the Antikythera mechanism, invented some time around 100 BC in ancient Greece, is the first known mechanical calculator utilizing gears of various sizes and configuration to perform calculations, which tracked the metonic cycle still used in lunar-to-solar calendars, and which is consistent for calculating the dates of the Olympiads.

The medieval scientist Al-Jazari built programmable automata in 1206 AD. One system employed in these devices was the use of pegs and cams placed into a wooden drum at specific locations, which would sequentially trigger levers that in turn operated percussion instruments. The output of this device was a small drummer playing various rhythms and drum patterns. The Jacquard loom, which Joseph Marie Jacquard developed in 1801, uses a series of pasteboard cards with holes punched in them. The hole pattern represented the pattern that the loom had to follow in weaving cloth. The loom could produce entirely different weaves using different sets of cards.

Charles Babbage adopted the use of punched cards around 1830 to control his Analytical Engine. Mathematician Ada Lovelace, a friend of Babbage, between 1842 and 1843 translated an article by Italian military engineer Luigi Menabrea on the engine, which she supplemented with a set of notes, simply called Notes. These notes include an algorithm to calculate a sequence of Bernoulli numbers, intended to be carried out by a machine. Despite controversy over scope of her contribution, many consider this algorithm to be the first computer program.

Data and instructions were once stored on external punched cards, which were kept in order and arranged in program decks.

In the 1880s, Herman Hollerith invented the recording of data on a medium that could then be read by a machine. Prior uses of machine readable media, above, had been for lists of instructions (not data) to drive programmed machines such as Jacquard looms and mechanized musical instruments. "After some initial trials with paper tape, he settled on punched cards..." To process these punched cards, first known as "Hollerith cards" he invented the keypunch, sorter, and tabulator unit record machines. These inventions were the foundation of the data processing industry. In 1896 he founded the *Tabulating Machine Company* (which later became the core of IBM). The addition of a control panel (plugboard) to his 1906 Type I Tabulator allowed it to do different jobs without having to be physically rebuilt. By the late 1940s, there were several unit record calculators, such as the IBM 602 and IBM 604, whose control panels specified a sequence (list) of operations and thus were programmable machines.

The invention of the von Neumann architecture allowed computer programs to be stored in computer memory. Early programs had to be painstakingly crafted using the instructions (elementary operations) of the particular machine, often in binary notation. Every model of computer would likely use different instructions (machine language) to do the same task. Later, assembly languages were developed that let the programmer specify each instruction in a text format, entering abbreviations for each operation code instead of a number and specifying addresses in symbolic form (e.g., ADD X, TOTAL). Entering a program in assembly language is usually more convenient, faster, and less prone to human error than using machine language, but because an assembly language is little more than a different notation for a machine language, any two machines with different instruction sets also have different assembly languages.

Wired control panel for an IBM 402 Accounting Machine

The synthesis of numerical calculation, predetermined operation and output, along with a way to organize and input instructions in a manner relatively easy for humans to conceive and produce, led to the modern development of computer programming. In 1954, FORTRAN was invented; it was the first widely used high level programming language to have a functional implementation, as opposed to just a design on paper. (A high-level language is, in very general terms, any programming language that allows the programmer to write programs in terms that are more abstract than assembly language instructions, i.e. at a level of abstraction "higher" than that of an assembly language.) It allowed programmers to specify calculations by entering a formula directly (e.g. $Y = X*2 + 5*X + 9$). The program text, or *source*, is converted into machine instructions using a special program called a compiler, which translates the FORTRAN program into machine language. In fact, the name FORTRAN stands for "Formula Translation". Many other languages were developed, including some for commercial programming, such as COBOL. Programs were mostly still entered using punched cards or paper tape. By the late 1960s, data storage devices and computer terminals became inexpensive enough that programs could be created by typing directly into the computers. Text editors were developed that allowed changes and corrections to be made much more easily than with punched cards. (Usually, an error in punching a card meant that the card had to be discarded and a new one punched to replace it.) As time has progressed, computers have made giant leaps in processing power, which have al-lowed the development of programming languages that are more abstracted from the underlying hardware. Popular programming languages of the modern era include ActionScript, C, C++, C#, Haskell, Java, JavaScript, Objective-C, Perl, PHP, Python, Ruby, Smalltalk, SQL, Visual Basic, and dozens more. Although these high-level languages usually incur greater overhead, the increase in speed of modern computers has made the use of these languages much more practical than in the past. These increasingly abstracted languages are typically easier to learn and allow the program-mer to develop applications much more efficiently and with less source code. However, high-level languages are still impractical for a few programs, such as those where low-level hardware control is necessary or where maximum processing speed is vital. Computer programming has become a popular career in the developed world, particularly in the United States, Europe, and Japan. Due to the high labor cost of programmers in these countries, some forms of programming have been increasingly subject to outsourcing (importing software and services from other countries, usually at a lower wage), making programming career decisions in developed countries more complicated, while increasing economic opportunities for programmers in less developed areas, particularly China and India.

Modern Programming

Quality Requirements

Whatever the approach to development may be, the final program must satisfy some fundamental properties. The following properties are among the most important:

- Reliability: how often the results of a program are correct. This depends on conceptual correctness of algorithms, and minimization of programming mistakes, such as mistakes in resource management (e.g., buffer overflows and race conditions) and logic errors (such as division by zero or off-by-one errors).

- Robustness: how well a program anticipates problems due to errors (not bugs). This includes situations such as incorrect, inappropriate or corrupt data, unavailability of needed resources such as memory, operating system services and network connections, user error, and unexpected power outages.

- Usability: the ergonomics of a program: the ease with which a person can use the program for its intended purpose or in some cases even unanticipated purposes. Such issues can make or break its success even regardless of other issues. This involves a wide range of textual, graphical and sometimes hardware elements that improve the clarity, intuitiveness, cohesiveness and completeness of a program's user interface.

- Portability: the range of computer hardware and operating system platforms on which the source code of a program can be compiled/interpreted and run. This depends on differences in the programming facilities provided by the different platforms, including hardware and operating system resources, expected behavior of the hardware and operating system, and availability of platform specific compilers (and sometimes libraries) for the language of the source code.

- Maintainability: the ease with which a program can be modified by its present or future developers in order to make improvements or customizations, fix bugs and security holes, or adapt it to new environments. Good practices during initial development make the difference in this regard. This quality may not be directly apparent to the end user but it can significantly affect the fate of a program over the long term.

- Efficiency/performance: Measure of system resources a program consumes (processor time, memory space, slow devices such as disks, network bandwidth and to some extent even user interaction): the less, the better. This also includes careful management of resources, for example cleaning up temporary files and eliminating memory leaks.

Readability of Source Code

In computer programming, readability refers to the ease with which a human reader can comprehend the purpose, control flow, and operation of source code. It affects the aspects of quality above, including portability, usability and most importantly maintainability.

Readability is important because programmers spend the majority of their time reading, trying to understand and modifying existing source code, rather than writing new source code. Unreadable code often leads to bugs, inefficiencies, and duplicated code. A study found that a few simple readability transformations made code shorter and drastically reduced the time to understand it.

Following a consistent programming style often helps readability. However, readability is more than just programming style. Many factors, having little or nothing to do with the ability of the computer to efficiently compile and execute the code, contribute to readability. Some of these factors include:

- Different indentation styles (whitespace)

- Comments

- Decomposition

- Naming conventions for objects (such as variables, classes, procedures, etc.)

Various visual programming languages have also been developed with the intent to resolve readability concerns by adopting non-traditional approaches to code structure and display. Techniques like Code refactoring can enhance readability.

Algorithmic Complexity

The academic field and the engineering practice of computer programming are both largely concerned with discovering and implementing the most efficient algorithms for a given class of problem. For this purpose, algorithms are classified into *orders* using so-called Big O notation, which expresses resource use, such as execution time or memory consumption, in terms of the size of an input. Expert programmers are familiar with a variety of well-established algorithms and their respective complexities and use this knowledge to choose algorithms that are best suited to the circumstances.

Methodologies

The first step in most formal software development processes is requirements analysis, followed by testing to determine value modeling, implementation, and failure elimination (debugging). There exist a lot of differing approaches for each of those tasks. One approach popular for requirements analysis is Use Case analysis. Many programmers use forms of Agile software development where the various stages of formal software development are more integrated together into short cycles that take a few weeks rather than years. There are many approaches to the Software development process.

Popular modeling techniques include Object-Oriented Analysis and Design (OOAD) and Model-Driven Architecture (MDA). The Unified Modeling Language (UML) is a notation used for both the OOAD and MDA.

A similar technique used for database design is Entity-Relationship Modeling (ER Modeling).

Implementation techniques include imperative languages (object-oriented or procedural), functional languages, and logic languages.

Measuring Language Usage

It is very difficult to determine what are the most popular of modern programming languages. Methods of measuring programming language popularity include: counting the number of job advertisements that mention the language, the number of books sold and courses teaching the language (this overestimates the importance of newer languages), and estimates of the number of existing lines of code written in the language (this underestimates the number of users of business languages such as COBOL).

Some languages are very popular for particular kinds of applications, while some languages are regularly used to write many different kinds of applications. For example, COBOL is still strong in corporate data centers often on large mainframe computers, Fortran in engineering applications, scripting languages in Web development, and C in embedded software. Many applications use a mix of several languages in their construction and use. New languages are generally designed around the syntax of a prior language with new functionality added, (for example C++ adds object-orientation to C, and Java adds memory management and bytecode to C++, but as a result, loses efficiency and the ability for low-level manipulation).

Debugging

Debugging is a very important task in the software development process since having defects in a program can have significant consequences for its users. Some languages are more prone to some kinds of faults because their specification does not require compilers to perform as much checking as other languages. Use of a static code analysis tool can help detect some possible problems.

Debugging is often done with IDEs like Eclipse, Visual Studio, Kdevelop, NetBeans and Code::-Blocks. Standalone debuggers like gdb are also used, and these often provide less of a visual environment, usually using a command line.

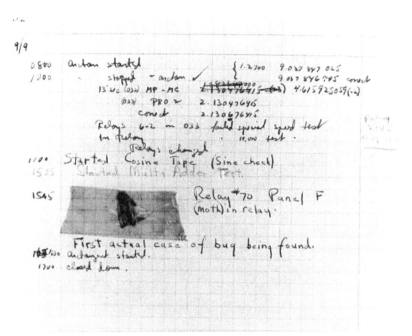

The bug from 1947 which is at the origin of a popular (but incorrect) etymology for the common term for a software defect.

Programming Languages

Different programming languages support different styles of programming (called *programming paradigms*). The choice of language used is subject to many considerations, such as company policy, suitability to task, availability of third-party packages, or individual preference. Ideally, the programming language best suited for the task at hand will be selected. Trade-offs from this ideal involve finding enough programmers who know the language to build a team, the availability of compilers for that language, and the efficiency with which programs written in a given language execute. Languages form an approximate spectrum from "low-level" to "high-level"; "low-level" languages are typically more machine-oriented and faster to execute, whereas "high-level" languages are more abstract and easier to use but execute less quickly. It is usually easier to code in "high-level" languages than in "low-level" ones.

Allen Downey, in his book *How To Think Like A Computer Scientist*, writes:

> The details look different in different languages, but a few basic instructions appear in just about every language:
>
> - Input: Gather data from the keyboard, a file, or some other device.
>
> - Output: Display data on the screen or send data to a file or other device.
>
> - Arithmetic: Perform basic arithmetical operations like addition and multiplication.
>
> - Conditional Execution: Check for certain conditions and execute the appropriate sequence of statements.
>
> - Repetition: Perform some action repeatedly, usually with some variation.

Many computer languages provide a mechanism to call functions provided by shared libraries. Provided the functions in a library follow the appropriate run time conventions (e.g., method of passing arguments), then these functions may be written in any other language.

Programmers

Computer programmers are those who write computer software. Their jobs usually involve:

- Coding
- Debugging
- Documentation
- Integration
- Maintenance
- Requirements analysis
- Software architecture
- Software testing
- Specification

Programming Paradigm

The notion of programming paradigms is a way to classify programming languages according to the style of computer programming. Features of various programming languages determine which paradigms they belong to; as a result, some languages fall into only one paradigm, while others fall into multiple paradigms. Some paradigms are concerned primarily with implications for the execution model of the language, such as allowing side effects, or whether the sequence of operations is defined by the execution model. Other paradigms are concerned primarily with the way that code is organized, such as grouping code into units along with the state that is modified by the code. Yet others are concerned primarily with the style of syntax and grammar.

Common programming paradigms include imperative which allows side effects, functional which does not allow side effects, declarative which does not state the order in which operations execute, object-oriented which groups code together with the state the code modifies, procedural which groups code into functions, logic which has a particular style of execution model coupled to a particular style of syntax and grammar, and symbolic programming which has a particular style of syntax and grammar.

For example, languages that fall into the imperative paradigm have two main features: they state the order in which operations take place, with constructs that explicitly control that order, and they allow side effects, in which state can be modified at one point in time, within one unit of code, and then later read at a different point in time inside a different unit of code. The communication between the units of code is not explicit. Meanwhile, in object-oriented programming, code is organized into objects that contain state that is only modified by the code that is part of the object. Most object oriented languages are also imperative languages. In contrast, languages that fit the declarative paradigm do not state the order in which to execute operations. Instead, they supply a number of operations that are available in the system, along with the conditions under which each is allowed to execute. The implementation of the language's execution model tracks which operations are free to execute and chooses the order on its own.

Overview

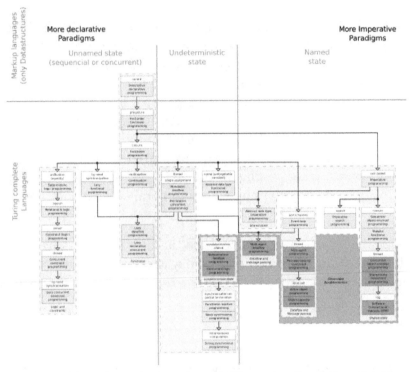

Overview of the various programming paradigms according to Peter Van Roy

Just as software engineering (as a process) is defined by differing *methodologies*, so the programming languages (as models of computation) are defined by differing *paradigms*. Some languages are designed to support one paradigm (Smalltalk supports object-oriented programming, Haskell supports functional programming), while other programming languages support multiple paradigms (such as Object Pascal, C++, Java, C#, Scala, Visual Basic, Common Lisp, Scheme, Perl, Python, Ruby, Oz and F#). For example, programs written in C++ or Object Pascal can be purely procedural, purely object-oriented, or they can contain elements of both or other paradigms. Software designers and programmers decide how to use those paradigm elements.

In object-oriented programming, programs are treated as a collection of interacting objects. In functional programming, programs are treated as a sequence of stateless function evaluations. When programming computers or systems with many processors, in process-oriented programming, programs are treated as sets of concurrent processes acting on logically shared data structures.

Many programming paradigms are as well known for the techniques they *forbid* as for those they *enable*. For instance, pure functional programming disallows use of side-effects, while structured programming disallows use of the goto statement. Partly for this reason, new paradigms are often regarded as doctrinaire or overly rigid by those accustomed to earlier styles. Yet, avoiding certain techniques can make it easier to prove theorems about the correctness of programs, or simply to understand the program behavior.

Programming paradigms can also be compared with *programming models* which allow invoking an external execution model by using only an API. Programming models can also be classified into paradigms, based on features of the execution model.

For parallel computing, using a programming model instead of a language is common. The reason is that details of the parallel hardware leak into the abstractions used to program the hardware. This causes the programmer to have to map patterns in the algorithm onto patterns in the execution model (which have been inserted due to leakage of hardware into the abstraction). As a consequence, no one parallel programming language fits well to all computation problems. It is thus more convenient to use a base sequential language and insert API calls to parallel execution models, via a programming model. Such parallel programming models can be classified according to abstractions that reflect the hardware, such as shared memory, distributed memory with message passing, notions of "place" visible in the code, and so forth. These can be considered flavors of programming paradigm that apply only to parallel languages and parallel programming models.

Some programming language researchers criticise the notion of paradigms as a classification of programming languages, e.g. Krishnamurthi. They argue that many programming languages cannot be strictly classified into one paradigm, but rather include features from several paradigms.

History

Different approaches to programming have developed over time, being identified as such either at the time or retrospectively. An early approach consciously identified as such is structured programming, advocated since the mid 1960s. The concept of a "programming paradigm" as such dates at least to 1978, in the Turing Award lecture of Robert W. Floyd, entitled *The Paradigms of Programming*, which cites the notion of paradigm as used by Thomas Kuhn in his *The Structure of Scientific Revolutions* (1962).

Machine Code

The lowest level programming paradigms are machine code, which directly represents the instructions (the contents of program memory) as a sequence of numbers, and assembly language where the machine instructions are represented by mnemonics and memory addresses can be given symbolic labels. These are sometimes called first- and second-generation languages.

In the 1960s, assembly languages were developed to support library COPY and quite sophisticated conditional macro generation and preprocessing abilities, CALL to (subroutines), external variables and common sections (globals), enabling significant code re-use and isolation from hardware specifics via use of logical operators such as READ/WRITE/GET/PUT. Assembly was, and still is, used for time critical systems and often in embedded systems as it gives the most direct control of what the machine does.

Procedural Languages

The next advance was the development of procedural languages. These third-generation languages (the first described as high-level languages) use vocabulary related to the problem being solved. For example,

- COmmon Business Oriented Language (COBOL) – uses terms like file, move and copy.

- FORmula TRANslation (FORTRAN) – using mathematical language terminology, it was developed mainly for scientific and engineering problems.

- ALGOrithmic Language (ALGOL) – focused on being an appropriate language to define algorithms, while using mathematical language terminology and targeting scientific and engineering problems just like FORTRAN.

- Programming Language One (PL/I) – a hybrid commercial/scientific general purpose language supporting pointers.

- Beginners All purpose Symbolic Instruction Code (BASIC) – it was developed to enable more people to write programs.

- C – a general-purpose programming language, initially developed by Dennis Ritchie between 1969 and 1973 at AT&T Bell Labs.

All these languages follow the procedural paradigm. That is, they describe, step by step, exactly the procedure that should, according to the particular programmer at least, be followed to solve a specific problem. The efficacy and efficiency of any such solution are both therefore entirely subjective and highly dependent on that programmer's experience, inventiveness, and ability.

Object-oriented Programming

Following the widespread use of procedural languages, object-oriented programming (OOP) languages were created, such as Simula, Smalltalk, C++, C#, Eiffel, and Java. In these languages, data and methods to manipulate it are kept as one unit called an object. The only way that another object or user can access the data is via the object's *methods*. Thus, the inner workings of an object may be changed without affecting any code that uses the object. There is still some controversy raised by Alexander Stepanov, Richard Stallman and other programmers, concerning the efficacy of the OOP paradigm versus the procedural paradigm. The need for every object to have associative methods leads some skeptics to associate OOP with software bloat; an attempt to resolve this dilemma came through polymorphism.

Because object-oriented programming is considered a paradigm, not a language, it is possible to create even an object-oriented assembler language. High Level Assembly (HLA) is an example of this that fully supports advanced data types and object-oriented assembly language programming – despite its early origins. Thus, differing programming paradigms can be seen rather like *motivational memes* of their advocates, rather than necessarily representing progress from one level to the next. Precise comparisons of the efficacy of competing paradigms are frequently made more difficult because of new and differing terminology applied to similar entities and processes together with numerous implementation distinctions across languages.

Further Paradigms

Literate programming, as a form of imperative programming, structures programs as a human-centered web, as in a hypertext essay: documentation is integral to the program, and the program is structured following the logic of prose exposition, rather than compiler convenience.

Independent of the imperative branch, declarative programming paradigms were developed. In these languages the computer is told what the problem is, not how to solve the problem – the program is structured as a collection of properties to find in the expected result, not as a procedure to follow. Given a database or a set of rules, the computer tries to find a solution matching all the desired properties. An archetype of a declarative language is the fourth generation language SQL, and the family of functional languages and logic programming.

Functional programming is a subset of declarative programming. Programs written using this paradigm use functions, blocks of code intended to behave like mathematical functions. Functional languages discourage changes in the value of variables through assignment, making a great deal of use of recursion instead.

The logic programming paradigm views computation as automated reasoning over a corpus of knowledge. Facts about the problem domain are expressed as logic formulae, and programs are executed by applying inference rules over them until an answer to the problem is found, or the collection of formulae is proved inconsistent.

Symbolic programming is a paradigm that describes programs able to manipulate formulas and program components as data. Programs can thus effectively modify themselves, and appear to "learn", making them suited for applications such as artificial intelligence, expert systems, natural language processing and computer games. Languages that support this paradigm include Lisp and Prolog.

Multi-paradigm

A *multi-paradigm programming language* is a programming language that supports more than one programming paradigm. The design goal of such languages is to allow programmers to use the most suitable programming style and associated language constructs for a given job, considering that no single paradigm solves all problems in the easiest or most efficient way.

One example is C#, which includes imperative and object-oriented paradigms, together with a certain level of support for functional programming with features like delegates (allowing functions to be treated as first-order objects), type inference, anonymous functions and Language Integrated Query. Other examples are F# and Scala, which provide similar functionality to C# but also include full support for functional programming (including currying, pattern matching, algebraic data types, lazy evaluation, tail recursion, immutability, etc.). Perhaps the most extreme example is Oz, which has subsets that adhere to logic (Oz descends from logic programming), functional, object-oriented, dataflow concurrent, and other paradigms. Oz was designed over a ten-year period to combine in a harmonious way concepts that are traditionally associated with different programming paradigms. Lisp, while often taught as a functional language, is known for its malleability and thus its ability to engulf many paradigms.

References

- "Programming 101: Tips to become a good programmer - Wisdom Geek". Wisdom Geek. 2016-05-19. Retrieved 2016-05-23.

- Peter Van Roy (2009-05-12). "Programming Paradigms for Dummies: What Every Programmer Should Know" (PDF). info.ucl.ac.be. Retrieved 2014-01-27.

- "Sketch of The Analytical Engine, with notes upon the Memoir by the Translator". Switzerland: fourmilab.ch. Retrieved 28 March 2014.

- Frans Coenen (1999-10-11). "Characteristics of declarative programming languages". cgi.csc.liv.ac.uk. Retrieved 2014-02-20.

- Michael A. Covington (2010-08-23). "CSCI/ARTI 4540/6540: First Lecture on Symbolic Programming and LISP" (PDF). University of Georgia. Retrieved 2013-11-20.

- Nørmark, Kurt. Overview of the four main programming paradigms. Aalborg University, 9 May 2011. Retrieved 22 September 2012.

Various Applications of Software Engineering

The digital breakthroughs that have been achieved through software engineering techniques have led to the development of hi-tech gadgets such as heads-up displays (HUD), speech recognition and logic based AI. Some of the categories explored by this chapter include artificial intelligence and augmented reality. The topics discussed in the chapter are of great importance to broaden the existing knowledge on software engineering.

Artificial Intelligence

Artificial intelligence (AI) is intelligence exhibited by machines. In computer science, an ideal "intelligent" machine is a flexible rational agent that perceives its environment and takes actions that maximize its chance of success at some goal. Colloquially, the term "artificial intelligence" is applied when a machine mimics "cognitive" functions that humans associate with other human minds, such as "learning" and "problem solving". As machines become increasingly capable, facilities once thought to require intelligence are removed from the definition. For example, optical character recognition is no longer perceived as an exemplar of "artificial intelligence" having become a routine technology. Capabilities still classified as AI include advanced Chess and Go systems and self-driving cars.

AI research is divided into subfields that focus on specific problems or on specific approaches or on the use of a particular tool or towards satisfying particular applications.

The central problems (or goals) of AI research include reasoning, knowledge, planning, learning, natural language processing (communication), perception and the ability to move and manipulate objects. General intelligence is among the field's long-term goals. Approaches include statistical methods, computational intelligence, soft computing (e.g. machine learning), and traditional symbolic AI. Many tools are used in AI, including versions of search and mathematical optimization, logic, methods based on probability and economics. The AI field draws upon computer science, mathematics, psychology, linguistics, philosophy, neuroscience and artificial psychology.

The field was founded on the claim that human intelligence "can be so precisely described that a machine can be made to simulate it." This raises philosophical arguments about the nature of the mind and the ethics of creating artificial beings endowed with human-like intelligence, issues which have been explored by myth, fiction and philosophy since antiquity. Attempts to create artificial intelligence has experienced many setbacks, including the ALPAC report of 1966, the abandonment of perceptrons in 1970, the Lighthill Report of 1973 and the collapse of the Lisp machine market in 1987. In the twenty-first century AI techniques became an essential part of the technology industry, helping to solve many challenging problems in computer science.

History

While the concept of artificial beings (some of which are capable of thought) appeared as storytelling devices in antiquity, the idea of actually trying to build a machine to perform useful reasoning may have begun with Ramon Lull (c. 1300 CE). The first known calculating machine was built around 1623 by scientist Wilhelm Schickard. Gottfried Leibniz then built a crude variant, intended to perform operations on concepts rather than numbers. Since the 19th century, artificial beings are common in fiction, as in Mary Shelley's *Frankenstein* or Karel Čapek's *R.U.R. (Rossum's Universal Robots)*.

Mechanical or "formal" reasoning began with philosophers and mathematicians in antiquity. In the 19th century, George Boole refined those ideas into propositional logic and Gottlob Frege developed a notational system for mechanical reasoning (a *"predicate calculus"*). Around the 1940s, Alan Turing's theory of computation suggested that a machine, by shuffling symbols as simple as "0" and "1", could simulate any conceivable act of mathematical deduction. This insight, that digital computers can simulate any process of formal reasoning, is known as the Church–Turing thesis. Along with concurrent discoveries in neurology, information theory and cybernetics, this led researchers to consider the possibility of building an electronic brain. The first work that is now generally recognized as AI was McCullough and Pitts' 1943 formal design for Turing-complete "artificial neurons".

The field of AI research was founded at a conference at Dartmouth College in 1956. The attendees, including John McCarthy, Marvin Minsky, Allen Newell, Arthur Samuel and Herbert Simon, became the leaders of AI research. They and their students wrote programs that were, to most people, simply astonishing: computers were winning at checkers, solving word problems in algebra, proving logical theorems and speaking English. By the middle of the 1960s, research in the U.S. was heavily funded by the Department of Defense and laboratories had been established around the world. AI's founders were optimistic about the future: Herbert Simon predicted that "machines will be capable, within twenty years, of doing any work a man can do". Marvin Minsky agreed, writing that "within a generation ... the problem of creating 'artificial intelligence' will substantially be solved".

They failed to recognize the difficulty of some of the remaining tasks. Progress slowed and in 1974, in response to the criticism of Sir James Lighthill and ongoing pressure from the US Congress to fund more productive projects, both the U.S. and British governments cut off exploratory research in AI. The next few years would later be called an "AI winter", a period when funding for AI projects was hard to find.

In the early 1980s, AI research was revived by the commercial success of expert systems, a form of AI program that simulated the knowledge and analytical skills of human experts. By 1985 the market for AI had reached over a billion dollars. At the same time, Japan's fifth generation computer project inspired the U.S and British governments to restore funding for academic research. However, beginning with the collapse of the Lisp Machine market in 1987, AI once again fell into disrepute, and a second, longer-lasting hiatus began.

In the late 1990s and early 21st century, AI began to be used for logistics, data mining, medical diagnosis and other areas. The success was due to increasing computational power, greater emphasis on solving specific problems, new ties between AI and other fields and a commitment by researchers to mathematical methods and scientific standards. Deep Blue became the first computer chess-playing system to beat a reigning world chess champion, Garry Kasparov on 11 May 1997.

Advanced statistical techniques (loosely known as deep learning), access to large amounts of data and faster computers enabled advances in machine learning and perception. By the mid 2010s, machine learning applications were used throughout the world. In a *Jeopardy!* quiz show exhibition match, IBM's question answering system, Watson, defeated the two greatest Jeopardy champions, Brad Rutter and Ken Jennings, by a significant margin. The Kinect, which provides a 3D body–motion interface for the Xbox 360 and the Xbox One use algorithms that emerged from lengthy AI research as do intelligent personal assistants in smartphones. In March 2016, AlphaGo won 4 out of 5 games of Go in a match with Go champion Lee Sedol, becoming the first computer Go-playing system to beat a professional Go player without handicaps.

Research

Goals

The general problem of simulating (or creating) intelligence has been broken down into sub-problems. These consist of particular traits or capabilities that researchers expect an intelligent system to display. The traits described below have received the most attention.

Deduction, Reasoning, Problem Solving

Early researchers developed algorithms that imitated step-by-step reasoning that humans use when they solve puzzles or make logical deductions (reason). By the late 1980s and 1990s, AI research had developed methods for dealing with uncertain or incomplete information, employing concepts from probability and economics.

For difficult problems, algorithms can require enormous computational resources—most experience a "combinatorial explosion": the amount of memory or computer time required becomes astronomical for problems of a certain size. The search for more efficient problem-solving algorithms is a high priority.

Human beings ordinarily use fast, intuitive judgments rather than step-by-step deduction that early AI research was able to model. AI has progressed using "sub-symbolic" problem solving: embodied agent approaches emphasize the importance of sensorimotor skills to higher reasoning; neural net research attempts to simulate the structures inside the brain that give rise to this skill; statistical approaches to AI mimic the human ability to guess.

Knowledge Representation

Knowledge representation and knowledge engineering are central to AI research. Many of the problems machines are expected to solve will require extensive knowledge about the world. Among the things that AI needs to represent are: objects, properties, categories and relations between objects; situations, events, states and time; causes and effects; knowledge about knowledge (what we know about what other people know); and many other, less well researched domains. A representation of "what exists" is an ontology: the set of objects, relations, concepts and so on that the machine knows about. The most general are called upper ontologies, which attempt to provide a foundation for all other knowledge.

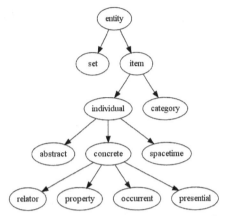

An ontology represents knowledge as a set of concepts within a domain and the relationships between those concepts.

Among the most difficult problems in knowledge representation are:

Default reasoning and the qualification problem

> Many of the things people know take the form of "working assumptions." For example, if a bird comes up in conversation, people typically picture an animal that is fist sized, sings, and flies. None of these things are true about all birds. John McCarthy identified this problem in 1969 as the qualification problem: for any commonsense rule that AI researchers care to represent, there tend to be a huge number of exceptions. Almost nothing is simply true or false in the way that abstract logic requires. AI research has explored a number of solutions to this problem.

The breadth of commonsense knowledge

> The number of atomic facts that the average person knows is astronomical. Research projects that attempt to build a complete knowledge base of commonsense knowledge (e.g., Cyc) require enormous amounts of laborious ontological engineering—they must be built, by hand, one complicated concept at a time. A major goal is to have the computer understand enough concepts to be able to learn by reading from sources like the Internet, and thus be able to add to its own ontology.

The subsymbolic form of some commonsense knowledge

> Much of what people know is not represented as "facts" or "statements" that they could express verbally. For example, a chess master will avoid a particular chess position because it "feels too exposed" or an art critic can take one look at a statue and instantly realize that it is a fake. These are intuitions or tendencies that are represented in the brain non-consciously and sub-symbolically. Knowledge like this informs, supports and provides a context for symbolic, conscious knowledge. As with the related problem of sub-symbolic reasoning, it is hoped that situated AI, computational intelligence, or statistical AI will provide ways to represent this kind of knowledge.

Planning

Intelligent agents must be able to set goals and achieve them. They need a way to visualize the future (they must have a representation of the state of the world and be able to make predictions about how their actions will change it) and be able to make choices that maximize the utility (or "value") of the available choices.

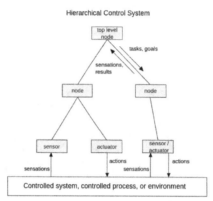

A hierarchical control system is a form of control system in which a set of devices and governing software is arranged in a hierarchy.

In classical planning problems, the agent can assume that it is the only thing acting on the world and it can be certain what the consequences of its actions may be. However, if the agent is not the only actor, it must periodically ascertain whether the world matches its predictions and it must change its plan as this becomes necessary, requiring the agent to reason under uncertainty.

Multi-agent planning uses the cooperation and competition of many agents to achieve a given goal. Emergent behavior such as this is used by evolutionary algorithms and swarm intelligence.

Learning

Machine learning is the study of computer algorithms that improve automatically through experience and has been central to AI research since the field's inception.

Unsupervised learning is the ability to find patterns in a stream of input. Supervised learning includes both classification and numerical regression. Classification is used to determine what category something belongs in, after seeing a number of examples of things from several categories. Regression is the attempt to produce a function that describes the relationship between inputs and outputs and predicts how the outputs should change as the inputs change. In reinforcement learning the agent is rewarded for good responses and punished for bad ones. The agent uses this sequence of rewards and punishments to form a strategy for operating in its problem space. These three types of learning can be analyzed in terms of decision theory, using concepts like utility. The mathematical analysis of machine learning algorithms and their performance is a branch of theoretical computer science known as computational learning theory.

Within developmental robotics, developmental learning approaches were elaborated for lifelong cumulative acquisition of repertoires of novel skills by a robot, through autonomous self-exploration and social interaction with human teachers, and using guidance mechanisms such as active learning, maturation, motor synergies, and imitation.

Natural Language Processing (Communication)

Natural language processing gives machines the ability to read and understand the languages that humans speak. A sufficiently powerful natural language processing system would enable natural language user interfaces and the acquisition of knowledge directly from human-written sources, such as newswire texts. Some straightforward applications of natural language processing include information retrieval, text mining, question answering and machine translation.

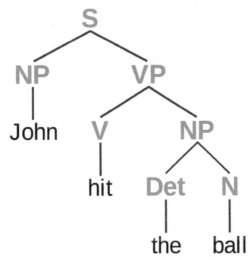

A parse tree represents the syntactic structure of a sentence according to some formal grammar.

A common method of processing and extracting meaning from natural language is through semantic indexing. Increases in processing speeds and the drop in the cost of data storage makes indexing large volumes of abstractions of the user's input much more efficient.

Perception

Machine perception is the ability to use input from sensors (such as cameras, microphones, tactile sensors, sonar and others more exotic) to deduce aspects of the world. Computer vision is the ability to analyze visual input. A few selected subproblems are speech recognition, facial recognition and object recognition.

Motion and manipulation

The field of robotics is closely related to AI. Intelligence is required for robots to be able to handle such tasks as object manipulation and navigation, with sub-problems of localization (knowing where you are, or finding out where other things are), mapping (learning what is around you, building a map of the environment), and motion planning (figuring out how to get there) or path planning (going from one point in space to another point, which may involve compliant motion – where the robot moves while maintaining physical contact with an object).

Long-term Goals

Among the long-term goals in the research pertaining to artificial intelligence are: (1) Social intelligence, (2) Creativity, and (3) General intelligence.

Social Intelligence

Affective computing is the study and development of systems and devices that can recognize, interpret, process, and simulate human affects. It is an interdisciplinary field spanning computer sciences, psychology, and cognitive science. While the origins of the field may be traced as far back as to early philosophical inquiries into emotion, the more modern branch of computer science originated with Rosalind Picard's 1995 paper on affective computing. A motivation for the research is the ability to simulate empathy. The machine should interpret the emotional state of humans and adapt its behaviour to them, giving an appropriate response for those emotions.

Kismet, a robot with rudimentary social skills

Emotion and social skills play two roles for an intelligent agent. First, it must be able to predict the actions of others, by understanding their motives and emotional states. (This involves elements of game theory, decision theory, as well as the ability to model human emotions and the perceptual skills to detect emotions.) Also, in an effort to facilitate human-computer interaction, an intelligent machine might want to be able to *display* emotions—even if it does not actually experience them itself—in order to appear sensitive to the emotional dynamics of human interaction.

Creativity

A sub-field of AI addresses creativity both theoretically (from a philosophical and psychological perspective) and practically (via specific implementations of systems that generate outputs that can be considered creative, or systems that identify and assess creativity). Related areas of computational research are Artificial intuition and Artificial thinking.

General Intelligence

Many researchers think that their work will eventually be incorporated into a machine with *general* intelligence (known as strong AI), combining all the skills above and exceeding human abilities at most or all of them. A few believe that anthropomorphic features like artificial consciousness or an artificial brain may be required for such a project.

Many of the problems above may require general intelligence to be considered solved. For example, even a straightforward, specific task like machine translation requires that the machine read and write in both languages (NLP), follow the author's argument (reason), know what is being talked about (knowledge), and faithfully reproduce the author's intention (social intelligence). A problem like machine translation is considered "AI-complete". In order to solve this particular problem, one must solve all the problems.

Approaches

There is no established unifying theory or paradigm that guides AI research. Researchers disagree about many issues. A few of the most long standing questions that have remained unanswered are these: should artificial intelligence simulate natural intelligence by studying psychology or neurology? Or is human biology as irrelevant to AI research as bird biology is to aeronautical engineering? Can intelligent behavior be described using simple, elegant principles (such as logic or optimization)? Or does it necessarily require solving a large number of completely unrelated problems? Can intelligence be reproduced using high-level symbols, similar to words and ideas? Or does it require "sub-symbolic" processing? John Haugeland, who coined the term GOFAI (Good Old-Fashioned Artificial Intelligence), also proposed that AI should more properly be referred to as synthetic intelligence, a term which has since been adopted by some non-GOFAI researchers.

Cybernetics and Brain Simulation

In the 1940s and 1950s, a number of researchers explored the connection between neurology, information theory, and cybernetics. Some of them built machines that used electronic networks to exhibit rudimentary intelligence, such as W. Grey Walter's turtles and the Johns Hopkins Beast. Many of these researchers gathered for meetings of the Teleological Society at Princeton University and the Ratio Club in England. By 1960, this approach was largely abandoned, although elements of it would be revived in the 1980s.

Symbolic

When access to digital computers became possible in the middle 1950s, AI research began to explore the possibility that human intelligence could be reduced to symbol manipulation. The research was centered in three institutions: Carnegie Mellon University, Stanford and MIT, and each one developed its own style of research. John Haugeland named these approaches to AI "good old fashioned AI" or "GOFAI". During the 1960s, symbolic approaches had achieved great success at simulating high-level thinking in small demonstration programs. Approaches based on cybernetics or neural networks were abandoned or pushed into the background. Researchers in the 1960s and the 1970s were convinced that symbolic approaches would eventually succeed in creating a machine with artificial general intelligence and considered this the goal of their field.

Cognitive simulation

> Economist Herbert Simon and Allen Newell studied human problem-solving skills and attempted to formalize them, and their work laid the foundations of the field of artificial intelligence, as well as cognitive science, operations research and management science. Their research team used the results of psychological experiments to develop programs that simulated the techniques that people used to solve problems. This tradition, centered at Carnegie Mellon University would eventually culminate in the development of the Soar architecture in the middle 1980s.

Logic-based

Unlike Newell and Simon, John McCarthy felt that machines did not need to simulate human thought, but should instead try to find the essence of abstract reasoning and problem solving, regardless of whether people used the same algorithms. His laboratory at Stanford (SAIL) focused on using formal logic to solve a wide variety of problems, including knowledge representation, planning and learning. Logic was also the focus of the work at the University of Edinburgh and elsewhere in Europe which led to the development of the programming language Prolog and the science of logic programming.

"Anti-logic" or "scruffy"

Researchers at MIT (such as Marvin Minsky and Seymour Papert) found that solving difficult problems in vision and natural language processing required ad-hoc solutions – they argued that there was no simple and general principle (like logic) that would capture all the aspects of intelligent behavior. Roger Schank described their "anti-logic" approaches as "scruffy" (as opposed to the "neat" paradigms at CMU and Stanford). Commonsense knowledge bases (such as Doug Lenat's Cyc) are an example of "scruffy" AI, since they must be built by hand, one complicated concept at a time.

Knowledge-based

When computers with large memories became available around 1970, researchers from all three traditions began to build knowledge into AI applications. This "knowledge revolution" led to the development and deployment of expert systems (introduced by Edward Feigenbaum), the first truly successful form of AI software. The knowledge revolution was also driven by the realization that enormous amounts of knowledge would be required by many simple AI applications.

Sub-symbolic

By the 1980s progress in symbolic AI seemed to stall and many believed that symbolic systems would never be able to imitate all the processes of human cognition, especially perception, robotics, learning and pattern recognition. A number of researchers began to look into "sub-symbolic" approaches to specific AI problems. Sub-symbolic methods manage to approach intelligence without specific representations of knowledge.

Bottom-up, embodied, situated, behavior-based or nouvelle AI

Researchers from the related field of robotics, such as Rodney Brooks, rejected symbolic AI and focused on the basic engineering problems that would allow robots to move and survive. Their work revived the non-symbolic viewpoint of the early cybernetics researchers of the 1950s and reintroduced the use of control theory in AI. This coincided with the development of the embodied mind thesis in the related field of cognitive science: the idea that aspects of the body (such as movement, perception and visualization) are required for higher intelligence.

Computational intelligence and soft computing

Interest in neural networks and "connectionism" was revived by David Rumelhart and others in the middle 1980s. Neural networks are an example of soft computing --- they are solutions to problems which cannot be solved with complete logical certainty, and where an approximate solution is often enough. Other soft computing approaches to AI include fuzzy systems, evolutionary computation and many statistical tools. The application of soft computing to AI is studied collectively by the emerging discipline of computational intelligence.

Statistical

In the 1990s, AI researchers developed sophisticated mathematical tools to solve specific subproblems. These tools are truly scientific, in the sense that their results are both measurable and verifiable, and they have been responsible for many of AI's recent successes. The shared mathematical language has also permitted a high level of collaboration with more established fields (like mathematics, economics or operations research). Stuart Russell and Peter Norvig describe this movement as nothing less than a "revolution" and "the victory of the neats." Critics argue that these techniques (with few exceptions) are too focused on particular problems and have failed to address the long-term goal of general intelligence. There is an ongoing debate about the relevance and validity of statistical approaches in AI, exemplified in part by exchanges between Peter Norvig and Noam Chomsky.

Integrating the Approaches

Intelligent agent paradigm

An intelligent agent is a system that perceives its environment and takes actions which maximize its chances of success. The simplest intelligent agents are programs that solve specific problems. More complicated agents include human beings and organizations of human beings (such as firms). The paradigm gives researchers license to study isolated problems and find solutions that are both verifiable and useful, without agreeing on one single approach. An agent that solves a specific problem can use any approach that works – some agents are symbolic and logical, some are sub-symbolic neural networks and others may use new approaches. The paradigm also gives researchers a common language to communicate with other fields—such as decision theory and economics—that also use concepts of abstract agents. The intelligent agent paradigm became widely accepted during the 1990s.

Agent architectures and cognitive architectures

Researchers have designed systems to build intelligent systems out of interacting intelligent agents in a multi-agent system. A system with both symbolic and sub-symbolic components is a hybrid intelligent system, and the study of such systems is artificial intelligence systems integration. A hierarchical control system provides a bridge between sub-symbolic AI at its lowest, reactive levels and traditional symbolic AI at its highest levels, where relaxed time constraints permit planning and world modelling. Rodney Brooks' subsumption architecture was an early proposal for such a hierarchical system.

Tools

In the course of 50 years of research, AI has developed a large number of tools to solve the most difficult problems in computer science. A few of the most general of these methods are discussed below.

Search and Optimization

Many problems in AI can be solved in theory by intelligently searching through many possible solutions: Reasoning can be reduced to performing a search. For example, logical proof can be viewed as searching for a path that leads from premises to conclusions, where each step is the application of an inference rule. Planning algorithms search through trees of goals and subgoals, attempting to find a path to a target goal, a process called means-ends analysis. Robotics algorithms for moving limbs and grasping objects use local searches in configuration space. Many learning algorithms use search algorithms based on optimization.

Simple exhaustive searches are rarely sufficient for most real world problems: the search space (the number of places to search) quickly grows to astronomical numbers. The result is a search that is too slow or never completes. The solution, for many problems, is to use "heuristics" or "rules of thumb" that eliminate choices that are unlikely to lead to the goal (called "pruning the search tree"). Heuristics supply the program with a "best guess" for the path on which the solution lies. Heuristics limit the search for solutions into a smaller sample size.

A very different kind of search came to prominence in the 1990s, based on the mathematical theory of optimization. For many problems, it is possible to begin the search with some form of a guess and then refine the guess incrementally until no more refinements can be made. These algorithms can be visualized as blind hill climbing: we begin the search at a random point on the landscape, and then, by jumps or steps, we keep moving our guess uphill, until we reach the top. Other optimization algorithms are simulated annealing, beam search and random optimization.

Evolutionary computation uses a form of optimization search. For example, they may begin with a population of organisms (the guesses) and then allow them to mutate and recombine, selecting only the fittest to survive each generation (refining the guesses). Forms of evolutionary computation include swarm intelligence algorithms (such as ant colony or particle swarm optimization) and evolutionary algorithms (such as genetic algorithms, gene expression programming, and genetic programming).

Logic

Logic is used for knowledge representation and problem solving, but it can be applied to other problems as well. For example, the satplan algorithm uses logic for planning and inductive logic programming is a method for learning.

Several different forms of logic are used in AI research. Propositional or sentential logic is the logic of statements which can be true or false. First-order logic also allows the use of quantifiers and predicates, and can express facts about objects, their properties, and their relations with each other. Fuzzy logic, is a version of first-order logic which allows the truth of a statement to be represented as a value between 0 and 1, rather than simply True (1) or False (0). Fuzzy systems can be used for uncertain reasoning and have been widely used in modern industrial and consumer product control systems. Subjective logic models uncertainty in a different and more explicit manner than fuzzy-logic: a given binomial opinion satisfies belief + disbelief + uncertainty = 1 within a Beta distribution. By this method, ignorance can be distinguished from probabilistic statements that an agent makes with high confidence.

Default logics, non-monotonic logics and circumscription are forms of logic designed to help with default reasoning and the qualification problem. Several extensions of logic have been designed to handle specific domains of knowledge, such as: description logics; situation calculus, event calculus and fluent calculus (for representing events and time); causal calculus; belief calculus; and modal logics.

Probabilistic Methods for Uncertain Reasoning

Many problems in AI (in reasoning, planning, learning, perception and robotics) require the agent to operate with incomplete or uncertain information. AI researchers have devised a number of powerful tools to solve these problems using methods from probability theory and economics.

Bayesian networks are a very general tool that can be used for a large number of problems: reasoning (using the Bayesian inference algorithm), learning (using the expectation-maximization algorithm), planning (using decision networks) and perception (using dynamic Bayesian networks). Probabilistic algorithms can also be used for filtering, prediction, smoothing and finding explanations for streams of data, helping perception systems to analyze processes that occur over time (e.g., hidden Markov models or Kalman filters).

A key concept from the science of economics is "utility": a measure of how valuable something is to an intelligent agent. Precise mathematical tools have been developed that analyze how an agent can make choices and plan, using decision theory, decision analysis, and information value theory. These tools include models such as Markov decision processes, dynamic decision networks, game theory and mechanism design.

Classifiers and Statistical Learning Methods

The simplest AI applications can be divided into two types: classifiers ("if shiny then diamond") and controllers ("if shiny then pick up"). Controllers do, however, also classify conditions before inferring actions, and therefore classification forms a central part of many AI systems. Classifiers are functions that use pattern matching to determine a closest match. They can be tuned according to examples, making them very attractive for use in AI. These examples are known as observations or patterns. In supervised learning, each pattern belongs to a certain predefined class. A class can be seen as a decision that has to be made. All the observations combined with their class labels are known as a data set. When a new observation is received, that observation is classified based on previous experience.

A classifier can be trained in various ways; there are many statistical and machine learning approaches. The most widely used classifiers are the neural network, kernel methods such as the support vector machine, k-nearest neighbor algorithm, Gaussian mixture model, naive Bayes classifier, and decision tree. The performance of these classifiers have been compared over a wide range of tasks. Classifier performance depends greatly on the characteristics of the data to be classified. There is no single classifier that works best on all given problems; this is also referred to as the "no free lunch" theorem. Determining a suitable classifier for a given problem is still more an art than science.

Neural Networks

The study of non-learning artificial neural networks began in the decade before the field of AI research was founded, in the work of Walter Pitts and Warren McCullough. Frank Rosenblatt invented the perceptron, a learning network with a single layer, similar to the old concept of linear regression. Early pioneers also include Alexey Grigorevich Ivakhnenko, Teuvo Kohonen, Stephen Grossberg, Kunihiko Fukushima, Christoph von der Malsburg, David Willshaw, Shun-Ichi Amari, Bernard Widrow, John Hopfield, and others.

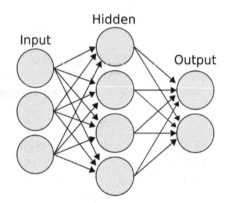

A neural network is an interconnected group of nodes, akin to the vast network of neurons in the human brain.

The main categories of networks are acyclic or feedforward neural networks (where the signal passes in only one direction) and recurrent neural networks (which allow feedback and short-term memories of previous input events). Among the most popular feedforward networks are perceptrons, multi-layer perceptrons and radial basis networks. Neural networks can be applied to the problem of intelligent control (for robotics) or learning, using such techniques as Hebbian learning, GMDH or competitive learning.

Today, neural networks are often trained by the backpropagation algorithm, which had been around since 1970 as the reverse mode of automatic differentiation published by Seppo Linnainmaa, and was introduced to neural networks by Paul Werbos.

Hierarchical temporal memory is an approach that models some of the structural and algorithmic properties of the neocortex.

Deep Feedforward Neural Networks

Deep learning in artificial neural networks with many layers has transformed many important subfields of artificial intelligence, including computer vision, speech recognition, natural language processing and others.

According to a survey, the expression "Deep Learning" was introduced to the Machine Learning community by Rina Dechter in 1986 and gained traction after Igor Aizenberg and colleagues introduced it to Artificial Neural Networks in 2000. The first functional Deep Learning networks were published by Alexey Grigorevich Ivakhnenko and V. G. Lapa in 1965. These networks are trained one layer at a time. Ivakhnenko's 1971 paper describes the learning of a deep feedforward multilayer perceptron with eight layers, already much deeper than many later networks. In 2006, a publication by Geoffrey Hinton and Ruslan Salakhutdinov introduced another way of pre-training many-layered feedforward neural networks (FNNs) one layer at a time, treating each layer in turn as an unsupervised restricted Boltzmann machine, then using supervised backpropagation for fine-tuning. Similar to shallow artificial neural networks, deep neural networks can model complex non-linear relationships. Over the last few years, advances in both machine learning algorithms and computer hardware have led to more efficient methods for training deep neural networks that contain many layers of non-linear hidden units and a very large output layer.

Deep learning often uses convolutional neural networks (CNNs), whose origins can be traced back to the Neocognitron introduced by Kunihiko Fukushima in 1980. In 1989, Yann LeCun and colleagues applied backpropagation to such an architecture. In the early 2000s, in an industrial application CNNs already processed an estimated 10% to 20% of all the checks written in the US. Since 2011, fast implementations of CNNs on GPUs have won many visual pattern recognition competitions.

Deep feedforward neural networks were used in conjunction with reinforcement learning by AlphaGo, Google Deepmind's program that was the first to beat a professional human player.

Deep Recurrent Neural Networks

Early on, deep learning was also applied to sequence learning with recurrent neural networks (RNNs) which are general computers and can run arbitrary programs to process arbitrary sequences of inputs. The depth of an RNN is unlimited and depends on the length of its input sequence. RNNs can be trained by gradient descent but suffer from the vanishing gradient problem. In 1992, it was shown that unsupervised pre-training of a stack of recurrent neural networks can speed up subsequent supervised learning of deep sequential problems.

Numerous researchers now use variants of a deep learning recurrent NN called the Long short term memory (LSTM) network published by Hochreiter & Schmidhuber in 1997. LSTM is often trained by Connectionist Temporal Classification (CTC). At Google, Microsoft and Baidu this approach has revolutionised speech recognition. For example, in 2015, Google's speech recognition experienced a dramatic performance jump of 49% through CTC-trained LSTM, which is now available through Google Voice to billions of smartphone users. Google also used LSTM to improve machine translation, Language Modeling and Multilingual Language Processing. LSTM combined with CNNs also improved automatic image captioning and a plethora of other applications.

Control Theory

Control theory, the grandchild of cybernetics, has many important applications, especially in robotics.

Languages

AI researchers have developed several specialized languages for AI research, including Lisp and Prolog.

Evaluating Progress

In 1950, Alan Turing proposed a general procedure to test the intelligence of an agent now known as the Turing test. This procedure allows almost all the major problems of artificial intelligence to be tested. However, it is a very difficult challenge and at present all agents fail.

Artificial intelligence can also be evaluated on specific problems such as small problems in chemistry, hand-writing recognition and game-playing. Such tests have been termed subject matter expert Turing tests. Smaller problems provide more achievable goals and there are an ever-increasing number of positive results.

One classification for outcomes of an AI test is:

1. Optimal: it is not possible to perform better.

2. Strong super-human: performs better than all humans.

3. Super-human: performs better than most humans.

4. Sub-human: performs worse than most humans.

For example, performance at draughts (i.e. checkers) is optimal, performance at chess is super-human and nearing strong super-human and per-formance at many everyday tasks (such as recognizing a face or crossing a room without bumping into something) is sub-human.

A quite different approach measures machine intelligence through tests which are developed from *mathematical* definitions of intelligence. Examples of these kinds of tests start in the late nineties devising intelligence tests using notions from Kolmogorov complexity and data compression. Two major advantages of mathematical definitions are their applicability to nonhuman intelligences and their absence of a requirement for human testers.

A derivative of the Turing test is the Completely Automated Public Turing test to tell Computers and Humans Apart (CAPTCHA). As the name implies, this helps to determine that a user is an actual person and not a computer posing as a human. In contrast to the standard Turing test, CAPTCHA administered by a machine and targeted to a human as opposed to being administered by a human and targeted to a machine. A computer asks a user to complete a simple test then generates a grade for that test. Computers are unable to solve the problem, so correct solutions are deemed to be the result of a person taking the test. A common type of CAPTCHA is the test that requires the typing of distorted letters, numbers or symbols that appear in an image undecipherable by a computer.

Applications

An automated online assistant providing customer service on a web page – one of many very primitive applications of artificial intelligence.

AI is relevant to any intellectual task. Modern artificial intelligence techniques are pervasive and are too numerous to list here. Frequently, when a technique reaches mainstream use, it is no longer considered artificial intelligence; this phenomenon is described as the AI effect.

High-profile examples of AI include autonomous vehicles (such as drones and self-driving cars), medical diagnosis, creating art (such as poetry), proving mathemetical theorems, playing games (such as Chess or Go), search engines (such as Google search), online assistants (such as Siri), image recognition in photographs, spam filtering, and targeting online advertisements.

Competitions and Prizes

There are a number of competitions and prizes to promote research in artificial intelligence. The main areas promoted are: general machine intelligence, conversational behavior, data-mining, robotic cars, robot soccer and games.

Platforms

A platform (or "computing platform") is defined as "some sort of hardware architecture or software framework (including application frameworks), that allows software to run." As Rodney Brooks pointed out many years ago, it is not just the artificial intelligence software that defines the AI features of the platform, but rather the actual platform itself that affects the AI that results, i.e., there needs to be work in AI problems on real-world platforms rather than in isolation.

A wide variety of platforms has allowed different aspects of AI to develop, ranging from expert systems such as Cyc to deep-learning frameworks to robot platforms such as the Roomba with open interface. Recent advances in deep artificial neural networks and distributed computing have led to a proliferation of software libraries, including Deeplearning4j, TensorFlow, Theano and Torch.

Philosophy and Ethics

There are three philosophical questions related to AI:

1. Is artificial general intelligence possible? Can a machine solve any problem that a human being can solve using intelligence? Or are there hard limits to what a machine can accomplish?

2. Are intelligent machines dangerous? How can we ensure that machines behave ethically and that they are used ethically?

3. Can a machine have a mind, consciousness and mental states in exactly the same sense that human beings do? Can a machine be sentient, and thus deserve certain rights? Can a machine intentionally cause harm?

The Limits of Artificial General Intelligence

Can a machine be intelligent? Can it "think"?

Turing's "polite convention"

> We need not decide if a machine can "think"; we need only decide if a machine can act as

intelligently as a human being. This approach to the philosophical problems associated with artificial intelligence forms the basis of the Turing test.

The Dartmouth proposal

"Every aspect of learning or any other feature of intelligence can be so precisely described that a machine can be made to simulate it." This conjecture was printed in the proposal for the Dartmouth Conference of 1956, and represents the position of most working AI researchers.

Newell and Simon's physical symbol system hypothesis

"A physical symbol system has the necessary and sufficient means of general intelligent action." Newell and Simon argue that intelligence consists of formal operations on symbols. Hubert Dreyfus argued that, on the contrary, human expertise depends on unconscious instinct rather than conscious symbol manipulation and on having a "feel" for the situation rather than explicit symbolic knowledge.

Gödelian arguments

Gödel himself, John Lucas (in 1961) and Roger Penrose (in a more detailed argument from 1989 onwards) argued that humans are not reducible to Turing machines. The detailed arguments are complex, but in essence they derive from Kurt Gödel's 1931 proof in his first incompleteness theorem that it is always possible to create statements that a formal system could not prove. A human being, however, can (with some thought) see the truth of these "Gödel statements". Any Turing program designed to search for these statements can have its methods reduced to a formal system, and so will always have a "Gödel statement" derivable from its program which it can never discover. However, if humans are indeed capable of understanding mathematical truth, it doesn't seem possible that we could be limited in the same way. This is quite a general result, if accepted, since it can be shown that hardware neural nets, and computers based on random processes (e.g. annealing approaches) and quantum computers based on entangled qubits (so long as they involve no new physics) can all be reduced to Turing machines. All they do is reduce the complexity of the tasks, not permit new types of problems to be solved. Roger Penrose speculates that there may be new physics involved in our brain, perhaps at the intersection of gravity and quantum mechanics at the Planck scale. This argument, if accepted does not rule out the possibility of true artificial intelligence, but means it has to be biological in basis or based on new physical principles. The argument has been followed up by many counter arguments, and then Roger Penrose has replied to those with counter counter examples, and it is now an intricate complex debate.

The artificial brain argument

The brain can be simulated by machines and because brains are intelligent, simulated brains must also be intelligent; thus machines can be intelligent. Hans Moravec, Ray Kurzweil and others have argued that it is technologically feasible to copy the brain directly into hardware and software, and that such a simulation will be essentially identical to the original.

The AI effect

Machines are *already* intelligent, but observers have failed to recognize it. When Deep Blue beat Garry Kasparov in chess, the machine was acting intelligently. However, onlookers commonly discount the behavior of an artificial intelligence program by arguing that it is not "real" intelligence after all; thus "real" intelligence is whatever intelligent behavior people can do that machines still can not. This is known as the AI Effect: "AI is whatever hasn't been done yet."

Intelligent Behaviour and Machine Ethics

As a minimum, an AI system must be able to reproduce aspects of human intelligence. This raises the issue of how ethically the machine should behave towards both humans and other AI agents. This issue was addressed by Wendell Wallach in his book titled *Moral Machines* in which he introduced the concept of artificial moral agents (AMA). For Wallach, AMAs have become a part of the research landscape of artificial intelligence as guided by its two central questions which he identifies as "Does Humanity Want Computers Making Moral Decisions" and "Can (Ro)bots Really Be Moral". For Wallach the question is not centered on the issue of *whether* machines can demonstrate the equivalent of moral behavior in contrast to the *constraints* which society may place on the development of AMAs.

Machine Ethics

The field of machine ethics is concerned with giving machines ethical principles, or a procedure for discovering a way to resolve the ethical dilemmas they might encounter, enabling them to function in an ethically responsible manner through their own ethical decision making. The field was delineated in the AAAI Fall 2005 Symposium on Machine Ethics: "Past research concerning the relationship between technology and ethics has largely focused on responsible and irresponsible use of technology by human beings, with a few people being interested in how human beings ought to treat machines. In all cases, only human beings have engaged in ethical reasoning. The time has come for adding an ethical dimension to at least some machines. Recognition of the ethical ramifications of behavior involving machines, as well as recent and potential developments in machine autonomy, necessitate this. In contrast to computer hacking, software property issues, privacy issues and other topics normally ascribed to computer ethics, machine ethics is concerned with the behavior of machines towards human users and other machines. Research in machine ethics is key to alleviating concerns with autonomous systems—it could be argued that the notion of autonomous machines without such a dimension is at the root of all fear concerning machine intelligence. Further, investigation of machine ethics could enable the discovery of problems with current ethical theories, advancing our thinking about Ethics." Machine ethics is sometimes referred to as machine morality, computational ethics or computational morality. A variety of perspectives of this nascent field can be found in the collected edition "Machine Ethics" that stems from the AAAI Fall 2005 Symposium on Machine Ethics. Some suggest that to ensure that AI-equipped machines (sometimes called "smart machines") will act ethically requires a new kind of AI. This AI would be able to monitor, supervise, and if need be, correct the first order AI.

Malevolent and Friendly AI

Political scientist Charles T. Rubin believes that AI can be neither designed nor guaranteed to be benevolent. He argues that "any sufficiently advanced benevolence may be indistinguishable from malevolence." Humans should not assume machines or robots would treat us favorably, because there is no *a priori* reason to believe that they would be sympathetic to our system of morality, which has evolved along with our particular biology (which AIs would not share). Hyper-intelligent software may not necessarily decide to support the continued existence of mankind, and would be extremely difficult to stop. This topic has also recently begun to be discussed in academic publications as a real source of risks to civilization, humans, and planet Earth.

Physicist Stephen Hawking, Microsoft founder Bill Gates and SpaceX founder Elon Musk have expressed concerns about the possibility that AI could evolve to the point that humans could not control it, with Hawking theorizing that this could "spell the end of the human race".

One proposal to deal with this is to ensure that the first generally intelligent AI is 'Friendly AI', and will then be able to control subsequently developed AIs. Some question whether this kind of check could really remain in place.

Leading AI researcher Rodney Brooks writes, "I think it is a mistake to be worrying about us developing malevolent AI anytime in the next few hundred years. I think the worry stems from a fundamental error in not distinguishing the difference between the very real recent advances in a particular aspect of AI, and the enormity and complexity of building sentient volitional intelligence."

Devaluation of Humanity

Joseph Weizenbaum wrote that AI applications can not, by definition, successfully simulate genuine human empathy and that the use of AI technology in fields such as customer service or psychotherapy was deeply misguided. Weizenbaum was also bothered that AI researchers (and some philosophers) were willing to view the human mind as nothing more than a computer program (a position now known as computationalism). To Weizenbaum these points suggest that AI research devalues human life.

Decrease in Demand for Human Labor

Martin Ford, author of *The Lights in the Tunnel: Automation, Accelerating Technology and the Economy of the Future*, and others argue that specialized artificial intelligence applications, robotics and other forms of automation will ultimately result in significant unemployment as machines begin to match and exceed the capability of workers to perform most routine and repetitive jobs. Ford predicts that many knowledge-based occupations—and in particular entry level jobs—will be increasingly susceptible to automation via expert systems, machine learning and other AI-enhanced applications. AI-based applications may also be used to amplify the capabilities of low-wage offshore workers, making it more feasible to outsource knowledge work.

Machine Consciousness, Sentience and Mind

If an AI system replicates all key aspects of human intelligence, will that system also be sentient – will it have a mind which has conscious experiences? This question is closely related to the philosophical problem as to the nature of human consciousness, generally referred to as the hard problem of consciousness.

Consciousness

Computationalism

Computationalism is the position in the philosophy of mind that the human mind or the human brain (or both) is an information processing system and that thinking is a form of computing. Computationalism argues that the relationship between mind and body is similar or identical to the relationship between software and hardware and thus may be a solution to the mind-body problem. This philosophical position was inspired by the work of AI researchers and cognitive scientists in the 1960s and was originally proposed by philosophers Jerry Fodor and Hillary Putnam.

Strong AI Hypothesis

Searle's strong AI hypothesis states that "The appropriately programmed computer with the right inputs and outputs would thereby have a mind in exactly the same sense human beings have minds." John Searle counters this assertion with his Chinese room argument, which asks us to look *inside* the computer and try to find where the "mind" might be.

Robot Rights

Mary Shelley's *Frankenstein* considers a key issue in the ethics of artificial intelligence: if a machine can be created that has intelligence, could it also *feel*? If it can feel, does it have the same rights as a human? The idea also appears in modern science fiction, such as the film *A.I.: Artificial Intelligence*, in which humanoid machines have the ability to feel emotions. This issue, now known as "robot rights", is currently being considered by, for example, California's Institute for the Future, although many critics believe that the discussion is premature. The subject is profoundly discussed in the 2010 documentary film *Plug & Pray*.

Superintelligence

Are there limits to how intelligent machines – or human-machine hybrids – can be? A superintelligence, hyperintelligence, or superhuman intelligence is a hypothetical agent that would possess intelligence far surpassing that of the brightest and most gifted human mind. "Superintelligence" may also refer to the form or degree of intelligence possessed by such an agent.

Technological Singularity

If research into Strong AI produced sufficiently intelligent software, it might be able to reprogram and improve itself. The improved software would be even better at improving itself, leading to recursive self-improvement. The new intelligence could thus increase exponentially and dramatically surpass humans. Science fiction writer Vernor Vinge named this scenario "singularity". Technological singularity is when accelerating progress in technologies will cause a runaway effect wherein artificial intelligence will exceed human intellectual capacity and control, thus radically changing or even ending civilization. Because the capabilities of such an intelligence may be impossible to comprehend, the technological singularity is an occurrence beyond which events are unpredictable or even unfathomable.

Ray Kurzweil has used Moore's law (which describes the relentless exponential improvement in digital technology) to calculate that desktop computers will have the same processing power as human brains by the year 2029, and predicts that the singularity will occur in 2045.

Transhumanism

You awake one morning to find your brain has another lobe functioning. Invisible, this auxiliary lobe answers your questions with information beyond the realm of your own memory, suggests plausible courses of action, and asks questions that help bring out relevant facts. You quickly come to rely on the new lobe so much that you stop wondering how it works. You just use it. This is the dream of artificial intelligence.

— BYTE, April 1985

Robot designer Hans Moravec, cyberneticist Kevin Warwick and inventor Ray Kurzweil have predicted that humans and machines will merge in the future into cyborgs that are more capable and powerful than either. This idea, called transhumanism, which has roots in Aldous Huxley and Robert Ettinger, has been illustrated in fiction as well, for example in the manga *Ghost in the Shell* and the science-fiction series *Dune*.

In the 1980s artist Hajime Sorayama's Sexy Robots series were painted and published in Japan depicting the actual organic human form with lifelike muscular metallic skins and later "the Gynoids" book followed that was used by or influenced movie makers including George Lucas and other creatives. Sorayama never considered these organic robots to be real part of nature but always unnatural product of the human mind, a fantasy existing in the mind even when realized in actual form.

Edward Fredkin argues that "artificial intelligence is the next stage in evolution", an idea first proposed by Samuel Butler's "Darwin among the Machines" (1863), and expanded upon by George Dyson in his book of the same name in 1998.

Existential Risk

The development of full artificial intelligence could spell the end of the human race. Once humans develop artificial intelligence, it will take off on its own and redesign itself at an ever-increasing rate. Humans, who are limited by slow biological evolution, couldn't compete and would be superseded.

— Stephen Hawking

A common concern about the development of artificial intelligence is the potential threat it could pose to mankind. This concern has recently gained attention after mentions by celebrities including Stephen Hawking, Bill Gates, and Elon Musk. A group of prominent tech titans including Peter Thiel, Amazon Web Services and Musk have committed $1billion to OpenAI a nonprofit company aimed at championing responsible AI development. The opinion of experts within the field of artificial intelligence is mixed, with sizable fractions both concerned and unconcerned by risk from eventual superhumanly-capable AI.

In his book *Superintelligence*, Nick Bostrom provides an argument that artificial intelligence will pose a threat to mankind. He argues that sufficiently intelligent AI, if it chooses actions based on achieving some goal, will exhibit convergent behavior such as acquiring resources or protecting itself from being shut down. If this AI's goals do not reflect humanity's - one example is an AI told to compute as many digits of pi as possible - it might harm humanity in order to acquire more resources or prevent itself from being shut down, ultimately to better achieve its goal.

For this danger to be realized, the hypothetical AI would have to overpower or out-think all of humanity, which a minority of experts argue is a possibility far enough in the future to not be worth researching. Other counterarguments revolve around humans being either intrinsically or convergently valuable from the perspective of an artificial intelligence.

Concern over risk from artificial intelligence has led to some high-profile donations and investments. In January 2015, Elon Musk donated ten million dollars to the Future of Life Institute to fund research on understanding AI decision making. The goal of the institute is to "grow wisdom with which we manage" the growing power of technology. Musk also funds companies developing artificial intelligence such as Google DeepMind and Vicarious to "just keep an eye on what's going on with artificial intelligence. I think there is potentially a dangerous outcome there."

Development of militarized artificial intelligence is a related concern. Currently, 50+ countries are researching battlefield robots, including the United States, China, Russia, and the United Kingdom. Many people concerned about risk from superintelligent AI also want to limit the use of artificial soldiers.

Moral Decision-making

To keep AI ethical, some have suggested teaching new technologies equipped with AI, such as driver-less cars, to render moral decisions on their own. Others argued that these technologies could learn to act ethically the way children do—by interacting with adults, in particular, with ethicists. Still others suggest these smart technologies can determine the moral preferences of those who use them (just the way one learns about consumer preferences) and then be programmed to heed these preferences.

In Fiction

The implications of artificial intelligence have been a persistent theme in science fiction. Early stories typically revolved around intelligent robots. The word "robot" itself was coined by Karel Čapek in his 1921 play *R.U.R.*, the title standing for "Rossum's Universal Robots". Later, the SF writer Isaac Asimov developed the Three Laws of Robotics which he subsequently explored in a long series of robot stories. These laws have since gained some traction in genuine AI research.

Other influential fictional intelligences include HAL, the computer in charge of the spaceship in *2001: A Space Odyssey*, released as both a film and a book in 1968 and written by Arthur C. Clarke.

AI has since become firmly rooted in popular culture and is in many films, such as *The Terminator* (1984) and *A.I. Artificial Intelligence* (2001).

Computational Neuroscience

Computational neuroscience (also theoretical neuroscience) is the study of brain function in terms of the information processing properties of the structures that make up the nervous system. It is an interdisciplinary science that links the diverse fields of neuroscience, cognitive science, and psychology with electrical engineering, computer science, mathematics, and physics.

Computational neuroscience is distinct from psychological connectionism and from learning theories of disciplines such as machine learning, neural networks, and computational learning theory in that it emphasizes descriptions of functional and biologically realistic neurons (and neural systems) and their physiology and dynamics. These models capture the essential features of the biological system at multiple spatial-temporal scales, from membrane currents, proteins, and chemical coupling to network oscillations, columnar and topographic architecture, and learning and memory.

These computational models are used to frame hypotheses that can be directly tested by biological or psychological experiments.

History

The term "computational neuroscience" was introduced by Eric L. Schwartz, who organized a conference, held in 1985 in Carmel, California, at the request of the Systems Development Foundation to provide a summary of the current status of a field which until that point was referred to by a variety of names, such as neural modeling, brain theory and neural networks. The proceedings of this definitional meeting were published in 1990 as the book *Computational Neuroscience*. The first open international meeting focused on Computational Neuroscience was organized by James M. Bower and John Miller in San Francisco, California in 1989 and has continued each year since as the annual CNS meeting The first graduate educational program in computational neuroscience was organized as the Computational and Neural Systems Ph.D. program at the California Institute of Technology in 1985.

The early historical roots of the field can be traced to the work of people such as Louis Lapicque, Hodgkin & Huxley, Hubel & Wiesel, and David Marr, to name a few. Lapicque introduced the integrate and fire model of the neuron in a seminal article published in 1907; this model is still one of the most popular models in computational neuroscience for both cellular and neural networks studies, as well as in mathematical neuroscience because of its simplicity. About 40 years later, Hodgkin & Huxley de-veloped the voltage clamp and created the first biophysical model of the action potential. Hubel & Wiesel discovered that neurons in the primary visual cortex, the first cortical area to process infor-mation coming from the retina, have oriented receptive fields and are organized in columns. David Marr's work focused on the interactions between neurons, suggesting computational approaches to the study of how functional groups of neurons within the hippocampus and neocortex interact, store, process, and transmit information. Computational modeling of biophysically realistic neu-rons and dendrites began with the work of Wilfrid Rall, with the first multicompartmental model using cable theory.

Major Topics

Research in computational neuroscience can be roughly categorized into several lines of inquiry. Most computational neuroscientists collaborate closely with experimentalists in analyzing novel data and synthesizing new models of biological phenomena.

Single-neuron Modeling

Even single neurons have complex biophysical characteristics and can perform computations (e.g.). Hodgkin and Huxley's original model only employed two voltage-sensitive currents (Voltage sensitive ion channels are glycoprotein molecules which extend through the lipid bilayer, allowing ions to traverse under certain conditions through the axolemma), the fast-acting sodium and the inward-rectifying potassium. Though successful in predicting the timing and qualitative features of the action potential, it nevertheless failed to predict a number of important features such as adaptation and shunting. Scientists now believe that there are a wide variety of voltage-sensitive currents, and the implications of the differing dynamics, modulations, and sensitivity of these currents is an important topic of computational neuroscience.

The computational functions of complex dendrites are also under intense investigation. There is a large body of literature regarding how different currents interact with geometric properties of neurons.

Some models are also tracking biochemical pathways at very small scales such as spines or synaptic clefts.

There are many software packages, such as GENESIS and NEURON, that allow rapid and systematic *in silico* modeling of realistic neurons. Blue Brain, a project founded by Henry Markram from the École Polytechnique Fédérale de Lausanne, aims to construct a biophysically detailed simulation of a cortical column on the Blue Gene supercomputer.

A problem in the field is that detailed neuron descriptions are computationally expensive and this can handicap the pursuit of realistic network investigations, where many neurons need to be simulated. So, researchers that study large neural circuits typically represent each neuron and synapse simply, ignoring much of the biological detail. This is unfortunate as there is evidence that the richness of biophysical properties on the single neuron scale can supply mechanisms that serve as the building blocks for network dynamics. Hence there is a drive to produce simplified neuron models that can retain significant biological fidelity at a low computational overhead. Algorithms have been developed to produce faithful, faster running, simplified surrogate neuron models from computationally expensive, detailed neuron models.

Development, Axonal Patterning, and Guidance

How do axons and dendrites form during development? How do axons know where to target and how to reach these targets? How do neurons migrate to the proper position in the central and peripheral systems? How do synapses form? We know from molecular biology that distinct parts of the nervous system release distinct chemical cues, from growth factors to hormones that modulate and influence the growth and development of functional connections between neurons.

Theoretical investigations into the formation and patterning of synaptic connection and morphology are still nascent. One hypothesis that has recently garnered some attention is the *minimal wiring hypothesis*, which postulates that the formation of axons and dendrites effectively minimizes resource allocation while maintaining maximal information storage.

Sensory Processing

Early models of sensory processing understood within a theoretical framework are credited to Horace Barlow. Somewhat similar to the minimal wiring hypothesis described in the preceding section, Barlow understood the processing of the early sensory systems to be a form of efficient coding, where the neurons encoded information which minimized the number of spikes. Experimental and computational work have since supported this hypothesis in one form or another.

Current research in sensory processing is divided among a biophysical modelling of different subsystems and a more theoretical modelling of perception. Current models of perception have suggested that the brain performs some form of Bayesian inference and integration of different sensory information in generating our perception of the physical world.

Memory and Synaptic Plasticity

Earlier models of memory are primarily based on the postulates of Hebbian learning. Biologically relevant models such as Hopfield net have been developed to address the properties of associative, rather than content-addressable, style of memory that occur in biological systems. These attempts are primarily focusing on the formation of medium- and long-term memory, localizing in the hippocampus. Models of working memory, relying on theories of network oscillations and persistent activity, have been built to capture some features of the prefrontal cortex in context-related memory.

One of the major problems in neurophysiological memory is how it is maintained and changed through multiple time scales. Unstable synapses are easy to train but also prone to stochastic disruption. Stable synapses forget less easily, but they are also harder to consolidate. One recent computational hypothesis involves cascades of plasticity that allow synapses to function at multiple time scales. Stereochemically detailed models of the acetylcholine receptor-based synapse with the Monte Carlo method, working at the time scale of microseconds, have been built. It is likely that computational tools will contribute greatly to our understanding of how synapses function and change in relation to external stimulus in the coming decades.

Behaviors of Networks

Biological neurons are connected to each other in a complex, recurrent fashion. These connections are, unlike most artificial neural networks, sparse and usually specific. It is not known how information is transmitted through such sparsely connected networks. It is also unknown what the computational functions of these specific connectivity patterns are, if any.

The interactions of neurons in a small network can be often reduced to simple models such as the Ising model. The statistical mechanics of such simple systems are well-characterized theoretically. There has been some recent evidence that suggests that dynamics of arbitrary neuronal networks can be reduced to pairwise interactions. It is not known, however, whether such descriptive dynamics impart any important computational function. With the emergence of two-photon microscopy and calcium imaging, we now have powerful experimental methods with which to test the new theories regarding neuronal networks.

In some cases the complex interactions between *inhibitory* and *excitatory* neurons can be simplified using mean field theory, which gives rise to the population model of neural networks. While many neurotheorists prefer such models with reduced complexity, others argue that uncovering structural functional relations depends on including as much neuronal and network structure as possible. Models of this type are typically built in large simulation platforms like GENESIS or NEURON. There have been some attempts to provide unified methods that bridge and integrate these levels of complexity.

Cognition, Discrimination, and Learning

Computational modeling of higher cognitive functions has only recently begun. Experimental data comes primarily from single-unit recording in primates. The frontal lobe and parietal lobe function as integrators of information from multiple sensory modalities. There are some tentative ideas regarding how simple mutually inhibitory functional circuits in these areas may carry out biologically relevant computation.

The brain seems to be able to discriminate and adapt particularly well in certain contexts. For instance, human beings seem to have an enormous capacity for memorizing and recognizing faces. One of the key goals of computational neuroscience is to dissect how biological systems carry out these complex computations efficiently and potentially replicate these processes in building intelligent machines.

The brain's large-scale organizational principles are illuminated by many fields, including biology, psychology, and clinical practice. Integrative neuroscience attempts to consolidate these observations through unified descriptive models and databases of behavioral measures and recordings. These are the bases for some quantitative modeling of large-scale brain activity.

The Computational Representational Understanding of Mind (CRUM) is another attempt at modeling human cognition through simulated processes like acquired rule-based systems in decision making and the manipulation of visual representations in decision making.

Consciousness

One of the ultimate goals of psychology/neuroscience is to be able to explain the everyday experience of conscious life. Francis Crick and Christof Koch made some attempts to formulate a consistent framework for future work in neural correlates of consciousness (NCC), though much of the work in this field remains speculative.

Computational Clinical Neuroscience

It is a field that brings together experts in neuroscience, neurology, psychiatry, decision sciences and computational modeling to quantitatively define and investigate problems in neurological and psychiatric diseases, and to train scientists and clinicians that wish to apply these models to diagnosis and treatment.

Augmented Reality

Samsung SARI AR SDK markerless tracker used in the *AR EdiBear* game (Android OS)

AR Tower Defense game on the Nokia N95 smartphone (Symbian OS) uses fiducial markers

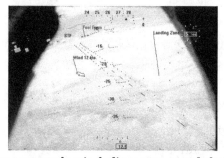

NASA X38 display showing video map overlays including runways and obstacles during flight test in 2000.

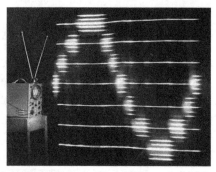

Early example of AR: Overlaying electromagnetic radio waves onto visual reality. Sequential Wave Imprinting Machine imprints visual images onto the human eye's retina or photographic film.

Augmented reality (AR) is a live direct or indirect view of a physical, real-world environment whose elements are *augmented* (or supplemented) by computer-generated sensory input such as sound, video, graphics or GPS data. It is related to a more general concept called mediated reality, in which a view of reality is modified (possibly even diminished rather than augmented) by a computer. As a result, the technology functions by enhancing one's current perception of reality. By contrast, virtual reality replaces the real world with a simulated one. Augmentation is conventionally in real-time and in semantic context with environmental elements, such as sports scores on TV during a match. With the help of advanced AR technology (e.g. adding computer vision and object recognition) the information about the surrounding real world of the user becomes interactive and digitally manipulable. Information about the environment and its objects is overlaid on the real world. This information can be virtual or real, e.g. seeing other real sensed or measured information such as electromagnetic radio waves overlaid in exact alignment with where they actually are in space.

Technology

Hardware

Hardware components for augmented reality are: processor, display, sensors and input devices. Modern mobile computing devices like smartphones and tablet computers contain these elements which often include a camera and MEMS sensors such as accelerometer, GPS, and solid state compass, making them suitable AR platforms.

Display

Various technologies are used in Augmented Reality rendering including optical projection systems, monitors, hand held devices, and display systems worn on the human body.

Head-mounted

A head-mounted display (HMD) is a display device paired to a headset such as a harness or helmet. HMDs place images of both the physical world and virtual objects over the user's field of view. Modern HMDs often employ sensors for six degrees of freedom monitoring that allow the system to align virtual information to the physical world and adjust accordingly with the user's head movements. HMDs can provide users immersive, mobile and collaborative AR experiences.

Meta 2 Headset

In January 2015, Meta launched a $23 million project led by Horizons Ventures, Tim Draper, Alexis Ohanian, BOE Optoelectronics and Garry Tan. On February 17, 2016, Meta announced their second-generation product at TED, Meta 2. The Meta 2 head-mounted display headset uses a sensory array for hand interactions and positional tracking, visual field view of 90 degrees (diagonal), and resolution display of 2560 x 1440 (20 pixels per degree), which is considered the largest field view (FOV) currently available.

Eyeglasses

AR displays can be rendered on devices resembling eyeglasses. Versions include eyewear that employ cameras to intercept the real world view and re-display its augmented view through the eye pieces and devices in which the AR imagery is projected through or reflected off the surfaces of the eyewear lens pieces.

HUD

Near eye augmented reality devices can be used as portable head-up displays as they can show data, information, and images while the user views the real world. Many definitions of augmented reality only define it as overlaying the information. This is basically what a head-up display does; however, practically speaking, augmented reality is expected to include tracking between the superimposed information, data, and images and some portion of the real world.

Microsoft HoloLens

CrowdOptic, an existing app for smartphones, applies algorithms and triangulation techniques to photo metadata including GPS position, compass heading, and a time stamp to arrive at a relative significance value for photo objects. CrowdOptic technology can be used by Google Glass users to learn where to look at a given point in time.

In January 2015, Microsoft introduced HoloLens, which is an independent smartglasses unit. Brian Blau, research director of consumer technology and markets at Gartner, said that "Out of all the head-mounted displays that I've tried in the past couple of decades, the HoloLens was the best in its class.". First impressions and opinions have been generally that HoloLens is a superior device to the Google Glass, and manages to do several things "right" in which Glass failed.

Contact Lenses

Contact lenses that display AR imaging are in development. These bionic contact lenses might contain the elements for display embedded into the lens including integrated circuitry, LEDs and an antenna for wireless communication. The first contact lens display was reported in 1999 and subsequently, 11 years later in 2010/2011 Another version of contact lenses, in development for the U.S. Military, is designed to function with AR spectacles, allowing soldiers to focus on close-to-the-eye AR images on the spectacles and distant real world objects at the same time. The futuristic short film *Sight* features contact lens-like augmented reality devices.

Virtual Retinal Display

A virtual retinal display (VRD) is a personal display device under development at the University of Washington's Human Interface Technology Laboratory. With this technology, a display is scanned directly onto the retina of a viewer's eye. The viewer sees what appears to be a conventional display floating in space in front of them.

EyeTap

The EyeTap (also known as Generation-2 Glass) captures rays of light that would otherwise pass through the center of a lens of an eye of the wearer, and substitutes synthetic computer-controlled light for each ray of real light. The Generation-4 Glass (Laser EyeTap) is similar to the VRD (i.e. it uses a computer controlled laser light source) except that it also has infinite depth of focus and causes the eye itself to, in effect, function as both a camera and a display, by way of exact alignment with the eye, and resynthesis (in laser light) of rays of light entering the eye.

Handheld

Handheld displays employ a small display that fits in a user's hand. All handheld AR solutions to date opt for video see-through. Initially handheld AR employed fiducial markers, and later GPS units and MEMS sensors such as digital compasses and six degrees of freedom accelerometer–gyroscope. Today SLAM markerless trackers such as PTAM are starting to come into use. Handheld display AR promises to be the first commercial success for AR technologies. The two main advantages of handheld AR is the portable nature of handheld devices and ubiquitous nature of camera phones. The disadvantages are the physical constraints of the user having to hold the handheld device out in front of them at all times as well as distorting effect of classically wide-angled mobile phone cameras when compared to the real world as viewed through the eye.

Spatial

Spatial Augmented Reality (SAR) augments real world objects and scenes without the use of special displays such as monitors, head mounted displays or hand-held devices. SAR makes use of digital projectors to display graphical information onto physical objects. The key difference in SAR is that the display is separated from the users of the system. Because the displays are not associated with each user, SAR scales naturally up to groups of users, thus allowing for collocated collaboration between users.

Examples include shader lamps, mobile projectors, virtual tables, and smart projectors. Shader lamps mimic and augment reality by projecting imagery onto neutral objects, providing the opportunity to enhance the object's appearance with materials of a simple unit- a projector, camera, and sensor.

Other applications include table and wall projections. One innovation, the Extended Virtual Table, separates the virtual from the real by including beam-splitter mirrors attached to the ceiling at an adjustable angle. Virtual showcases, which employ beam-splitter mirrors together with multiple graphics displays, provide an interactive means of simultaneously engaging with the virtual and the real. Many more implementations and configurations make spatial augmented reality display an increasingly attractive interactive alternative.

A SAR system can display on any number of surfaces of an indoor setting at once. SAR supports both a graphical visualisation and passive haptic sensation for the end users. Users are able to touch physical objects in a process that provides passive haptic sensation.

Tracking

Modern mobile augmented reality systems use one or more of the following tracking technologies: digital cameras and/or other optical sensors, accelerometers, GPS, gyroscopes, solid state compasses, RFID and wireless sensors. These technologies offer varying levels of accuracy and precision. Most important is the position and orientation of the user's head. Tracking the user's hand(s) or a handheld input device can provide a 6DOF interaction technique.

Input Devices

Techniques include speech recognition systems that translate a user's spoken words into computer instructions and gesture recognition systems that can interpret a user's body movements by visual detection or from sensors embedded in a peripheral device such as a wand, stylus, pointer, glove or other body wear. Some of the products which are trying to serve as a controller of AR Headsets include Wave by Seebright Inc. and Nimble by Intugine Technologies.

Computer

The computer analyzes the sensed visual and other data to synthesize and position augmentations.

Software and Algorithms

A key measure of AR systems is how realistically they integrate augmentations with the real world. The software must derive real world coordinates, independent from the camera, from camera images. That process is called image registration which uses different methods of computer vision, mostly related to video tracking. Many computer vision methods of augmented reality are inherited from visual odometry. Usually those methods consist of two parts.

First detect interest points, or fiducial markers, or optical flow in the camera images. First stage can use feature detection methods like corner detection, blob detection, edge detection or thresholding and/or other image processing methods. The second stage restores a real world coordinate system from the data obtained in the first stage. Some methods assume objects with known geometry (or fiducial markers) present in the scene. In some of those cases the scene 3D structure should be precalculated beforehand. If part of the scene is unknown simultaneous localization and mapping (SLAM) can map relative positions. If no information about scene geometry is available, structure from motion methods like bundle adjustment are used. Mathematical methods used in the second stage include projective (epipolar) geometry, geometric algebra, rotation representation with exponential map, kalman and particle filters, nonlinear optimization, robust statistics.

Augmented Reality Markup Language (ARML) is a data standard developed within the Open Geospatial Consortium (OGC), which consists of an XML grammar to describe the location and appearance of virtual objects in the scene, as well as ECMAScript bindings to allow dynamic access to properties of virtual objects.

To enable rapid development of Augmented Reality Application, some software development kits (SDK) have emerged. A few SDK such as CloudRidAR leverage cloud computing for performance improvement. Some of the well known AR SDKs are offered by Vuforia, ARToolKit, Catchoom CraftAR, Mobinett AR, Wikitude, Blippar Layar, and Meta.

Applications

Augmented reality has many applications. First used for military, industrial, and medical applications, it has also been applied to commercial and entertainment areas.

Literature

In 2011, there were works using AR poetry made by ni_ka from the Sekai Camera in Japan, Tokyo. The rose of these works come from Paul Celan, "Die Niemandsrose", and express the mourning of 3.11, 2011 Tōhoku earthquake and tsunami. In these works, there is a rose on the top of the Tokyo Tower, and touching Kitty float poetry words, and we can write the reply of this insteration. Pokémon Go make people know Augmented Reality, however ni_ka is a pioneer of AR literature.

AR Poetry

Archaeology

AR can be used to aid archaeological research, by augmenting archaeological features onto the modern landscape, enabling archaeologists to formulate conclusions about site placement and configuration.

Another application given to AR in this field is the possibility for users to rebuild ruins, buildings, landscapes or even ancient characters as they formerly existed.

Architecture

AR can aid in visualizing building projects. Computer-generated images of a structure can be superimposed into a real life local view of a property before the physical building is constructed there; this was demonstrated publicly by Trimble Navigation in 2004. AR can also be employed within an architect's work space, rendering into their view animated 3D visualizations of their 2D drawings. Architecture sight-seeing can be enhanced with AR applications allowing users viewing a building's exterior to virtually see through its walls, viewing its interior objects and layout.

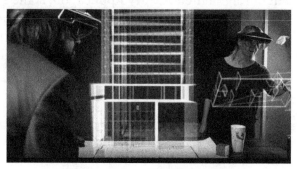

Meta 2 used for collaborative design

Visual Art

AR technology has helped disabled individuals create visual art by using eye tracking to translate a user's eye movements into drawings on a screen. An item such as a commemorative coin can be designed so that when scanned by an AR-enabled device it displays additional objects and layers of information that were not visible in a real world view of it. In 2013, L'Oreal used CrowdOptic technology to create an augmented reality at the seventh annual Luminato Festival in Toronto, Canada.

iGreet's augmented reality greeting card suddenly becomes alive and hidden digital content appears when being viewed through the app.

AR in visual art opens the possibility of multidimensional experiences and interpretations of reality. Augmenting people, objects, and landscapes is becoming an art form in itself. In 2011, artist

Amir Bardaran's *Frenchising the Mona Lisa* infiltrates Da Vinci's painting using an AR mobile application called Junaio. Aim a Junaio loaded smartphone camera at any image of the Mona Lisa and watch as Leonardo's subject places a scarf made of a French flag around her head. The AR app allows the user to train his or her smartphone on Da Vinci's *Mona Lisa* and watch the mysterious Italian lady loosen her hair and wrap a French flag around her in the form a (currently banned) Islamic *hijab*.

Greeting Cards

AR technology has been used in conjunction with greeting cards. They can be implemented with digital content which users are able to discover by viewing the illustrations with certain mobile applications or devices using augmented reality technology. The digital content could be 2D & 3D animations, standard video and 3D objects with which the users can interact.

In 2015, the Bulgarian startup iGreet developed its own AR technology and used it to make the first premade "live" greeting card. It looks like traditional paper card, but contains hidden digital content which only appears when users scan the greeting card with the iGreet app.

Commerce

AR can enhance product previews such as allowing a customer to view what's inside a product's packaging without opening it. AR can also be used as an aid in selecting products from a catalog or through a kiosk. Scanned images of products can activate views of additional content such as customization options and additional images of the product in its use. AR is used to integrate print and video marketing. Printed marketing material can be designed with certain "trigger" images that, when scanned by an AR enabled device using image recognition, activate a video version of the promotional material. A major difference between Augmented Reality and straight forward image recognition is that you can overlay multiple media at the same time in the view screen, such as social media share buttons, in-page video even audio and 3D objects. Traditional print only publications are using Augmented Reality to connect many different types of media.

View Description image 1

Construction

With the continual improvements to GPS accuracy, businesses are able to use augmented reality to visualize georeferenced models of construction sites, underground structures, cables and pipes using mobile devices. Augmented reality is applied to present new projects, to solve on-site construction challenges, and to enhance promotional materials. Examples include the Daqri Smart Helmet, an Android-powered hard hat used to create augmented reality for the industrial worker, including visual instructions, real time alerts, and 3D mapping.

Following the Christchurch earthquake, the University of Canterbury released, CityViewAR, which enabled city planners and engineers to visualize buildings that were destroyed in the earthquake. Not only did this provide planners with tools to reference the previous cityscape, but it also served as a reminder to the magnitude of the devastation caused, as entire buildings were demolished.

Education

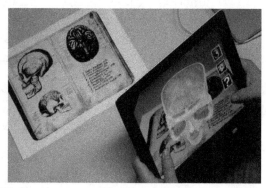

App iSkull, an augmented human skull for education (iOS OS)

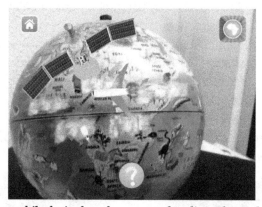

App iWow, a mobile device based augmented reality enhanced world globe

Augmented reality applications can complement a standard curriculum. Text, graphics, video and audio can be superimposed into a student's real time environment. Textbooks, flashcards and other educational reading material can contain embedded "markers" that, when scanned by an AR device, produce supplementary information to the student rendered in a multimedia format. Students can participate interactively with computer generated simulations of historical events, exploring and learning details of each significant area of the event site. On higher education, there are some applications that can be used. For instance, Construct3D, a Studierstube system, allows students to learn mechanical engineering concepts, math or geometry. This is an active learning process in which students learn to learn with technology. AR can aid students in understanding chemistry by allowing them to visualize the spatial structure of a molecule and interact with a virtual model of it that appears, in a camera image, positioned at a marker held in their hand. It can also enable students of physiology to visualize different systems of the human body in three dimensions. Augmented reality technology also permits learning via remote collaboration, in which students and instructors not at the same physical location can share a common virtual learning environment populated by virtual objects and learning materials and interact with another within that setting.

This resource could also be of advantage in Primary School. Children can learn through experiences, and visuals can be used to help them learn. For instance, they can learn new knowledge about astronomy, which can be difficult to understand, and children might better understand the solar system when using AR devices and being able to see it in 3D. Further, learners could change the illustrations in their science books by using this resource. For teaching anatomy, teachers could visualize bones and organs using augmented reality to display them on the body of a person.

Mobile apps using augmented reality are emerging in the classroom. The mix of real life and virtual reality displayed by the apps using the mobile phone's camera allows information to be manipulated and seen like never before. Many such apps have been designed to create a highly engaging environment and transform the learning experience. Examples of the mobile apps, that leverage augmented reality to aid learning, include SkyView for studying astronomy and AR Circuits for building simple electric circuits.

Emergency management / Search and Rescue

Augmented reality systems are used in public safety situations - from super storms to suspects at large. Two interesting articles from *Emergency Management* magazine discuss the power of the technology for emergency management. The first is "Augmented Reality--Emerging Technology for Emergency Management" by Gerald Baron. Per Adam Crowe: "Technologies like augmented reality (ex: Google Glass) and the growing expectation of the public will continue to force professional emergency managers to radically shift when, where, and how technology is deployed before, during, and after disasters.".

LandForm+ is a geographic augmented reality system used for search and rescue, and emergency management.

Another example, a search aircraft is looking for a lost hiker in rugged mountain terrain. Augmented reality systems provide aerial camera operators with a geographic awareness of forest road names and locations blended with the camera video. As a result, the camera operator is better able to search for the hiker knowing the geographic context of the camera image. Once found, the operator can more efficiently direct rescuers to the hiker's location.

Everyday

Since the 1970s and early 1980s, Steve Mann has been developing technologies meant for everyday use i.e. "horizontal" across all applications rather than a specific "vertical" market. Examples include Mann's "EyeTap Digital Eye Glass", a general-purpose seeing aid that does dynamic-range management (HDR vision) and overlays, underlays, simultaneous augmentation and diminishment (e.g. diminishing the electric arc while looking at a welding torch).

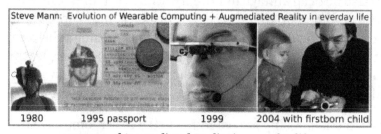

30 years of Augmediated Reality in everyday life.

Video Games

Augmented reality allows video game players to experience digital game play in a real world environment. Companies and platforms like Niantic and LyteShot emerged as augmented reality gaming creators.

Lyteshot in action

Merchlar's mobile game Get On Target uses a trigger image as fiducial marker

Industrial Design

AR can help industrial designers experience a product's design and operation before completion. Volkswagen uses AR for comparing calculated and actual crash test imagery. AR can be used to visualize and modify a car body structure and engine layout. AR can also be used to compare digital mock-ups with physical mock-ups for finding discrepancies between them.

Medical

Since 2005, a device that films subcutaneous veins, processes and projects the image of the veins onto the skin has been used to locate veins. This device is called VeinViewer

Augmented Reality can provide the surgeon with information, which are otherwise hidden, such as showing the heartbeat rate, the blood pressure, the state of the patient's organ, etc. AR can be used to let a doctor look inside a patient by combining one source of images such as an X-ray with another such as video.

Examples include a virtual X-ray view based on prior tomography or on real time images from ultrasound and confocal microscopy probes, visualizing the position of a tumor in the video of an endoscope, or radiation exposure risks from X-ray imaging devices. AR can enhance viewing a fetus inside a mother's womb. It has been also used for cockroach phobia treatment. Also, patients wearing augmented reality glasses can be reminded to take medications.

Beauty

In 2014 the company L'Oreal Paris started developing a smartphone and tablet application called "Makeup Genius", which lets users try out make-up and beauty styles utilizing the front-facing camera of the endpoint and its display.

Spatial Immersion and Interaction

Augmented reality applications, running on handheld devices utilized as virtual reality headsets, can also digitalize human presence in space and provide a computer generated model of them, in a virtual space where they can interact and perform various actions. Such capabilities are demonstrated by "project Anywhere" developed by a post graduate student at ETH Zurich, which was dubbed as an "out-of-body experience".

Military

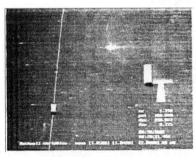

Rockwell WorldView Console showing space surveillance telescope video map overlay of satellite flight tracks from a 1993 paper.

In combat, AR can serve as a networked communication system that renders useful battlefield data onto a soldier's goggles in real time. From the soldier's viewpoint, people and various objects can be marked with special indicators to warn of potential dangers. Virtual maps and 360° view camera imaging can also be rendered to aid a soldier's navigation and battlefield perspective, and this can be transmitted to military leaders at a remote command center.

An interesting application of AR occurred when Rockwell International created video map overlays of satellite and orbital debris tracks to aid in space observations at Air Force Maui Optical System. In their 1993 paper "Debris Correlation Using the Rockwell WorldView System" the authors describe the use of map overlays applied to video from space surveillance telescopes. The map overlays indicated the trajectories of various objects in geographic coordinates. This allowed telescope operators to identify satellites, and also to identify - and catalog - potentially dangerous space debris.

Screen capture of SmartCam3D in picture in picture (PIP) mode. This helps sensor operators maintain a broader situation awareness than a telescopic camera "soda-straw". It was shown to essentially double the speed at which points can be located on the ground.

Starting in 2003 the US Army integrated the SmartCam3D augmented reality system into the Shadow Unmanned Aerial System to aid sensor operators using telescopic cameras to locate people or points of interest. The system combined both fixed geographic information including street names, points of interest, airports and railroads with live video from the camera system. The system offered "picture in picture" mode that allows the system to show a synthetic view of the area surrounding the camera's field of view. This helps solve a problem in which the field of view is so narrow that it excludes important context, as if "looking through a soda straw". The system displays real-time friend/foe/neutral location markers blended with live video, providing the operator with improved situation awareness.

Researchers at USAF Research Lab (Calhoun, Draper et al.) found an approximately two-fold increase in the speed at which UAV sensor operators found points of interest using this technology. This ability to maintain geographic awareness quantitatively enhances mission efficiency. The system is in use on the US Army RQ-7 Shadow and the MQ-1C Gray Eagle Unmanned Aerial Systems.

Navigation

LandForm video map overlay marking runways, road, and buildings during 1999 helicopter flight test.

Augmented reality map on iPhone

AR can augment the effectiveness of navigation devices. Information can be displayed on an automobile's windshield indicating destination directions and meter, weather, terrain, road conditions and traffic information as well as alerts to potential hazards in their path. Aboard maritime vessels, AR can allow bridge watch-standers to continuously monitor important information such as a ship's heading and speed while moving throughout the bridge or performing other tasks.

The NASA X-38 was flown using a Hybrid Synthetic Vision system that overlaid map data on video to provide enhanced navigation for the spacecraft during flight tests from 1998 to 2002. It used the LandForm software and was useful for times of limited visibility, including an instance when the video camera window frosted over leaving astronauts to rely on the map overlays. The LandForm software was also test flown at the Army Yuma Proving Ground in 1999. In the photo at right one can see the map markers indicating runways, air traffic control tower, taxiways, and hangars overlaid on the video.

Office Workplace

AR can help facilitate collaboration among distributed team members in a work force via conferences with real and virtual participants. AR tasks can include brainstorming and discussion meetings utilizing common visualization via touch screen tables, interactive digital whiteboards, shared design spaces, and distributed control rooms.

Sports and Entertainment

AR has become common in sports telecasting. Sports and entertainment venues are provided with see-through and overlay augmentation through tracked camera feeds for enhanced viewing by the audience. Examples include the yellow "first down" line seen in television broadcasts of American football games showing the line the offensive team must cross to receive a first down. AR is also used in association with football and other sporting events to show commercial advertisements overlaid onto the view of the playing area. Sections of rugby fields and cricket pitches also display sponsored images. Swimming telecasts often add a line across the lanes to indicate the position of the current record holder as a race proceeds to allow viewers to compare the current race to the best performance. Other examples include hockey puck tracking and annotations of racing car performance and snooker ball trajectories.

AR can enhance concert and theater performances. For example, artists can allow listeners to augment their listening experience by adding their performance to that of other bands/groups of users.

The gaming industry has benefited a lot from the development of this technology. A number of games have been developed for prepared indoor environments. Early AR games also include AR air hockey, collaborative combat against virtual enemies, and an AR-enhanced pool games. A significant number of games incorporate AR in them and the introduction of the smartphone has made a bigger impact.

Task Support

Complex tasks such as assembly, maintenance, and surgery can be simplified by inserting additional information into the field of view. For example, labels can be displayed on parts of a system to clarify operating instructions for a mechanic who is performing maintenance on the system. Assembly lines gain many benefits from the usage of AR. In addition to Boeing, BMW and Volkswagen are known for incorporating this technology in their assembly line to improve their manufacturing and assembly processes. Big machines are difficult to maintain because of the multiple layers or structures they have. With the use of AR the workers can complete their job in a much easier way because AR permits them to look through the machine as if it was with x-ray, pointing them to the problem right away.

Television

Weather visualizations were the first application of augmented reality to television. It has now become common in weathercasting to display full motion video of images captured in real-time from multiple cameras and other imaging devices. Coupled with 3D graphics symbols and mapped to a common virtual geo-space model, these animated visualizations constitute the first true application of AR to TV.

Augmented reality has also become common in sports telecasting. Sports and entertainment venues are provided with see-through and overlay augmentation through tracked camera feeds for enhanced viewing by the audience. Examples include the yellow "first down" line seen in television broadcasts of American football games showing the line the offensive team must cross to receive a first down. AR is also used in association with football and other sporting events to show commercial advertisements overlaid onto the view of the playing area. Sections of rugby fields and cricket pitches also display sponsored images. Swimming telecasts often add a line across the lanes to indicate the position of the current record holder as a race proceeds to allow viewers to compare the current race to the best performance. Other examples include hockey puck tracking and annotations of racing car performance and snooker ball trajectories.

Augmented reality is starting to allow Next Generation TV viewers to interact with the programs they are watching. They can place objects into an existing program and interact with these objects, such as moving them around. Avatars of real persons in real time who are also watching the same program.

Tourism and Sightseeing

Augmented reality applications can enhance a user's experience when traveling by providing real time informational displays regarding a location and its features, including comments made by previous visitors of the site. AR applications allow tourists to experience simulations of historical events, places and objects by rendering them into their current view of a landscape. AR applications can also present location information by audio, announcing features of interest at a particular site as they become visible to the user.

Translation

AR systems can interpret foreign text on signs and menus and, in a user's augmented view, re-display the text in the user's language. Spoken words of a foreign language can be translated and displayed in a user's view as printed subtitles.

Privacy Concerns

The concept of modern augmented reality depends on the ability of the device to record and analyze the environment in real time. Because of this, there are potential legal concerns over privacy. While the First Amendment to the United States Constitution allows for such recording in the name of public interest, the constant recording of an AR device makes it difficult to do so without also recording outside of the public domain. Legal complications would be found in areas where a right to certain amount of privacy is expected or where copyrighted media are displayed. In terms of individual privacy, there exists the ease of access to information that one should not readily possess about a given person. This is accomplished through facial recognition technology. Assuming that AR automatically passes information about persons that the user sees, there could be anything seen from social media, criminal record, and marital status.

Notable Researchers

- Ivan Sutherland invented the first AR head-mounted display at Harvard University.

- Steven Feiner, Professor at Columbia University, is a leading pioneer of augmented reality, and author of the first paper on an AR system prototype, KARMA (the Knowledge-based Augmented Reality Maintenance Assistant), along with Blair MacIntyre and Doree Seligmann. He is also an advisor to Meta.

- Meron Gribetz, conceptualized the Meta mounted display headset. He is also founder and CEO of Meta, a Silicon Valley company that is known for producing innovative Augmented Reality products.

- S. Ravela, B. Draper, J. Lim and A. Hanson develop marker/fixture-less augmented reality system with computer vision in 1994. They augmented an engine block observed from a single video camera with annotations for repair. They use model-based pose estimation, aspect graphs and visual feature tracking to dynamically register model with the observed video.

- Steve Mann formulated an earlier concept of Mediated reality in the 1970s and 1980s, using cameras, processors, and display systems to modify visual reality to help people see better (dynamic range management), building computerized welding helmets, as well as "Augmediated Reality" vision systems for use in everyday life. He is also an adviser to Meta.

- Louis Rosenberg developed one of the first known AR systems, called Virtual Fixtures, while working at the U.S. Air Force Armstrong Labs in 1991, and published the first study of how an AR system can enhance human performance. Rosenberg's subsequent work at Stanford University in the early 90's, was the first proof that virtual overlays, when registered and presented over a user's direct view of the real physical world, could significantly enhance human performance.

- Mike Abernathy pioneered one of the first successful augmented reality applications of video overlay using map data for space debris in 1993, while at Rockwell International. He co-founded Rapid Imaging Software, Inc. and was the primary author of the LandForm system in 1995, and the SmartCam3D system. LandForm augmented reality was successfully flight tested in 1999 aboard a helicopter and SmartCam3D was used to fly the NASA X-38 from 1999-2002. He and NASA colleague Francisco Delgado received the National Defense Industries Association Top5 awards in 2004.

- Francisco "Frank" Delgado is a NASA engineer and project manager specializing in human interface research and development. Starting 1998 he conducted research into displays that combined video with synthetic vision systems (called hybrid synthetic vision at the time) that we recognize today as augmented reality systems for the control of aircraft and spacecraft. In 1999 he and colleague Mike Abernathy flight-tested the LandForm system aboard a US Army helicopter. Delgado oversaw integration of the LandForm and SmartCam3D systems into the X-38 Crew Return Vehicle. In 2001, Aviation Week reported NASA astronaut's successful use of hybrid synthetic vision (augmented reality) to fly the X-38 during a flight test at Dryden Flight Research Center. The technology was used in all subsequent flights of the X-38. Delgado was co-recipient of the National Defense Industries Association 2004 Top 5 software of the year award for SmartCam3D.

- Dieter Schmalstieg and Daniel Wagner jump started the field of AR on mobile phones. They developed the first marker tracking systems for mobile phones and PDAs.

- Bruce H. Thomas and Wayne Piekarski develop the Tinmith system in 1998. They along with Steve Feiner with his MARS system pioneer outdoor augmented reality.

- Dr. Mark Billinghurst is one of the world's leading augmented reality researchers, focusing on innovative computer interfaces that explore how virtual and real worlds can be merged. Director of the HIT Lab New Zealand (HIT Lab NZ) at the University of Canterbury in New Zealand, he has produced over 250 technical publications and presented demonstrations and courses at a wide variety of conferences.

- Reinhold Behringer performed important early work in image registration for augmented reality, and prototype wearable testbeds for augmented reality. He also co-organized the First IEEE International Symposium on Augmented Reality in 1998 (IWAR'98), and co-edited one of the first books on augmented reality.

History

- 1901: L. Frank Baum, an author, first mentions the idea of an electronic display/spectacles that overlays data onto real life (in this case 'people'), it is named a 'character marker'.

- 1957–62: Morton Heilig, a cinematographer, creates and patents a simulator called Sensorama with visuals, sound, vibration, and smell.

- 1968: Ivan Sutherland invents the head-mounted display and positions it as a window into a virtual world.

- 1975: Myron Krueger creates Videoplace to allow users to interact with virtual objects for the first time.

- 1980: Steve Mann creates the first wearable computer, a computer vision system with text and graphical overlays on a photographically mediated reality, or Augmediated Reality.

- 1981: Dan Reitan geospatially maps multiple weather radar images and space-based and studio cameras to virtual reality Earth maps and abstract symbols for television weather broadcasts, bringing Augmented Reality to TV.

- 1989: Jaron Lanier coins the phrase Virtual Reality and creates the first commercial business around virtual worlds.

- 1990: The term 'Augmented Reality' is attributed to Thomas P. Caudell, a former Boeing researcher.

- 1992: Louis Rosenberg develops one of the first functioning AR systems, called Virtual Fixtures, at the U.S. Air Force Research Laboratory—Armstrong, and demonstrates benefits to human performance.

- 1992: Steven Feiner, Blair MacIntyre and Doree Seligmann present the first major paper on an AR system prototype, KARMA, at the Graphics Interface conference.

- 1993: Mike Abernathy, et al., report the first use of augmented reality in identifying space debris using Rockwell WorldView by overlaying satellite geographic trajectories on live telescope video.

- 1993 A widely cited version of the paper above is published in Communications of the ACM – Special issue on computer augmented environments, edited by Pierre Wellner, Wendy Mackay, and Rich Gold.

- 1993: Loral WDL, with sponsorship from STRICOM, performed the first demonstration combining live AR-equipped vehicles and manned simulators. Unpublished paper, J. Barrilleaux, "Experiences and Observations in Applying Augmented Reality to Live Training", 1999.

- 1994: Julie Martin creates first 'Augmented Reality Theater production', Dancing In Cyberspace, funded by the Australia Council for the Arts, features dancers and acrobats manipulating body–sized virtual object in real time, projected into the same physical space and performance plane. The acrobats appeared immersed within the virtual object and environments. The installation used Silicon Graphics computers and Polhemus sensing system.

- 1995: S. Ravela et al. at University of Massachusetts introduce a vision-based system using monocular cameras to track objects (engine blocks) across views for augmented reality.

- 1998: Spatial Augmented Reality introduced at University of North Carolina at Chapel Hill by Ramesh Raskar, Welch, Henry Fuchs.

- 1999: Frank Delgado, Mike Abernathy et al. report successful flight test of LandForm software video map overlay from a helicopter at Army Yuma Proving Ground overlaying video with runways, taxiways, roads and road names.

- 1999: The US Naval Research Laboratory engage on a decade long research program called the Battlefield Augmented Reality System (BARS) to prototype some of the early wearable systems for dismounted soldier operating in urban environment for situation awareness and training NRL BARS Web page

- 1999: Hirokazu Kato (加藤 博一) created ARToolKit at HITLab, where AR later was further developed by other HITLab scientists, demonstrating it at SIGGRAPH.

- 2000: Bruce H. Thomas develops ARQuake, the first outdoor mobile AR game, demonstrating it in the International Symposium on Wearable Computers.

- 2001: NASA X-38 flown using LandForm software video map overlays at Dryden Flight Research Center.

- 2004: Outdoor helmet-mounted AR system demonstrated by Trimble Navigation and the Human Interface Technology Laboratory.

- 2008: Wikitude AR Travel Guide launches on 20 Oct 2008 with the G1 Android phone.

- 2009: ARToolkit was ported to Adobe Flash (FLARToolkit) by Saqoosha, bringing augmented reality to the web browser.

- 2012: Launch of Lyteshot, an interactive AR gaming platform that utilizes smartglasses for game data

- 2013: Meta announces the Meta 1 developer kit, the first to market AR see-through display

- 2013: Google announces an open beta test of its Google Glass augmented reality glasses. The glasses reach the Internet through Bluetooth, which connects to the wireless service on a user's cellphone. The glasses respond when a user speaks, touches the frame or moves the head.

- 2014: Mahei creates the first generation of augmented reality enhanced educational toys.

- 2015: Microsoft announces Windows Holographic and the HoloLens augmented reality headset. The headset utilizes various sensors and a processing unit to blend high definition "holograms" with the real world.

- 2016: Niantic released Pokémon Go for iOS and Android in July 2016. The game quickly became one of the most used applications and has brought augmented reality to the mainstream.

References

- Shapiro, Stuart C. (1992). "Artificial Intelligence". In Shapiro, Stuart C. Encyclopedia of Artificial Intelligence (PDF) (2nd ed.). New York: John Wiley. pp. 54–57. ISBN 0-471-50306-1.

- Wu, Samuel Miao-sin; Johnston, Daniel (1995). Foundations of cellular neurophysiology. Cambridge, Mass: MIT Press. ISBN 0-262-10053-3.

- Koch, Christof (1999). Biophysics of computation: information processing in single neurons. Oxford [Oxfordshire]: Oxford University Press. ISBN 0-19-510491-9.

- R. Behringer, G. Klinker,. D. Mizell. Augmented Reality – Placing Artificial Objects in Real Scenes. Proceedings of IWAR '98. A.K.Peters, Natick, 1999. ISBN 1-56881-098-9.

- Bond, Sarah (July 17, 2016). "After the Success Of Pokémon Go, How Will Augmented Reality Impact Archaeological Sites?". Retrieved July 17, 2016.

- Chapman, Lizette (2015-01-28). "Augmented-Reality Headset Maker Meta Secures $23 Million". Wall Street Journal. Retrieved 2016-02-29.

- Matney, Lucas (2016-03-02). "Hands-on with the $949 mind-bending Meta 2 augmented reality headset". TechCrunch. Retrieved 2016-03-02.

- "augmented reality: definition of augmented reality in Oxford dictionary (American English) (US)". www.oxforddictionaries.com. Retrieved 2015-10-08.

- "What is Augmented Reality (AR): Augmented Reality Defined, iPhone Augmented Reality Apps and Games and More". Digital Trends. Retrieved 2015-10-08.

- Berinato, Scott (January 29, 2015). "What HoloLens Has That Google Glass Didn't". Harward Business Preview. Retrieved 15 February 2015.

- Lee, Kangdon (March 2012). "Augmented Reality in Education and Training" (PDF). Techtrends: Linking Research & Practice To Improve Learning. 56 (2). Retrieved 2014-05-15.

- Wadhwa, Tarun. "CrowdOptic and L'Oreal To Make History By Demonstrating How Augmented Reality Can Be A Shared Experience". Forbes. Retrieved 6 June 2013.

- O'Neil, Lauren. "LCD contact lenses could display text messages in your eye". CBC. Archived from the original on 11 December 2012. Retrieved 2012-12-12.

- Stuart Eve. "Augmenting Phenomenology: Using Augmented Reality to Aid Archaeological Phenomenology in the Landscape". Retrieved 2012-09-25.

- Noelle, S. (2002). "Stereo augmentation of simulation results on a projection wall". Mixed and Augmented Reality, 2002. ISMAR 2002. Proceedings.: 271–322. Retrieved 2012-10-07.

- Verlinden, Jouke; Horvath, Imre. "Augmented Prototyping as Design Means in Industrial Design Engineering". Delft University of Technology. Retrieved 2012-10-07.

- Pang, Y; Nee, A; Youcef-Toumie, Kamal; Ong, S.K; Yuan, M.L (November 18, 2004). "Assembly Design and Evaluation in an Augmented Reality Environment". National University of Singapore, M.I.T. Retrieved 2012-10-07.

Languages used in Computer Programming

Computer languages were developed with a view to ensure the system adheres to certain actions and patterns. Computer languages perform a variety of functions. Some popular languages are FORTRAN and COBOL. Software engineering is best understood in confluence with the major topics listed in the following chapter.

Programming Language

A programming language is a formal computer language or constructed language designed to communicate instructions to a machine, particularly a computer. Programming languages can be used to create programs to control the behavior of a machine or to express algorithms.

```
1  /* This line basically imports the "stdio" header file, part of
2   * the standard library. It provides input and output functionality
3   * to the program.
4   */
5  #include <stdio.h>
6
7  /*
8   * Function (method) declaration. This outputs "Hello, world" to
9   * standard output when invoked.
10  */
11 void sayHello() {
12     // printf() in C outputs the specified text (with optional
13     // formatting options) when invoked.
14     printf("Hello, world!");
15 }
16
17 /*
18  * This is a "main function". The compiled program will run the code
19  * defined here.
20  */
21 void main() {
22     // Invoke the sayHello() function.
23     sayHello();
24 }
```

Source code of a simple computer program written in the C programming language, which will output the "Hello, world!" message when compiled and run

The earliest known programmable machine preceded the invention of the digital computer and is the automatic flute player described in the 9th century by the brothers Musa in Baghdad, at the time a major centre of knowledge. From the early 1800s, "programs" were used to direct the behavior of machines such as Jacquard looms and player pianos. Thousands of different programming languages have been created, mainly in the computer field, and many more still are being created every year. Many programming languages require computation to be specified in an imperative form (i.e., as a sequence of operations to perform), while other languages use other forms of program specification such as the declarative form (i.e. the desired result is specified, not how to achieve it).

The description of a programming language is usually split into the two components of syntax (form) and semantics (meaning). Some languages are defined by a specification document (for example, the C programming language is specified by an ISO Standard), while other languages (such as Perl) have a dominant implementation that is treated as a reference. Some languages have both, with the basic language defined by a standard and extensions taken from the dominant implementation being common.

Definitions

A programming language is a notation for writing programs, which are specifications of a computation or algorithm. Some, but not all, authors restrict the term "programming language" to those languages that can express *all* possible algorithms. Traits often considered important for what constitutes a programming language include:

Function and target

A *computer programming language* is a language used to write computer programs, which involve a computer performing some kind of computation or algorithm and possibly control external devices such as printers, disk drives, robots, and so on. For example, PostScript programs are frequently created by another program to control a computer printer or display. More generally, a programming language may describe computation on some, possibly abstract, machine. It is generally accepted that a complete specification for a programming language includes a description, possibly idealized, of a machine or processor for that language. In most practical contexts, a programming language involves a computer; consequently, programming languages are usually defined and studied this way. Programming languages differ from natural languages in that natural languages are only used for interaction between people, while programming languages also allow humans to communicate instructions to machines.

Abstractions

Programming languages usually contain abstractions for defining and manipulating data structures or controlling the flow of execution. The practical necessity that a programming language support adequate abstractions is expressed by the abstraction principle; this principle is sometimes formulated as recommendation to the programmer to make proper use of such abstractions.

Expressive power

The theory of computation classifies languages by the computations they are capable of expressing. All Turing complete languages can implement the same set of algorithms. ANSI/ISO SQL-92 and Charity are examples of languages that are not Turing complete, yet often called programming languages.

Markup languages like XML, HTML or troff, which define structured data, are not usually considered programming languages. Programming languages may, however, share the syntax with markup languages if a computational semantics is defined. XSLT, for example, is a Turing complete XML dialect. Moreover, LaTeX, which is mostly used for structuring documents, also contains a Turing complete subset.

The term *computer language* is sometimes used interchangeably with programming language. However, the usage of both terms varies among authors, including the exact scope of each. One usage describes programming languages as a subset of computer languages. In this vein, languages used in computing that have a different goal than expressing computer programs are generically designated computer languages. For instance, markup languages are sometimes referred to as computer languages to emphasize that they are not meant to be used for programming.

Another usage regards programming languages as theoretical constructs for programming abstract machines, and computer languages as the subset thereof that runs on physical computers, which have finite hardware resources. John C. Reynolds emphasizes that formal specification languages are just as much programming languages as are the languages intended for execution. He also argues that textual and even graphical input formats that affect the behavior of a computer are programming languages, despite the fact they are commonly not Turing-complete, and remarks that ignorance of programming language concepts is the reason for many flaws in input formats.

History

Early Developments

The earliest computers were often programmed without the help of a programming language, by writing programs in absolute machine language. The programs, in decimal or binary form, were read in from punched cards or magnetic tape, or toggled in on switches on the front panel of the computer. Absolute machine languages were later termed *first-generation programming languages* (1GL).

The next step was development of so-called *second-generation programming languages* (2GL) or assembly languages, which were still closely tied to the instruction set architecture of the specific computer. These served to make the program much more human-readable, and relieved the programmer of tedious and error-prone address calculations.

The first *high-level programming languages*, or *third-generation programming languages* (3GL), were written in the 1950s. An early high-level programming language to be designed for a computer was Plankalkül, developed for the German Z3 by Konrad Zuse between 1943 and 1945. However, it was not implemented until 1998 and 2000.

John Mauchly's Short Code, proposed in 1949, was one of the first high-level languages ever developed for an electronic computer. Unlike machine code, Short Code statements represented mathematical expressions in understandable form. However, the program had to be translated into machine code every time it ran, making the process much slower than running the equivalent machine code.

At the University of Manchester, Alick Glennie developed Autocode in the early 1950s. A programming language, it used a compiler to automatically convert the language into machine code. The first code and compiler was developed in 1952 for the Mark 1 computer at the University of Manchester and is considered to be the first compiled high-level programming language.

The second autocode was developed for the Mark 1 by R. A. Brooker in 1954 and was called the "Mark 1 Autocode". Brooker also developed an autocode for the Ferranti Mercury in the 1950s in conjunction with the University of Manchester. The version for the EDSAC 2 was devised by D. F.

Hartley of University of Cambridge Mathematical Laboratory in 1961. Known as EDSAC 2 Autocode, it was a straight development from Mercury Autocode adapted for local circumstances, and was noted for its object code optimisation and source-language diagnostics which were advanced for the time. A contemporary but separate thread of development, Atlas Autocode was developed for the University of Manchester Atlas 1 machine.

In 1954, language FORTRAN was invented at IBM by John Backus; it was the first widely used high level general purpose programming language to have a functional implementation, as opposed to just a design on paper. It is still popular language for high-performance computing and is used for programs that benchmark and rank the world's fastest supercomputers.

Another early programming language was devised by Grace Hopper in the US, called FLOW-MATIC. It was developed for the UNIVAC I at Remington Rand during the period from 1955 until 1959. Hopper found that business data processing customers were uncomfortable with mathematical notation, and in early 1955, she and her team wrote a specification for an English programming language and implemented a prototype. The FLOW-MATIC compiler became publicly available in early 1958 and was substantially complete in 1959. Flow-Matic was a major influence in the design of COBOL, since only it and its direct descendant AIMACO were in actual use at the time.

Refinement

The increased use of high-level languages introduced a requirement for *low-level programming languages* or *system programming languages*. These languages, to varying degrees, provide facilities between assembly languages and high-level languages, and can be used to perform tasks which require direct access to hardware facilities but still provide higher-level control structures and error-checking.

The period from the 1960s to the late 1970s brought the development of the major language paradigms now in use:

- APL introduced *array programming* and influenced functional programming.

- ALGOL refined both *structured procedural programming* and the discipline of language specification; the "Revised Report on the Algorithmic Language ALGOL 60" became a model for how later language specifications were written.

- Lisp, implemented in 1958, was the first dynamically typed *functional programming* language

- In the 1960s, Simula was the first language designed to support *object-oriented programming*; in the mid-1970s, Smalltalk followed with the first "purely" object-oriented language.

- C was developed between 1969 and 1973 as a system programming language for the Unix operating system, and remains popular.

- Prolog, designed in 1972, was the first *logic programming* language.

- In 1978, ML built a polymorphic type system on top of Lisp, pioneering *statically typed functional programming* languages.

Each of these languages spawned descendants, and most modern programming languages count at least one of them in their ancestry.

The 1960s and 1970s also saw considerable debate over the merits of *structured programming*, and whether programming languages should be designed to support it. Edsger Dijkstra, in a famous 1968 letter published in the Communications of the ACM, argued that GOTO statements should be eliminated from all "higher level" programming languages.

Consolidation and Growth

A selection of textbooks that teach programming, in languages both popular and obscure. These are only a few of the thousands of programming languages and dialects that have been designed in history.

The 1980s were years of relative consolidation. C++ combined object-oriented and systems programming. The United States government standardized Ada, a systems programming language derived from Pascal and intended for use by defense contractors. In Japan and elsewhere, vast sums were spent investigating so-called "fifth generation" languages that incorporated logic programming constructs. The functional languages community moved to standardize ML and Lisp. Rather than inventing new paradigms, all of these movements elaborated upon the ideas invented in the previous decades.

One important trend in language design for programming large-scale systems during the 1980s was an increased focus on the use of *modules*, or large-scale organizational units of code. Modula-2, Ada, and ML all developed notable module systems in the 1980s, which were often wedded to generic programming constructs.

The rapid growth of the Internet in the mid-1990s created opportunities for new languages. Perl, originally a Unix scripting tool first released in 1987, became common in dynamic websites. Java came to be used for server-side programming, and bytecode virtual machines became popular again in commercial settings with their promise of "Write once, run anywhere" (UCSD Pascal had been popular for a time in the early 1980s). These developments were not fundamentally novel, rather they were refinements of many existing languages and paradigms (although their syntax was often based on the C family of programming languages).

Programming language evolution continues, in both industry and research. Current directions include security and reliability verification, new kinds of modularity (mixins, delegates, aspects), and database integration such as Microsoft's LINQ.

Fourth-generation programming languages (4GL) are a computer programming languages which aim to provide a higher level of abstraction of the internal computer hardware details than 3GLs. *Fifth generation programming languages* (5GL) are programming languages based on solving problems using constraints given to the program, rather than using an algorithm written by a programmer.

Elements

All programming languages have some primitive building blocks for the description of data and the processes or transformations applied to them (like the addition of two numbers or the selection of an item from a collection). These primitives are defined by syntactic and semantic rules which describe their structure and meaning respectively.

Syntax

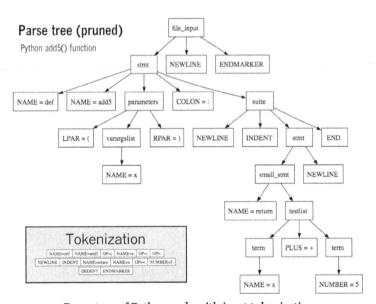

Parse tree of Python code with inset tokenization

A programming language's surface form is known as its syntax. Most programming languages are purely textual; they use sequences of text including words, numbers, and punctuation, much like written natural languages. On the other hand, there are some programming languages which are more graphical in nature, using visual relationships between symbols to specify a program.

The syntax of a language describes the possible combinations of symbols that form a syntactically correct program. The meaning given to a combination of symbols is handled by semantics (either formal or hard-coded in a reference implementation). Since most languages are textual, this article discusses textual syntax.

Programming language syntax is usually defined using a combination of regular expressions (for lexical structure) and Backus–Naur Form (for grammatical structure). Below is a simple grammar, based on Lisp:

expression   :: = atom | list

atom   :: = number | symbol

number   :: = [+-]?['0'-'9']+

symbol   :: = ['A'-'Z''a'-'z'].*

list   :: = '(' expression* ')'

This grammar specifies the following:

- an *expression* is either an *atom* or a *list*;

- an *atom* is either a *number* or a *symbol*;

- a *number* is an unbroken sequence of one or more decimal digits, optionally preceded by a plus or minus sign;

- a *symbol* is a letter followed by zero or more of any characters (excluding whitespace); and

- a *list* is a matched pair of parentheses, with zero or more *expressions* inside it.

The following are examples of well-formed token sequences in this grammar: 12345, () and (a b c232 (1)).

Not all syntactically correct programs are semantically correct. Many syntactically correct programs are nonetheless ill-formed, per the language's rules; and may (depending on the language specification and the soundness of the implementation) result in an error on translation or execution. In some cases, such programs may exhibit undefined behavior. Even when a program is well-defined within a language, it may still have a meaning that is not intended by the person who wrote it.

Using natural language as an example, it may not be possible to assign a meaning to a grammatically correct sentence or the sentence may be false:

- "Colorless green ideas sleep furiously." is grammatically well-formed but has no generally accepted meaning.

- "John is a married bachelor." is grammatically well-formed but expresses a meaning that cannot be true.

The following C language fragment is syntactically correct, but performs operations that are not semantically defined (the operation *p >> 4 has no meaning for a value having a complex type and p->im is not defined because the value of p is the null pointer):

complex *p = NULL;

complex abs_p = sqrt(*p >> 4 + p->im);

If the type declaration on the first line were omitted, the program would trigger an error on compilation, as the variable "p" would not be defined. But the program would still be syntactically correct, since type declarations provide only semantic information.

The grammar needed to specify a programming language can be classified by its position in the Chomsky hierarchy. The syntax of most programming languages can be specified using a Type-2 grammar, i.e., they are context-free grammars. Some languages, including Perl and Lisp, contain constructs that allow execution during the parsing phase. Languages that have constructs that allow the programmer to alter the behavior of the parser make syntax analysis an undecidable problem, and generally blur the distinction between parsing and execution. In contrast to Lisp's macro system and Perl's BEGIN blocks, which may contain general computations, C macros are merely string replacements, and do not require code execution.

Semantics

The term Semantics refers to the meaning of languages, as opposed to their form (syntax).

Static Semantics

The static semantics defines restrictions on the structure of valid texts that are hard or impossible to express in standard syntactic formalisms. For compiled languages, static semantics essentially include those semantic rules that can be checked at compile time. Examples include checking that every identifier is declared before it is used (in languages that require such declarations) or that the labels on the arms of a case statement are distinct. Many important restrictions of this type, like checking that identifiers are used in the appropriate context (e.g. not adding an integer to a function name), or that subroutine calls have the appropriate number and type of arguments, can be enforced by defining them as rules in a logic called a type system. Other forms of static analyses like data flow analysis may also be part of static semantics. Newer programming languages like Java and C# have definite assignment analysis, a form of data flow analysis, as part of their static semantics.

Dynamic Semantics

Once data has been specified, the machine must be instructed to perform operations on the data. For example, the semantics may define the strategy by which expressions are evaluated to values, or the manner in which control structures conditionally execute statements. The *dynamic semantics* (also known as *execution semantics*) of a language defines how and when the various constructs of a language should produce a program behavior. There are many ways of defining execution semantics. Natural language is often used to specify the execution semantics of languages commonly used in practice. A significant amount of academic research went into formal semantics of programming languages, which allow execution semantics to be specified in a formal manner. Results from this field of research have seen limited application to programming language design and implementation outside academia.

Type System

A type system defines how a programming language classifies values and expressions into *types*, how it can manipulate those types and how they interact. The goal of a type system is to verify and usually enforce a certain level of correctness in programs written in that language by detecting certain incorrect operations. Any decidable type system involves a trade-off: while it rejects many incorrect programs, it can also prohibit some correct, albeit unusual programs. In order to bypass this downside, a number of languages have *type loopholes*, usually unchecked casts that may be used by the programmer to explicitly allow a normally disallowed operation between different types. In most typed languages, the type system is used only to type check programs, but a number of languages, usually functional ones, infer types, relieving the programmer from the need to write type annotations. The formal design and study of type systems is known as *type theory*.

Typed Versus Untyped Languages

A language is *typed* if the specification of every operation defines types of data to which the operation is applicable, with the implication that it is not applicable to other types. For example, the data represented by "this text between the quotes" is a string, and in many programming languages dividing a number by a string has no meaning and will be rejected by the compilers. The invalid operation may be detected when the program is compiled ("static" type checking) and will be rejected by the compiler with a compilation error message, or it may be detected when the program is run ("dynamic" type checking), resulting in a run-time exception. Many languages allow a function called an exception handler to be written to handle this exception and, for example, always return "-1" as the result.

A special case of typed languages are the *single-type* languages. These are often scripting or markup languages, such as REXX or SGML, and have only one data type—most commonly character strings which are used for both symbolic and numeric data.

In contrast, an *untyped language*, such as most assembly languages, allows any operation to be performed on any data, which are generally considered to be sequences of bits of various lengths. High-level languages which are untyped include BCPL, Tcl, and some varieties of Forth.

In practice, while few languages are considered typed from the point of view of type theory (verifying or rejecting *all* operations), most modern languages offer a degree of typing. Many production languages provide means to bypass or subvert the type system, trading type-safety for finer control over the program's execution.

Static Versus Dynamic Typing

In *static typing*, all expressions have their types determined prior to when the program is executed, typically at compile-time. For example, 1 and (2+2) are integer expressions; they cannot be passed to a function that expects a string, or stored in a variable that is defined to hold dates.

Statically typed languages can be either *manifestly typed* or *type-inferred*. In the first case, the programmer must explicitly write types at certain textual positions (for example, at variable declarations). In the second case, the compiler *infers* the types of expressions and declarations based on context. Most mainstream statically typed languages, such as C++, C# and Java, are manifestly typed. Complete type inference has traditionally been associated with less mainstream languages, such as Haskell and ML. However, many manifestly typed languages support partial type inference; for example, Java and C# both infer types in certain limited cases. Additionally, some programming languages allow for some types to be automatically converted to other types; for example, an int can be used where the program expects a float.

Dynamic typing, also called *latent typing*, determines the type-safety of operations at run time; in other words, types are associated with *run-time values* rather than *textual expressions*. As with type-inferred languages, dynamically typed languages do not require the programmer to write explicit type annotations on expressions. Among other things, this may permit a single variable to refer to values of different types at different points in the program execution. However, type errors cannot be automatically detected until a piece of code is actually executed, potentially making debugging more difficult. Lisp, Smalltalk, Perl, Python, JavaScript, and Ruby are dynamically typed.

Weak and Strong Typing

Weak typing allows a value of one type to be treated as another, for example treating a string as a number. This can occasionally be useful, but it can also allow some kinds of program faults to go undetected at compile time and even at run time.

Strong typing prevents the above. An attempt to perform an operation on the wrong type of value raises an error. Strongly typed languages are often termed *type-safe* or *safe*.

An alternative definition for "weakly typed" refers to languages, such as Perl and JavaScript, which permit a large number of implicit type conversions. In JavaScript, for example, the expression 2 * x implicitly converts x to a number, and this conversion succeeds even if x is null, undefined, an Array, or a string of letters. Such implicit conversions are often useful, but they can mask programming errors. *Strong* and *static* are now generally considered orthogonal concepts, but usage in the literature differs. Some use the term *strongly typed* to mean *strongly, statically typed*, or, even more confusingly, to mean simply *statically typed*. Thus C has been called both strongly typed and weakly, statically typed.

It may seem odd to some professional programmers that C could be "weakly, statically typed". However, notice that the use of the generic pointer, the void* pointer, does allow for casting of pointers to other pointers without needing to do an explicit cast. This is extremely similar to somehow casting an array of bytes to any kind of datatype in C without using an explicit cast, such as (int) or (char).

Standard Library and Run-Time System

Most programming languages have an associated core library (sometimes known as the 'standard library', especially if it is included as part of the published language standard), which is conventionally made available by all implementations of the language. Core libraries typically include definitions for commonly used algorithms, data structures, and mechanisms for input and output.

The line between a language and its core library differs from language to language. In some cases, the language designers may treat the library as a separate entity from the language. However, a language's core library is often treated as part of the language by its users, and some language specifications even require that this library be made available in all implementations. Indeed, some languages are designed so that the meanings of certain syntactic constructs cannot even be described without referring to the core library. For example, in Java, a string literal is defined as an instance of the java.lang.String class; similarly, in Smalltalk, an anonymous function expression (a "block") constructs an instance of the library's BlockContext class. Conversely, Scheme contains multiple coherent subsets that suffice to construct the rest of the language as library macros, and so the language designers do not even bother to say which portions of the language must be implemented as language constructs, and which must be implemented as parts of a library.

Design and ImpLementation

Programming languages share properties with natural languages related to their purpose as vehicles for communication, having a syntactic form separate from its semantics, and showing *language families* of related languages branching one from another. But as artificial constructs, they also differ in fundamental ways from languages that have evolved through usage. A significant difference is that a programming language can be fully described and studied in its entirety, since it has a precise and finite definition. By contrast, natural languages have changing meanings given by their users in different communities. While constructed languages are also artificial languages designed from the ground up with a specific purpose, they lack the precise and complete semantic definition that a programming language has.

Many programming languages have been designed from scratch, altered to meet new needs, and combined with other languages. Many have eventually fallen into disuse. Although there have been attempts to design one "universal" programming language that serves all purposes, all of them have failed to be generally accepted as filling this role. The need for diverse programming languages arises from the diversity of contexts in which languages are used:

- Programs range from tiny scripts written by individual hobbyists to huge systems written by hundreds of programmers.

- Programmers range in expertise from novices who need simplicity above all else, to experts who may be comfortable with considerable complexity.

- Programs must balance speed, size, and simplicity on systems ranging from microcontrollers to supercomputers.

- Programs may be written once and not change for generations, or they may undergo continual modification.

- Programmers may simply differ in their tastes: they may be accustomed to discussing problems and expressing them in a particular language.

One common trend in the development of programming languages has been to add more ability to solve problems using a higher level of abstraction. The earliest programming languages were tied very closely to the underlying hardware of the computer. As new programming languages have developed, features have been added that let programmers express ideas that are more remote from simple translation into underlying hardware instructions. Because programmers are less tied to the complexity of the computer, their programs can do more computing with less effort from the programmer. This lets them write more functionality per time unit.

Natural language programming has been proposed as a way to eliminate the need for a specialized language for programming. However, this goal remains distant and its benefits are open to debate. Edsger W. Dijkstra took the position that the use of a formal language is essential to prevent the introduction of meaningless constructs, and dismissed natural language programming as "foolish". Alan Perlis was similarly dismissive of the idea. Hybrid approaches have been taken in Structured English and SQL.

A language's designers and users must construct a number of artifacts that govern and enable the practice of programming. The most important of these artifacts are the language *specification* and *implementation*.

Specification

The specification of a programming language is an artifact that the language users and the implementors can use to agree upon whether a piece of source code is a valid program in that language, and if so what its behavior shall be.

A programming language specification can take several forms, including the following:

- An explicit definition of the syntax, static semantics, and execution semantics of the language. While syntax is commonly specified using a formal grammar, semantic definitions may be written in natural language (e.g., as in the C language), or a formal semantics (e.g., as in Standard ML and Scheme specifications).

- A description of the behavior of a translator for the language (e.g., the C++ and Fortran specifications). The syntax and semantics of the language have to be inferred from this description, which may be written in natural or a formal language.

- A *reference* or *model* implementation, sometimes written in the language being specified (e.g., Prolog or ANSI REXX). The syntax and semantics of the language are explicit in the behavior of the reference implementation.

Implementation

An *implementation* of a programming language provides a way to write programs in that language and execute them on one or more configurations of hardware and software. There are, broadly, two approaches to programming language implementation: *compilation* and *interpretation*. It is generally possible to implement a language using either technique.

The output of a compiler may be executed by hardware or a program called an interpreter. In some implementations that make use of the interpreter approach there is no distinct boundary between compiling and interpreting. For instance, some implementations of BASIC compile and then execute the source a line at a time.

Programs that are executed directly on the hardware usually run several orders of magnitude faster than those that are interpreted in software.

One technique for improving the performance of interpreted programs is just-in-time compilation. Here the virtual machine, just before execution, translates the blocks of bytecode which are going to be used to machine code, for direct execution on the hardware.

Proprietary Languages

Although most of the most commonly used programming languages have fully open specifications and implementations, many programming languages exist only as proprietary programming languages with the implementation available only from a single vendor, which may claim that such a proprietary language is their intellectual property. Proprietary programming languages are commonly domain specific languages or internal scripting languages for a single product; some proprietary languages are used only internally within a vendor, while others are available to external users.

Some programming languages exist on the border between proprietary and open; for example, Oracle Corporation asserts proprietary rights to some aspects of the Java programming language, and Microsoft's C# programming language, which has open implementations of most parts of the system, also has Common Language Runtime (CLR) as a closed environment.

Many proprietary languages are widely used, in spite of their proprietary nature; examples include MATLAB and VBScript. Some languages may make the transition from closed to open; for example, Erlang was originally an Ericsson's internal programming language.

Usage

Thousands of different programming languages have been created, mainly in the computing field. Software is commonly built with 5 programming languages or more.

Programming languages differ from most other forms of human expression in that they require a greater degree of precision and completeness. When using a natural language to communicate with other people, human authors and speakers can be ambiguous and make small errors, and still expect their intent to be understood. However, figuratively speaking, computers "do exactly what they are told to do", and cannot "understand" what code the programmer intended to write. The combination of the language definition, a program, and the program's inputs must fully specify the external behavior that occurs when the program is executed, within the domain of control of that program. On the other hand, ideas about an algorithm can be communicated to humans without the precision required for execution by using pseudocode, which interleaves natural language with code written in a programming language.

A programming language provides a structured mechanism for defining pieces of data, and the operations or transformations that may be carried out automatically on that data. A programmer uses the abstractions present in the language to represent the concepts involved in a computation. These concepts are represented as a collection of the simplest elements available (called primitives). *Programming* is the process by which programmers combine these primitives to compose new programs, or adapt existing ones to new uses or a changing environment.

Programs for a computer might be executed in a batch process without human interaction, or a user might type commands in an interactive session of an interpreter. In this case the "commands" are simply programs, whose execution is chained together. When a language can run its commands through an interpreter (such as a Unix shell or other command-line interface), without compiling, it is called a scripting language.

Measuring Language Usage

It is difficult to determine which programming languages are most widely used, and what usage means varies by context. One language may occupy the greater number of programmer hours, a different one have more lines of code, and a third may consume the most CPU time. Some languages are very popular for particular kinds of applications. For example, COBOL is still strong in the corporate data center, often on large mainframes; Fortran in scientific and engineering applications; Ada in aerospace, transportation, military, real-time and embedded applications; and C in embedded applications and operating systems. Other languages are regularly used to write many different kinds of applications.

Various methods of measuring language popularity, each subject to a different bias over what is measured, have been proposed:

- counting the number of job advertisements that mention the language

- the number of books sold that teach or describe the language

- estimates of the number of existing lines of code written in the language – which may underestimate languages not often found in public searches

- counts of language references (i.e., to the name of the language) found using a web search engine.

Combining and averaging information from various internet sites, langpop.com claims that in 2013 the ten most popular programming languages are (in descending order by overall popularity): C, Java, PHP, JavaScript, C++, Python, Shell, Ruby, Objective-C and C#.

Taxonomies

There is no overarching classification scheme for programming languages. A given programming language does not usually have a single ancestor language. Languages commonly arise by combining the elements of several predecessor languages with new ideas in circulation at the time. Ideas that originate in one language will diffuse throughout a family of related languages, and then leap suddenly across familial gaps to appear in an entirely different family.

The task is further complicated by the fact that languages can be classified along multiple axes. For example, Java is both an object-oriented language (because it encourages object-oriented organization) and a concurrent language (because it contains built-in constructs for running multiple threads in parallel). Python is an object-oriented scripting language.

In broad strokes, programming languages divide into *programming paradigms* and a classification by *intended domain of use,* with general-purpose programming languages distinguished from domain-specific programming languages. Traditionally, programming languages have been regarded as describing computation in terms of imperative sentences, i.e. issuing commands. These are generally called imperative programming languages. A great deal of research in programming languages has been aimed at blurring the distinction between a program as a set of instructions and a program as an assertion about the desired answer, which is the main feature of declarative programming. More refined paradigms include procedural programming, object-oriented programming, functional programming, and logic programming; some languages are hybrids of paradigms or multi-paradigmatic. An assembly language is not so much a paradigm as a direct model of an underlying machine architecture. By purpose, programming languages might be considered general purpose, system programming languages, scripting languages, domain-specific languages, or concurrent/distributed languages (or a combination of these). Some general purpose languages were designed largely with educational goals.

A programming language may also be classified by factors unrelated to programming paradigm. For instance, most programming languages use English language keywords, while a minority do not. Other languages may be classified as being deliberately esoteric or not.

Modeling Language

A modeling language is any artificial language that can be used to express information or knowledge or systems in a structure that is defined by a consistent set of rules. The rules are used for interpretation of the meaning of components in the structure.

Overview

A modeling language can be graphical or textual.

- *Graphical* modeling languages use a diagram technique with named symbols that represent concepts and lines that connect the symbols and represent relationships and various other graphical notation to represent constraints.

- *Textual* modeling languages may use standardized keywords accompanied by parameters or natural language terms and phrases to make computer-interpretable expressions.

An example of a graphical modeling language and a corresponding textual modeling language is EXPRESS.

Not all modeling languages are executable, and for those that are, the use of them doesn't necessarily mean that programmers are no longer required. On the contrary, executable modeling languages are intended to amplify the productivity of skilled programmers, so that they can address more challenging problems, such as parallel computing and distributed systems.

A large number of modeling languages appear in the literature.

Type of modeling languages

Graphical types

Example of graphical modeling languages in the field of computer science, project management and systems engineering:

- Behavior Trees are a formal, graphical modeling language used primarily in systems and software engineering. Commonly used to unambiguously represent the hundreds or even thousands of natural language requirements that are typically used to express the stakeholder needs for a large-scale software-integrated system.

- Business Process Modeling Notation (BPMN, and the XML form BPML) is an example of a Process Modeling language.

- C-K theory consists of a modeling language for design processes.

- DRAKON is a general-purpose algorithmic modeling language for specifying software-intensive systems, a schematic representation of an algorithm or a stepwise process, and a family of programming languages.

- EXPRESS and EXPRESS-G (ISO 10303-11) is an international standard general-purpose data modeling language.

- Extended Enterprise Modeling Language (EEML) is commonly used for business process modeling across a number of layers.

- Flowchart is a schematic representation of an algorithm or a stepwise process.

- Fundamental Modeling Concepts (FMC) modeling language for software-intensive systems.

- IDEF is a family of modeling languages, which include IDEF0 for functional modeling, IDEF1X for information modeling, IDEF3 for business process modeling, IDEF4 for Object-Oriented Design and IDEF5 for modeling ontologies.

- Jackson Structured Programming (JSP) is a method for structured programming based on correspondences between data stream structure and program structure.

- LePUS3 is an object-oriented visual Design Description Language and a formal specification language that is suitable primarily for modeling large object-oriented (Java, C++, C#) programs and design patterns.

- Object-Role Modeling (ORM) in the field of software engineering is a method for conceptual modeling, and can be used as a tool for information and rules analysis.

- Petri nets use variations on exactly one diagramming technique and topology, namely the bipartite graph. The simplicity of its basic user interface easily enabled extensive tool support over the years, particularly in the areas of model checking, graphically oriented simulation, and software verification.

- Southbeach Notation is a visual modeling language used to describe situations in terms of agents that are considered useful or harmful from the modeler's perspective. The notation shows how the agents interact with each other and whether this interaction improves or worsens the situation.

- Specification and Description Language (SDL) is a specification language targeted at the unambiguous specification and description of the behavior of reactive and distributed systems.

- SysML is a Domain-Specific Modeling language for systems engineering that is defined as a UML profile (customization).

- Unified Modeling Language (UML) is a general-purpose modeling language that is an industry standard for specifying software-intensive systems. UML 2.0, the current version, supports thirteen different diagram techniques, and has widespread tool support.

- Service-oriented modeling framework (SOMF) is a holistic language for designing enterprise and application level architecture models in the space of enterprise architecture, virtualization, service-oriented architecture (SOA), cloud computing, and more.

- Architecture description language (ADL) is a language used to describe and represent the systems architecture of a system.

- AADL (AADL) is a modeling language that supports early and repeated analyses of a system's architecture with respect to performance-critical properties through an exetendable notation, a tool framework, and precisely defined semantics.

Examples of graphical modeling languages in other fields of science.

- EAST-ADL is a Domain-Specific Modeling language dedicated to automotive system design.

- Energy Systems Language (ESL), a language that aims to model ecological energetics & global economics.

Textual Types

Information models can also be expressed in formalized natural languages, such as Gellish. Gellish has natural language variants such as Gellish Formal English and Gellish Formal Dutch (Gellish Formeel Nederlands), etc. Gellish Formal English is an information representation language or semantic modeling language that is defined in the Gellish English Dictionary-Taxonomy, which has the form of a Taxonomy-Ontology (similarly for Dutch). Gellish Formal English is not only suitable to express knowledge, requirements and dictionaries, taxonomies and ontologies, but also information about individual things. All that information is expressed in one language and therefore it can all be integrated, independent of the question whether it is stored in central or distributed or in federated databases. Information models in Gellish Formal English consists of collections of Gellish Formal English expressions, that use natural language terms and formalized phrases. For example, a geographic information model might consist of a number of Gellish Formal English expressions, such as:

- the Eiffel tower <is located in> Paris

- Paris <is classified as a> city

whereas information requirements and knowledge can be expressed for example as follows:

- tower <shall be located in a> geographical area

- city <is a kind of> geographical area

Such Gellish Formal English expressions use names of concepts (such as 'city') and phrases that represent relation types (such as <is located in> and <is classified as a>) that should be selected from the Gellish English Dictionary-Taxonomy (or of your own domain dictionary). The Gellish English Dictionary-Taxonomy enables the creation of semantically rich information models, because the dictionary more than 600 standard relation types and contains definitions of more than 40000 concepts. An information model in Gellish can express facts or make statements, queries and answers.

More Specific Types

In the field of computer science recently more specific types of modeling languages have emerged.

Algebraic

Algebraic Modeling Languages (AML) are high-level programming languages for describing and solving high complexity problems for large scale mathematical computation (i.e. large scale optimization type problems). One particular advantage of AMLs like AIMMS, AMPL, GAMS, LPL, MPL, OPL and OptimJ is the similarity of its syntax to the mathematical notation of optimization problems. This allows for a very concise and readable definition of problems in the domain of optimization, which is supported by certain language elements like sets, indices, algebraic expressions, powerful sparse index and data handling variables, constraints with arbitrary names. The algebraic formulation of a model does not contain any hints how to process it.

Behavioral

Behavioral languages are designed to describe the observable behavior of complex systems consisting of components that execute concurrently. These languages focus on the description of key concepts such as: concurrency, nondeterminism, synchronization, and communication. The semantic foundations of Behavioral languages are process calculus or process algebra.

Discipline-Specific

A discipline-specific modeling (DspM) language is focused on deliverables affiliated with a specific software development life cycle stage. Therefore, such language offers a distinct vocabulary, syntax, and notation for each stage, such as discovery, analysis, design, architecture, contraction, etc. For example, for the analysis phase of a project, the modeler employs specific analysis notation to deliver an analysis proposition diagram. During the design phase, however, logical design notation is used to depict relationship between software entities. In addition, the discipline-specific modeling language best practices does not preclude practitioners from combining the various notations in a single diagram.

Domain-specific

Domain-specific modeling (DSM) is a software engineering methodology for designing and developing systems, most often IT systems such as computer software. It involves systematic use of a graphical domain-specific language (DSL) to represent the various facets of a system. DSM languages tend to support higher-level abstractions than General-purpose modeling languages, so they require less effort and fewer low-level details to specify a given system.

Framework-Specific

A framework-specific modeling language (FSML) is a kind of domain-specific modeling language which is designed for an object-oriented application framework. FSMLs define framework-provided abstractions as FSML concepts and decompose the abstractions into features. The features represent implementation steps or choices.

A FSML concept can be configured by selecting features and providing values for features. Such a concept configuration represents how the concept should be implemented in the code. In other words, concept configuration describes how the framework should be completed in order to create the implementation of the concept.

Object-Oriented

Object modeling language are modeling languages based on a standardized set of symbols and ways of arranging them to model (part of) an object oriented software design or system design.

Some organizations use them extensively in combination with a software development methodology to progress from initial specification to an implementation plan and to communicate that plan to an entire team of developers and stakeholders. Because a modeling language is visual and at a higher-level of abstraction than code, using models encourages the generation of a shared vision that may prevent problems of differing interpretation later in development. Often software modeling tools are used to construct these models, which may then be capable of automatic translation to code.

Virtual Reality

Virtual Reality Modeling Language (VRML), before 1995 known as the Virtual Reality Markup Language is a standard file format for representing 3-dimensional (3D) interactive vector graphics, designed particularly with the World Wide Web in mind.

Others

- Architecture Description Language
- Face Modeling Language
- Generative Modelling Language
- Java Modeling Language
- Promela
- Rebeca Modeling Language
- Service Modeling Language
- Web Services Modeling Language
- X3D

Applications

Various kinds of modeling languages are applied in different disciplines, including computer science, information management, business process modeling, software engineering, and systems engineering. Modeling languages can be used to specify:

- system requirements,
- structures and
- behaviors.

Modeling languages are intended to be used to precisely specify systems so that stakeholders (e.g., customers, operators, analysts, designers) can better understand the system being modeled.

The more mature modeling languages are precise, consistent and executable. Informal diagramming techniques applied with drawing tools are expected to produce useful pictorial representations of system requirements, structures and behaviors, but not much else. Executable modeling languages applied with proper tool support, however, are expected to automate system verification and validation, simulation and code generation from the same representations.

Quality

A review of modelling languages is essential to be able to assign which languages are appropriate for different modelling settings. In the term settings we include stakeholders, domain and the knowledge connected. Assessing the language quality is a means that aims to achieve better models.

Framework for Evaluation

Here language quality is stated in accordance with the SEQUAL framework for quality of models developed by Krogstie, Sindre and Lindland (2003), since this is a framework that connects the language quality to a framework for general model quality. Five areas are used in this framework to describe language quality and these are supposed to express both the conceptual as well as the visual notation of the language. We will not go into a thoroughly explanation of the underlying quality framework of models but concentrate on the areas used to explain the language quality framework.

Domain Appropriateness

The framework states the ability to represent the domain as domain appropriateness. The statement *appropriateness* can be a bit vague, but in this particular context it means *able to express*. You should ideally only be able to express things that are in the domain but be powerful enough to include everything that is in the domain. This requirement might seem a bit strict, but the aim is to get a visually expressed model which includes everything relevant to the domain and excludes everything not appropriate for the domain. To achieve this, the language has to have a good distinction of which notations and syntaxes that are advantageous to present.

Participant Appropriateness

To evaluate the participant appropriateness we try to identify how well the language expresses the knowledge held by the stakeholders. This involves challenges since a stakeholder's knowledge is subjective. The knowledge of the stakeholder is both tacit and explicit. Both types of knowledge are of dynamic character. In this framework only the explicit type of knowledge is taken into account. The language should to a large extent express all the explicit knowledge of the stakeholders relevant to the domain.

Modeller Appropriateness

Last paragraph stated that knowledge of the stakeholders should be presented in a good way. In addition it is imperative that the language should be able to express all possible explicit knowledge of the stakeholders. No knowledge should be left unexpressed due to lacks in the language.

Comprehensibility Appropriateness

Comprehensibility appropriateness makes sure that the social actors understand the model due to a consistent use of the language. To achieve this the framework includes a set of criteria. The general importance that these express is that the language should be flexible, easy to organize and easy to distinguish different parts of the language internally as well as from other languages. In addition to this, the goal should be as simple as possible and that each symbol in the language has a unique representation.

Tool Appropriateness

To ensure that the domain actually modelled is usable for analyzing and further processing, the language has to ensure that it is possible to reason in an automatic way. To achieve this it has to include formal syntax and semantics. Another advantage by formalizing is the ability to discover errors in an early stage. It is not always that the language best fitted for the technical actors is the same as for the social actors.

Organizational Appropriateness

The language used is appropriate for the organizational context, e.g. that the language is standardized within the organization, or that it is supported by tools that are chosen as standard in the organization.

History of Programming Languages

This article discusses the major developments in the **history of programming languages**.

Early History

During a nine-month period in 1842–1843, Ada Lovelace translated the memoir of Italian mathematician, Luigi Menabrea about Charles Babbage's newest proposed machine, the Analytical

Engine. With the article she appended a set of notes which specified in complete detail a method for calculating Bernoulli numbers with the Analytical Engine, recognized by some historians as the world's first computer program.

Herman Hollerith realized that he could encode information on punch cards when he observed that train conductors encode the appearance of the ticket holders on the train tickets using the position of punched holes on the tickets. Hollerith then encoded the 1890 census data on punch cards.

The first computer codes were specialized for their applications. In the first decades of the 20th century, numerical calculations were based on decimal numbers. Eventually it was realized that logic could be represented with numbers, not only with words. For example, Alonzo Church was able to express the lambda calculus in a formulaic way. The Turing machine was an abstraction of the operation of a tape-marking machine, for example, in use at the telephone companies. Turing machines set the basis for storage of programs as data in the von Neumann architecture of computers by representing a machine through a finite number. However, unlike the lambda calculus, Turing's code does not serve well as a basis for higher-level languages—its principal use is in rigorous analyses of algorithmic complexity.

Like many "firsts" in history, the first modern programming language is hard to identify. From the start, the restrictions of the hardware defined the language. Punch cards allowed 80 columns, but some of the columns had to be used for a sorting number on each card. FORTRAN included some keywords which were the same as English words, such as "IF", "GOTO" (go to) and "CONTINUE". The use of a magnetic drum for memory meant that computer programs also had to be interleaved with the rotations of the drum. Thus the programs were more hardware-dependent.

To some people, what was the first modern programming language depends on how much power and human-readability is required before the status of "programming language" is granted. Jacquard looms and Charles Babbage's Difference Engine both had simple, extremely limited languages for describing the actions that these machines should perform. One can even regard the punch holes on a player piano scroll as a limited domain-specific language, albeit not designed for human consumption.

First Programming Languages

In the 1940s, the first recognizably modern electrically powered computers were created. The limited speed and memory capacity forced programmers to write hand tuned assembly language programs. It was eventually realized that programming in assembly language required a great deal of intellectual effort and was error-prone.

The first programming languages designed to communicate instructions to a computer were written in the 1950s. An early high-level programming language to be designed for a computer was Plankalkül, developed by the Germans for Z3 by Konrad Zuse between 1943 and 1945. However, it was not implemented until 1998 and 2000.

John Mauchly's Short Code, proposed in 1949, was one of the first high-level languages ever developed for an electronic computer. Unlike machine code, Short Code statements represented mathematical expressions in understandable form. However, the program had to be translated into machine code every time it ran, making the process much slower than running the equivalent machine code.

The Manchester Mark 1 ran programs written in Autocode from 1952.

At the University of Manchester, Alick Glennie developed Autocode in the early 1950s. A programming language, it used a compiler to automatically convert the language into machine code. The first code and compiler was developed in 1952 for the Mark 1 computer at the University of Manchester and is considered to be the first compiled high-level programming language.

The second autocode was developed for the Mark 1 by R. A. Brooker in 1954 and was called the "Mark 1 Autocode". Brooker also developed an autocode for the Ferranti Mercury in the 1950s in conjunction with the University of Manchester. The version for the EDSAC 2 was devised by D. F. Hartley of University of Cambridge Mathematical Laboratory in 1961. Known as EDSAC 2 Autocode, it was a straight development from Mercury Autocode adapted for local circumstances, and was noted for its object code optimisation and source-language diagnostics which were advanced for the time. A contemporary but separate thread of development, Atlas Autocode was developed for the University of Manchester Atlas 1 machine.

In 1954, language FORTRAN was invented at IBM by John Backus; it was the first widely used high level general purpose programming language to have a functional implementation, as opposed to just a design on paper. It is still popular language for high-performance computing and is used for programs that benchmark and rank the world's fastest supercomputers.

Another early programming language was devised by Grace Hopper in the US, called FLOW-MATIC. It was developed for the UNIVAC I at Remington Rand during the period from 1955 until 1959. Hopper found that business data processing customers were uncomfortable with mathematical notation, and in early 1955, she and her team wrote a specification for an English programming language and implemented a prototype. The FLOW-MATIC compiler became publicly available in early 1958 and was substantially complete in 1959. Flow-Matic was a major influence in the design of COBOL, since only it and its direct descendent AIMACO were in actual use at the time.

Other languages still in use today include LISP (1958), invented by John McCarthy and COBOL (1959), created by the Short Range Committee. Another milestone in the late 1950s was the publication, by a committee of American and European computer scientists, of "a new language for algorithms"; the *ALGOL 60 Report* (the "ALGOrithmic Language"). This report consolidated many ideas circulating at the time and featured three key language innovations:

- nested block structure: code sequences and associated declarations could be grouped into blocks without having to be turned into separate, explicitly named procedures;

- lexical scoping: a block could have its own private variables, procedures and functions, invisible to code outside that block, that is, information hiding.

Another innovation, related to this, was in how the language was described:

- a mathematically exact notation, Backus-Naur Form (BNF), was used to describe the language's syntax. Nearly all subsequent programming languages have used a variant of BNF to describe the context-free portion of their syntax.

Algol 60 was particularly influential in the design of later languages, some of which soon became more popular. The Burroughs large systems were designed to be programmed in an extended subset of Algol.

Algol's key ideas were continued, producing ALGOL 68:

- syntax and semantics became even more orthogonal, with anonymous routines, a recursive typing system with higher-order functions, etc.;

- not only the context-free part, but the full language syntax and semantics were defined formally, in terms of Van Wijngaarden grammar, a formalism designed specifically for this purpose.

Algol 68's many little-used language features (for example, concurrent and parallel blocks) and its complex system of syntactic shortcuts and automatic type coercions made it unpopular with implementers and gained it a reputation of being *difficult*. Niklaus Wirth actually walked out of the design committee to create the simpler Pascal language.

Fortran

Some notable languages that were developed in this period include:

• 1951 – Regional Assembly Language	• 1959 – RPG
• 1952 – Autocode	• 1962 – APL
• 1954 – IPL (forerunner to LISP)	• 1962 – Simula
• 1955 – FLOW-MATIC (led to COBOL)	• 1962 – SNOBOL
• 1957 – FORTRAN (First compiler)	• 1963 – CPL (forerunner to C)
• 1957 – COMTRAN (precursor to COBOL)	• 1964 – Speakeasy (computational environment)
• 1958 – LISP	• 1964 – BASIC
• 1958 – ALGOL 58	• 1964 – PL/I
• 1959 – FACT (forerunner to COBOL)	• 1966 – JOSS
• 1959 – COBOL	• 1967 – BCPL (forerunner to C)

Establishing Fundamental Paradigms

Smalltalk

Scheme

The period from the late 1960s to the late 1970s brought a major flowering of programming languages. Most of the major language paradigms now in use were invented in this period:

- Speakeasy (computational environment), developed in 1964 at Argonne National Laboratory (ANL) by Stanley Cohen, is an OOPS (object-oriented programming, much like the later MATLAB, IDL (programming language) and Mathematica) numerical package. Speakeasy has a clear Fortran foundation syntax. It first addressed efficient physics computation internally at ANL, was modified for research use (as "Modeleasy") for the Federal Reserve Board in the early 1970s and then was made available commercially; Speakeasy and Modeleasy are still in use currently.

- Simula, invented in the late 1960s by Nygaard and Dahl as a superset of Algol 60, was the first language designed to support object-oriented programming.

- C, an early systems programming language, was developed by Dennis Ritchie and Ken Thompson at Bell Labs between 1969 and 1973.

- Smalltalk (mid-1970s) provided a complete ground-up design of an object-oriented language.

- Prolog, designed in 1972 by Colmerauer, Roussel, and Kowalski, was the first logic programming language.

- ML built a polymorphic type system (invented by Robin Milner in 1973) on top of Lisp, pioneering statically typed functional programming languages.

Each of these languages spawned an entire family of descendants, and most modern languages count at least one of them in their ancestry.

The 1960s and 1970s also saw considerable debate over the merits of "structured programming", which essentially meant programming without the use of Goto. This debate was closely related to language design: some languages did not include GOTO, which forced structured programming on the programmer. Although the debate raged hotly at the time, nearly all programmers now agree that, even in languages that provide GOTO, it is bad programming style to use it except in rare circumstances. As a result, later generations of language designers have found the structured programming debate tedious and even bewildering.

To provide even faster compile times, some languages were structured for "one-pass compilers" which expect subordinate routines to be defined first, as with Pascal, where the main routine, or driver function, is the final section of the program listing.

Some notable languages that were developed in this period include:

• 1968 – Logo	• 1972 – Smalltalk
• 1969 – B (forerunner to C)	• 1972 – Prolog
• 1970 – Pascal	• 1973 – ML
• 1970 – Forth	• 1975 – Scheme
• 1972 – C	• 1978 – SQL (a query language, later extended)

1980s: Consolidation, Modules, Performance

MATLAB

Erlang

Tcl

The 1980s were years of relative consolidation in imperative languages. Rather than inventing new paradigms, all of these movements elaborated upon the ideas invented in the previous decade. C++ combined object-oriented and systems programming. The United States government standardized Ada, a systems programming language intended for use by defense contractors. In Japan and elsewhere, vast sums were spent investigating so-called fifth-generation programming languages that incorporated logic programming constructs. The functional languages community moved to standardize ML and Lisp. Research in Miranda, a functional language with lazy evaluation, began to take hold in this decade.

One important new trend in language design was an increased focus on programming for large-scale systems through the use of *modules*, or large-scale organizational units of code. Modula, Ada, and ML all developed notable module systems in the 1980s. Module systems were often wedded to generic programming constructs---generics being, in essence, parametrized modules.

Although major new paradigms for imperative programming languages did not appear, many researchers expanded on the ideas of prior languages and adapted them to new contexts. For example, the languages of the Argus and Emerald systems adapted object-oriented programming to distributed systems.

The 1980s also brought advances in programming language implementation. The RISC movement in computer architecture postulated that hardware should be designed for compilers rather than for human assembly programmers. Aided by processor speed improvements that enabled increasingly aggressive compilation techniques, the RISC movement sparked greater interest in compilation technology for high-level languages.

Language technology continued along these lines well into the 1990s.

Some notable languages that were developed in this period include:

• 1980 – C++ (as C with classes, renamed in 1983)	• 1986 – Erlang
• 1983 – Ada	• 1987 – Perl
• 1984 – Common Lisp	• 1988 – Tcl
• 1984 – MATLAB	• 1988 – Wolfram Language (as part of Mathematica, only got a separate name in June 2013)
• 1985 – Eiffel	
• 1986 – Objective-C	• 1989 – FL (Backus)

1990s: The Internet Age

Haskell

Lua

Rebol

D Programming Language

The rapid growth of the Internet in the mid-1990s was the next major historic event in programming languages. By opening up a radically new platform for computer systems, the Internet created an opportunity for new languages to be adopted. In particular, the JavaScript programming language rose to popularity because of its early integration with the Netscape Navigator web browser. Various other scripting languages achieved widespread use in developing customized applications for web servers such as PHP. The 1990s saw no fundamental novelty in imperative languages, but much recombination and maturation of old ideas. This era began the spread of functional languages. A big driving philosophy was programmer productivity. Many "rapid application development" (RAD) languages emerged, which usually came with an IDE, garbage collection, and were descendants of older languages. All such languages were object-oriented. These included Object Pascal, Visual Basic, and Java. Java in particular received much attention. More radical and innovative than the RAD languages were the new scripting languages. These did not directly descend from other languages and featured new syntaxes and more liberal incorporation of features. Many consider these scripting languages to be more productive than even the RAD languages, but often because of choices that make small programs simpler but large programs more difficult to write and maintain. Nevertheless, scripting languages came to be the most prominent ones used in connection with the Web.

Some notable languages that were developed in this period include:

• 1990 – Haskell	• 1995 – Ada 95
• 1991 – Python	• 1995 – Java
• 1991 – Visual Basic	• 1995 – Delphi (Object Pascal)
• 1993 – Ruby	• 1995 – JavaScript
• 1993 – Lua	• 1995 – PHP
• 1993 – R	• 1997 – Rebol
• 1994 – CLOS (part of ANSI Common Lisp)	• 1999 – D

Current Trends

Programming language evolution continues, in both industry and research. Some of the recent trends have included:

- Increasing support for functional programming in mainstream languages used commercially, including pure functional programming for making code easier to reason about and easier to parallelise (at both micro- and macro- levels)

- Constructs to support concurrent and distributed programming.

- Mechanisms for adding security and reliability verification to the language: extended static checking, dependent typing, information flow control, static thread safety.

- Alternative mechanisms for composability and modularity: mixins, traits, delegates, aspects.

- Component-oriented software development.

- Metaprogramming, reflection or access to the abstract syntax tree

    o AOP or Aspect Oriented Programming allowing developers to insert code in another module or class at "join points"

    o Domain specific languages and code generation

        ▪ XML for graphical interface (XUL, XAML)

- Increased interest in distribution and mobility.

- Integration with databases, including XML and relational databases.

- Open source as a developmental philosophy for languages, including the GNU Compiler Collection and languages such as Python, Ruby, and Scala.

- Massively parallel languages for coding 2000 processor GPU graphics processing units and supercomputer arrays including OpenCL

- Early research into (as-yet-unimplementable) quantum computing programming languages

Groovy

Rust

Some notable languages developed during this period include:

• 2000 – ActionScript	• 2007 – Clojure
• 2001 – C#	• 2009 – Go
• 2003 – Apache Groovy	• 2011 – Dart
• 2003 – Scala	• 2012 – Julia
• 2005 – F#	• 2014 – Swift
• 2006 – Windows PowerShell	• 2015 – Rust

Prominent People

Anders Hejlsberg

Yukihiro Matsumoto

Grace M. Hopper

Bjarne Stroustrup

Niklaus Wirth

Some key people who helped develop programming languages:

- Joe Armstrong, creator of Erlang.

- John Backus, inventor of Fortran and cooperated in the design of ALGOL 58 and ALGOL 60.

- Jeff Bezanson, got a PhD for the Julia language, one of the designers, and one of the core developers (and only developer of FemtoLisp).

- Alan Cooper, developer of Visual Basic.

- Ole-Johan Dahl, pioneered object-oriented programming, co-invented Simula.

- Edsger W. Dijkstra, developed the framework for structured programming.

- Jean-Yves Girard, co-inventor of the polymorphic lambda calculus (System F).

- James Gosling, developer of Oak, the precursor of Java.

- Anders Hejlsberg, developer of Turbo Pascal, Delphi, C#, and TypeScript.

- Rich Hickey, creator of Clojure.

- Grace Hopper, inventor of the first compiler and developer of Flow-Matic, influencing CO-BOL. Popularized machine-independent programming languages and the term "debugging".

- Jean Ichbiah, chief designer of Ada, Ada 83

- Kenneth E. Iverson, developer of APL, and co-developer of J along with Roger Hui.

- Alan Kay, pioneering work on object-oriented programming, and originator of Smalltalk.

- Brian Kernighan, co-author of the first book on the C programming language with Dennis Ritchie, coauthor of the AWK and AMPL programming languages.

- Yukihiro Matsumoto, creator of Ruby.

- John McCarthy, inventor of LISP.

- Bertrand Meyer, inventor of Eiffel.

- Robin Milner, inventor of ML, and sharing credit for Hindley–Milner polymorphic type inference.

- John von Neumann, originator of the operating system concept.

- Kristen Nygaard, pioneered object-oriented programming, co-invented Simula.

- Martin Odersky, creator of Scala, and previously a contributor to the design of Java.

- John C. Reynolds, co-inventor of the polymorphic lambda calculus (System F).

- Dennis Ritchie, inventor of C. Unix Operating System, Plan 9 Operating System.

- Nathaniel Rochester, inventor of first assembler (IBM 701).

- Guido van Rossum, creator of Python.

- Bjarne Stroustrup, developer of C++.

- Ken Thompson, inventor of B, Go Programming Language, Inferno Programming Language, and Unix Operating System co-author.

- Larry Wall, creator of the Perl programming language.

- Niklaus Wirth, inventor of Pascal, Modula and Oberon.

- Stephen Wolfram, creator of Mathematica.

- Konrad Zuse, designed the first high-level programming language, Plankalkül (which influenced ALGOL 58).

References

- Rojas, Raúl; Hashagen, Ulf (2002). The First Computers: History and Architectures. MIT Press. p. 292. ISBN 978-0262681377. Retrieved October 25, 2013.

- In mathematical terms, this means the programming language is Turing-complete MacLennan, Bruce J. (1987). Principles of Programming Languages. Oxford University Press. p. 1. ISBN 0-19-511306-3.

- Scott, Michael (2006). Programming Language Pragmatics. Morgan Kaufmann. p. 802. ISBN 0-12-633951-1. XSLT, though highly specialized to the transformation of XML, is a Turing-complete programming language.

- Syropoulos, Apostolos; Antonis Tsolomitis; Nick Sofroniou (2003). Digital typography using LaTeX. Springer-Verlag. p. 213. ISBN 0-387-95217-9. TeX is not only an excellent typesetting engine but also a real programming language.

- Milner, R.; M. Tofte, R. Harper and D. MacQueen. (1997). The Definition of Standard ML (Revised). MIT Press. ISBN 0-262-63181-4. Cite uses deprecated parameter |coauthors= (help)

- Wirth, Niklaus (1993). "Recollections about the development of Pascal". Proc. 2nd ACM SIGPLAN conference on history of programming languages: 333–342. doi:10.1145/154766.155378. ISBN 0-89791-570-4. Retrieved 30 June 2006.

- Bell, Michael (2008). "Introduction to Service-Oriented Modeling". Service-Oriented Modeling: Service Analysis, Design, and Architecture. Wiley & Sons. ISBN 978-0-470-14111-3.

- "HPL - A Portable Implementation of the High-Performance Linpack Benchmark for Distributed-Memory Computers". Retrieved 2015-02-21.

- "HPL - A Portable Implementation of the High-Performance Linpack Benchmark for Distributed-Memory Computers". Retrieved 2015-02-21.

- Dijkstra, Edsger W. (March 1968). "Go To Statement Considered Harmful" (PDF). Communications of the ACM 11 (3): 147–148. doi:10.1145/362929.362947. Retrieved 2014-05-22.

- Nicholas Enticknap. "SSL/Computer Weekly IT salary survey: finance boom drives IT job growth". Computerweekly.com. Retrieved 2013-06-14.

Automatic Programming: An Integrated Study

Automatic programming uses artificially created source code that can be further developed by software programmers. It allows for quicker program development and easy optimization of programs. Program architecture becomes easier to visualize and multi-platform code can be created simultaneously. This chapter will provide an integrated understanding of automatic programming.

Automatic Programming

In computer science, the term automatic programming identifies a type of computer programming in which some mechanism generates a computer program to allow human programmers to write the code at a higher abstraction level.

There has been little agreement on the precise definition of automatic programming, mostly because its meaning has changed over time. David Parnas, tracing the history of "automatic programming" in published research, noted that in the 1940s it described automation of the manual process of punching paper tape. Later it referred to translation of high-level programming languages like Fortran and ALGOL. In fact, one of the earliest programs identifiable as a compiler was called Autocode. Parnas concluded that "automatic programming has always been a euphemism for programming in a higher-level language than was then available to the programmer."

Program synthesis is one type of automatic programming where a procedure is created from scratch, based on mathematical requirements.

Origin

Mildred Koss, an early UNIVAC programmer, explains: "Writing machine code involved several tedious steps—breaking down a process into discrete instructions, assigning specific memory locations to all the commands, and managing the I/O buffers. After following these steps to implement mathematical routines, a sub-routine library, and sorting programs, our task was to look at the larger programming process. We needed to understand how we might reuse tested code and have the machine help in programming. As we programmed, we examined the process and tried to think of ways to abstract these steps to incorporate them into higher-level language. This led to the development of interpreters, assemblers, compilers, and generators—programs designed to operate on or produce other programs, that is, *automatic programming*."

Generative Programming

Generative programming is a style of computer programming that uses automated source code creation through generic frames, classes, prototypes, templates, aspects, and code generators to improve programmer productivity. It is often related to code-reuse topics such as component-based software engineering and product family engineering.

Source Code Generation

Source code generation is the process of generating source code based on an ontological model such as a template and is accomplished with a programming tool such as a template processor or an integrated development environment (IDE). These tools allow the generation of source code through any of various means. A macro processor, such as the C preprocessor, which replaces patterns in source code according to relatively simple rules, is a simple form of source code generator.

Implementations

Some IDEs for Java and other languages have more advanced forms of source code generation, with which the programmer can interactively select and customize "snippets" of source code. Program "wizards", which allow the programmer to design graphical user interfaces interactively while the compiler invisibly generates the corresponding source code, are another common form of source code generation. This may be contrasted with, for example, user interface markup languages, which define user interfaces declaratively.

Besides the generation of code from a wizard or template, IDEs can also generate and manipulate code to automate code refactorings that would require multiple (error prone) manual steps, thereby improving developer productivity. Examples of such features in IDEs are the refactoring class browsers for Smalltalk and those found in Java IDEs like Eclipse.

A specialized alternative involves the generation of *optimized* code for quantities defined mathematically within a Computer algebra system (CAS). Compiler optimization consisting of finding common intermediates of a vector of size n requires a complexity of $O(n^2)$ or $O(n^3)$ operations whereas the very design of a computer algebra system requires only $O(n)$ operations. These facilities can be used as pre-optimizer before processing by the compiler. This option has been used for handling mathematically large expressions in e.g. computational (quantum) chemistry.

Examples:

- Acceleo is an open source code generator for Eclipse used to generate any textual language (Java, PHP, Python, etc.) from EMF models defined from any metamodel (UML, SysML, etc.).

- Actifsource is a plugin for Eclipse that allows graphical modelling and model-based code generation using custom templates.

- Altova MapForce is a graphical data mapping, conversion, and integration tool capable of generating application code in Java, C#, or C++ for executing recurrent transformations.

- CodeFluent Entities from SoftFluent is a graphical tool integrated into Microsoft Visual Studio that generates .NET source code, in C# or Visual Basic.

- DMS Software Reengineering Toolkit is a system for defining arbitrary domain specific languages and translating them to other languages.

· HPRCARCHITECT (from MNB Technologies, Inc) is an artificial intelligence-based software development tool with a Virtual Whiteboard human interface. Language and technology agnostic, the tool's development was funded by the US Air Force to solve the problem of code generation for systems targeting mixed processor technologies.

· Spring Roo is an open source active code generator for Spring Framework based Java applications. It uses AspectJ mixins to provide separation of concerns during round-trip maintenance.

· RISE is a free information modeling suite for system development using ERD or UML. Database code generation for MySQL, PostgreSQL and Microsoft SQL Server. Persistence code generation for C# (.NET) and PHP including both SOAP and JSON style web services and AJAX proxy code.

· The Maple computer algebra system offers code generators optimizers with Fortran, MATLAB, C and Java. Wolfram Language (Mathematica), and MuPAD have comparable interfaces.

· Screen Sculptor, SoftCode, UI Programmer, and Genifer are examples of pioneering program generators that arose during the mid-1980s through the early 1990s. They developed and advanced the technology of extendable, template based source code generators on a mass market scale.

· GeneXus is a Cross-Platform, knowledge representation-based, development tool, mainly oriented to enterprise-class applications for Web applications, smart devices and the Microsoft Windows platform. A developer describes an application in a high-level, mostly declarative language, from which native code is generated for multiple environments.

· Bidji is an Apache Ant project for code generation and data transformation.

Explaining Computer Networks and Networking

Software distribution, usage and development has greatly benefitted from the development of computer networks and the Internet. Programs can be quickly distributed, tested and edited with fast computing and networking technology. This chapter looks at themes such as network topology, network packet and computer network.

Computer Network

A computer network or data network is a telecommunications network which allows computers to exchange data. In computer networks, networked computing devices exchange data with each other using a data link. The connections between nodes are established using either cable media or wireless media. The best-known computer network is the Internet.

Network computer devices that originate, route and terminate the data are called network nodes. Nodes can include hosts such as personal computers, phones, servers as well as networking hardware. Two such devices can be said to be networked together when one device is able to exchange information with the other device, whether or not they have a direct connection to each other.

Computer networks differ in the transmission medium used to carry their signals, the communications protocols to organize network traffic, the network's size, topology and organizational intent.

Computer networks support an enormous number of applications such as access to the World Wide Web, video, digital audio, shared use of application and storage servers, printers, and fax machines, and use of email and instant messaging applications as well as many others. In most cases, application-specific communications protocols are layered (i.e. carried as payload) over other more general communications protocols.

History

The chronology of significant computer-network developments includes:

- In the late 1950s early networks of computers included the military radar system Semi-Automatic Ground Environment (SAGE).

- In 1959 Anatolii Ivanovich Kitov proposed to the Central Committee of the Communist Party of the Soviet Union a detailed plan for the re-organisation of the control of the Soviet armed forces and of the Soviet economy on the basis of a network of computing centres.

- In 1960 the commercial airline reservation system semi-automatic business research environment (SABRE) went online with two connected mainframes.

- In 1962 J.C.R. Licklider developed a working group he called the "Intergalactic Computer Network", a precursor to the ARPANET, at the Advanced Research Projects Agency (ARPA).

- In 1964 researchers at Dartmouth College developed the Dartmouth Time Sharing System for distributed users of large computer systems. The same year, at Massachusetts Institute of Technology, a research group supported by General Electric and Bell Labs used a computer to route and manage telephone connections.

- Throughout the 1960s, Leonard Kleinrock, Paul Baran, and Donald Davies independently developed network systems that used packets to transfer information between computers over a network.

- In 1965, Thomas Marill and Lawrence G. Roberts created the first wide area network (WAN). This was an immediate precursor to the ARPANET, of which Roberts became program manager.

- Also in 1965, Western Electric introduced the first widely used telephone switch that implemented true computer control.

- In 1969 the University of California at Los Angeles, the Stanford Research Institute, the University of California at Santa Barbara, and the University of Utah became connected as the beginning of the ARPANET network using 50 kbit/s circuits.

- In 1972 commercial services using X.25 were deployed, and later used as an underlying infrastructure for expanding TCP/IP networks.

- In 1973, Robert Metcalfe wrote a formal memo at Xerox PARC describing Ethernet, a networking system that was based on the Aloha network, developed in the 1960s by Norman Abramson and colleagues at the University of Hawaii. In July 1976, Robert Metcalfe and David Boggs published their paper "Ethernet: Distributed Packet Switching for Local Computer Networks" and collaborated on several patents received in 1977 and 1978. In 1979 Robert Metcalfe pursued making Ethernet an open standard.

- In 1976 John Murphy of Datapoint Corporation created ARCNET, a token-passing network first used to share storage devices.

- In 1995 the transmission speed capacity for Ethernet increased from 10 Mbit/s to 100 Mbit/s. By 1998, Ethernet supported transmission speeds of a Gigabit. Subsequently, higher speeds of up to 100 Gbit/s were added (as of 2016[update]). The ability of Ethernet to scale easily (such as quickly adapting to support new fiber optic cable speeds) is a contributing factor to its continued use.

Properties

Computer networking may be considered a branch of electrical engineering, telecommunications, computer science, information technology or computer engineering, since it relies upon the theoretical and practical application of the related disciplines.

A computer network facilitates interpersonal communications allowing users to communicate efficiently and easily via various means: email, instant messaging, chat rooms, telephone, video telephone calls, and video conferencing. Providing access to information on shared storage devices is an important feature of many networks. A network allows sharing of files, data, and other types of information giving authorized users the ability to access information stored on other computers on the network. A network allows sharing of network and computing resources. Users may access and use resources provided by devices on the network, such as printing a document on a shared network printer. Distributed computing uses computing resources across a network to accomplish tasks. A computer network may be used by computer crackers to deploy computer viruses or computer worms on devices connected to the network, or to prevent these devices from accessing the network via a denial of service attack.

Network Packet

Computer communication links that do not support packets, such as traditional point-to-point telecommunication links, simply transmit data as a bit stream. However, most information in computer networks is carried in *packets*. A network packet is a formatted unit of data (a list of bits or bytes, usually a few tens of bytes to a few kilobytes long) carried by a packet-switched network.

In packet networks, the data is formatted into packets that are sent through the network to their destination. Once the packets arrive they are reassembled into their original message. With packets, the bandwidth of the transmission medium can be better shared among users than if the network were circuit switched. When one user is not sending packets, the link can be filled with packets from others users, and so the cost can be shared, with relatively little interference, provided the link isn't overused.

Packets consist of two kinds of data: control information, and user data(payload). The control information provides data the network needs to deliver the user data, for example: source and destination network addresses, error detection codes, and sequencing information. Typically, control information is found in packet headers and trailers, with payload data in between.

Often the route a packet needs to take through a network is not immediately available. In that case the packet is queued and waits until a link is free.

Network Topology

The physical layout of a network is usually less important than the topology that connects network nodes. Most diagrams that describe a physical network are therefore topological, rather than geographic. The symbols on these diagrams usually denote network links and network nodes.

Network Links

The transmission media (often referred to in the literature as the *physical media*) used to link devices to form a computer network include electrical cable (Ethernet, HomePNA, power line communication, G.hn), optical fiber (fiber-optic communication), and radio waves (wireless networking). In the OSI model, these are defined at layers 1 and 2 — the physical layer and the data link layer.

A widely adopted *family* of transmission media used in local area network (LAN) technology is collectively known as Ethernet. The media and protocol standards that enable communication between networked devices over Ethernet are defined by IEEE 802.3. Ethernet transmits data over both copper and fiber cables. Wireless LAN standards (e.g. those defined by IEEE 802.11) use radio waves, or others use infrared signals as a transmission medium. Power line communication uses a building's power cabling to transmit data.

Wired Technologies

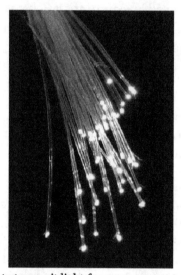

Fiber optic cables are used to transmit light from one computer/network node to another

The orders of the following wired technologies are, roughly, from slowest to fastest transmission speed.

- *Coaxial cable* is widely used for cable television systems, office buildings, and other work-sites for local area networks. The cables consist of copper or aluminum wire surrounded by an insulating layer (typically a flexible material with a high dielectric constant), which itself is surrounded by a conductive layer. The insulation helps minimize interference and distortion. Transmission speed ranges from 200 million bits per second to more than 500 million bits per second.

- ITU-T G.hn technology uses existing home wiring (coaxial cable, phone lines and power lines) to create a high-speed (up to 1 Gigabit/s) local area network

- *Twisted pair wire* is the most widely used medium for all telecommunication. Twisted-pair cabling consist of copper wires that are twisted into pairs. Ordinary telephone wires consist of two insulated copper wires twisted into pairs. Computer network cabling (wired Ethernet as defined by IEEE 802.3) consists of 4 pairs of copper cabling that can be utilized for both voice and data transmission. The use of two wires twisted together helps to reduce crosstalk and electromagnetic induction. The transmission speed ranges from 2 million bits per second to 10 billion bits per second. Twisted pair cabling comes in two forms:

unshielded twisted pair (UTP) and shielded twisted-pair (STP). Each form comes in several category ratings, designed for use in various scenarios.

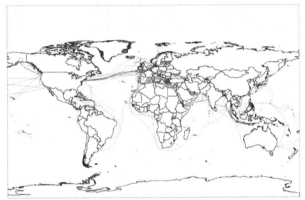

2007 map showing submarine optical fiber telecommunication cables around the world.

- An *optical fiber* is a glass fiber. It carries pulses of light that represent data. Some advantages of optical fibers over metal wires are very low transmission loss and immunity from electrical interference. Optical fibers can simultaneously carry multiple wavelengths of light, which greatly increases the rate that data can be sent, and helps enable data rates of up to trillions of bits per second. Optic fibers can be used for long runs of cable carrying very high data rates, and are used for undersea cables to interconnect continents.

Price is a main factor distinguishing wired- and wireless-technology options in a business. Wireless options command a price premium that can make purchasing wired computers, printers and other devices a financial benefit. Before making the decision to purchase hard-wired technology products, a review of the restrictions and limitations of the selections is necessary. Business and employee needs may override any cost considerations.

Wireless Technologies

Computers are very often connected to networks using wireless links

- *Terrestrial microwave* – Terrestrial microwave communication uses Earth-based transmitters and receivers resembling satellite dishes. Terrestrial microwaves are in the low-gigahertz range, which limits all communications to line-of-sight. Relay stations are spaced approximately 48 km (30 mi) apart.

- *Communications satellites* – Satellites communicate via microwave radio waves, which are not deflected by the Earth›s atmosphere. The satellites are stationed in space, typically in geosynchronous orbit 35,400 km (22,000 mi) above the equator. These Earth-orbiting systems are capable of receiving and relaying voice, data, and TV signals.

- *Cellular and PCS systems* use several radio communications technologies. The systems divide the region covered into multiple geographic areas. Each area has a low-power transmitter or radio relay antenna device to relay calls from one area to the next area.

- *Radio and spread spectrum technologies* – Wireless local area networks use a high-frequency radio technology similar to digital cellular and a low-frequency radio technology. Wireless LANs use spread spectrum technology to enable communication between multiple devices in a limited area. IEEE 802.11 defines a common flavor of open-standards wireless radio-wave technology known as Wifi.

- *Free-space optical communication* uses visible or invisible light for communications. In most cases, line-of-sight propagation is used, which limits the physical positioning of communicating devices.

Exotic Technologies

There have been various attempts at transporting data over exotic media:

- IP over Avian Carriers was a humorous April fool's Request for Comments, issued as RFC 1149. It was implemented in real life in 2001.

- Extending the Internet to interplanetary dimensions via radio waves.

Both cases have a large round-trip delay time, which gives slow two-way communication, but doesn't prevent sending large amounts of information.

Network Nodes

Apart from any physical transmission medium there may be, networks comprise additional basic system building blocks, such as network interface controller (NICs), repeaters, hubs, bridges, switches, routers, modems, and firewalls.

Network Interfaces

An ATM network interface in the form of an accessory card. A lot of network interfaces are built-in.

A network interface controller (NIC) is computer hardware that provides a computer with the ability to access the transmission media, and has the ability to process low-level network information. For example, the NIC may have a connector for accepting a cable, or an aerial for wireless transmission and reception, and the associated circuitry.

The NIC responds to traffic addressed to a network address for either the NIC or the computer as a whole.

In Ethernet networks, each network interface controller has a unique Media Access Control (MAC) address—usually stored in the controller's permanent memory. To avoid address conflicts between network devices, the Institute of Electrical and Electronics Engineers (IEEE) maintains and administers MAC address uniqueness. The size of an Ethernet MAC address is six octets. The three most significant octets are reserved to identify NIC manufacturers. These manufacturers, using only their assigned prefixes, uniquely assign the three least-significant octets of every Ethernet interface they produce.

Repeaters and Hubs

A repeater is an electronic device that receives a network signal, cleans it of unnecessary noise and regenerates it. The signal is retransmitted at a higher power level, or to the other side of an obstruction, so that the signal can cover longer distances without degradation. In most twisted pair Ethernet configurations, repeaters are required for cable that runs longer than 100 meters. With fiber optics, repeaters can be tens or even hundreds of kilometers apart.

A repeater with multiple ports is known as a hub. Repeaters work on the physical layer of the OSI model. Repeaters require a small amount of time to regenerate the signal. This can cause a propagation delay that affects network performance. As a result, many network architectures limit the number of repeaters that can be used in a row, e.g., the Ethernet 5-4-3 rule.

Hubs have been mostly obsoleted by modern switches; but repeaters are used for long distance links, notably undersea cabling.

Bridges

A network bridge connects and filters traffic between two network segments at the data link layer (layer 2) of the OSI model to form a single network. This breaks the network's collision domain but maintains a unified broadcast domain. Network segmentation breaks down a large, congested network into an aggregation of smaller, more efficient networks.

Bridges come in three basic types:

- Local bridges: Directly connect LANs

- Remote bridges: Can be used to create a wide area network (WAN) link between LANs. Remote bridges, where the connecting link is slower than the end networks, largely have been replaced with routers.

- Wireless bridges: Can be used to join LANs or connect remote devices to LANs.

Switches

A network switch is a device that forwards and filters OSI layer 2 datagrams (frames) between ports based on the destination MAC address in each frame. A switch is distinct from a hub in that it only forwards the frames to the physical ports involved in the communication rather than all ports connected. It can be thought of as a multi-port bridge. It learns to associate physical ports to MAC addresses by examining the source addresses of received frames. If an unknown destination is targeted, the switch broadcasts to all ports but the source. Switches normally have numerous ports, facilitating a star topology for devices, and cascading additional switches.

Multi-layer switches are capable of routing based on layer 3 addressing or additional logical levels. The term *switch* is often used loosely to include devices such as routers and bridges, as well as devices that may distribute traffic based on load or based on application content (e.g., a Web URL identifier).

Routers

A typical home or small office router showing the ADSL telephone line and Ethernet network cable connections

A router is an internetworking device that forwards packets between networks by processing the routing information included in the packet or datagram (Internet protocol information from layer 3). The routing information is often processed in conjunction with the routing table (or forwarding table). A router uses its routing table to determine where to forward packets. A destination in a routing table can include a "null" interface, also known as the "black hole" interface because data can go into it, however, no further processing is done for said data, i.e. the packets are dropped.

Modems

Modems (MOdulator-DEModulator) are used to connect network nodes via wire not originally designed for digital network traffic, or for wireless. To do this one or more carrier signals are modulated by the digital signal to produce an analog signal that can be tailored to give the required properties for transmission. Modems are commonly used for telephone lines, using a Digital Subscriber Line technology.

Firewalls

A firewall is a network device for controlling network security and access rules. Firewalls are typically configured to reject access requests from unrecognized sources while allowing actions from recognized ones. The vital role firewalls play in network security grows in parallel with the constant increase in cyber attacks.

Network Structure

Network topology is the layout or organizational hierarchy of interconnected nodes of a computer network. Different network topologies can affect throughput, but reliability is often more critical. With many technologies, such as bus networks, a single failure can cause the network to fail entirely. In general the more interconnections there are, the more robust the network is; but the more expensive it is to install.

Common Layouts

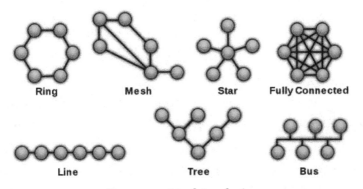

Common network topologies

Common Layouts are:

- A bus network: all nodes are connected to a common medium along this medium. This was the layout used in the original Ethernet, called 10BASE5 and 10BASE2.

- A star network: all nodes are connected to a special central node. This is the typical layout found in a Wireless LAN, where each wireless client connects to the central Wireless access point.

- A ring network: each node is connected to its left and right neighbour node, such that all nodes are connected and that each node can reach each other node by traversing nodes left- or rightwards. The Fiber Distributed Data Interface (FDDI) made use of such a topology.

- A mesh network: each node is connected to an arbitrary number of neighbours in such a way that there is at least one traversal from any node to any other.

- A fully connected network: each node is connected to every other node in the network.

- A tree network: nodes are arranged hierarchically.

Note that the physical layout of the nodes in a network may not necessarily reflect the network topology. As an example, with FDDI, the network topology is a ring (actually two counter-rotating rings), but the physical topology is often a star, because all neighboring connections can be routed via a central physical location.

Overlay Network

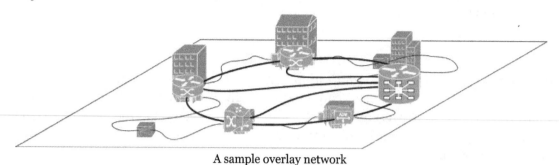

A sample overlay network

An overlay network is a virtual computer network that is built on top of another network. Nodes in the overlay network are connected by virtual or logical links. Each link corresponds to a path, perhaps through many physical links, in the underlying network. The topology of the overlay network may (and often does) differ from that of the underlying one. For example, many peer-to-peer networks are overlay networks. They are organized as nodes of a virtual system of links that run on top of the Internet.

Overlay networks have been around since the invention of networking when computer systems were connected over telephone lines using modems, before any data network existed.

The most striking example of an overlay network is the Internet itself. The Internet itself was initially built as an overlay on the telephone network. Even today, each Internet node can communicate with virtually any other through an underlying mesh of sub-networks of wildly different topologies and technologies. Address resolution and routing are the means that allow mapping of a fully connected IP overlay network to its underlying network.

Another example of an overlay network is a distributed hash table, which maps keys to nodes in the network. In this case, the underlying network is an IP network, and the overlay network is a table (actually a map) indexed by keys.

Overlay networks have also been proposed as a way to improve Internet routing, such as through quality of service guarantees to achieve higher-quality streaming media. Previous proposals such as IntServ, DiffServ, and IP Multicast have not seen wide acceptance largely because they require modification of all routers in the network. On the other hand, an overlay network can be incrementally deployed on end-hosts running the overlay protocol software, without cooperation from Internet service providers. The overlay network has no control over how packets are routed in the underlying network between two overlay nodes, but it can control, for example, the sequence of overlay nodes that a message traverses before it reaches its destination.

For example, Akamai Technologies manages an overlay network that provides reliable, efficient content delivery (a kind of multicast). Academic research includes end system multicast, resilient routing and quality of service studies, among others.

Communications Protocols

A communications protocol is a set of rules for exchanging information over network links. In a protocol stack, each protocol leverages the services of the protocol below it. An important example of a protocol stack is HTTP (the World Wide Web protocol) running over TCP over IP (the Internet protocols) over IEEE 802.11 (the Wi-Fi protocol). This stack is used between the wireless router and the home user's personal computer when the user is surfing the web.

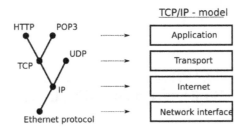

The TCP/IP model or Internet layering scheme and its relation to common protocols often layered on top of it.

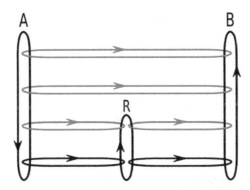

Figure 4. Message flows (A-B) in the presence of a router (R), red flows are effective communication paths, black paths are the actual paths.

Whilst the use of protocol layering is today ubiquitous across the field of computer networking, it has been historically criticized by many researchers for two principal reasons. Firstly, abstracting the protocol stack in this way may cause a higher layer to duplicate functionality of a lower layer, a prime example being error recovery on both a per-link basis and an end-to-end basis. Secondly, it is common that a protocol implementation at one layer may require data, state or addressing information that is only present at another layer, thus defeating the point of separating the layers in the first place. For example, TCP uses the ECN field in the IPv4 header as an indication of congestion; IP is a network layer protocol whereas TCP is a transport layer protocol.

Communication protocols have various characteristics. They may be connection-oriented or connectionless, they may use circuit mode or packet switching, and they may use hierarchical addressing or flat addressing.

There are many communication protocols, a few of which are described below.

IEEE 802

The complete IEEE 802 protocol suite provides a diverse set of networking capabilities. The protocols have a flat addressing scheme. They operate mostly at levels 1 and 2 of the OSI model.

For example, MAC bridging (IEEE 802.1D) deals with the routing of Ethernet packets using a Spanning Tree Protocol. IEEE 802.1Q describes VLANs, and IEEE 802.1X defines a port-based Network Access Control protocol, which forms the basis for the authentication mechanisms used in VLANs (but it is also found in WLANs) – it is what the home user sees when the user has to enter a "wireless access key".

Ethernet

Ethernet, sometimes simply called *LAN*, is a family of protocols used in wired LANs, described by a set of standards together called IEEE 802.3 published by the Institute of Electrical and Electronics Engineers.

Wireless LAN

Wireless LAN, also widely known as WLAN or WiFi, is probably the most well-known member of the IEEE 802 protocol family for home users today. It is standarized by IEEE 802.11 and shares many properties with wired Ethernet.

Internet Protocol Suite

The Internet Protocol Suite, also called TCP/IP, is the foundation of all modern networking. It offers connection-less as well as connection-oriented services over an inherently unreliable network traversed by data-gram transmission at the Internet protocol (IP) level. At its core, the protocol suite defines the addressing, identification, and routing specifications for Internet Protocol Version 4 (IPv4) and for IPv6, the next generation of the protocol with a much enlarged addressing capability.

SONET/SDH

Synchronous optical networking (SONET) and Synchronous Digital Hierarchy (SDH) are standardized multiplexing protocols that transfer multiple digital bit streams over optical fiber using lasers. They were originally designed to transport circuit mode communications from a variety of different sources, primarily to support real-time, uncompressed, circuit-switched voice encoded in PCM (Pulse-Code Modulation) format. However, due to its protocol neutrality and transport-oriented features, SONET/SDH also was the obvious choice for transporting Asynchronous Transfer Mode (ATM) frames.

Asynchronous Transfer Mode

Asynchronous Transfer Mode (ATM) is a switching technique for telecommunication networks. It uses asynchronous time-division multiplexing and encodes data into small, fixed-sized cells. This differs from other protocols such as the Internet Protocol Suite or Ethernet that use variable sized packets or frames. ATM has similarity with both circuit and packet switched networking. This makes it a good choice for a network that must handle both traditional high-throughput data traffic, and real-time, low-latency content such as voice and video. ATM uses a connection-oriented model in which a virtual circuit must be established between two endpoints before the actual data exchange begins.

While the role of ATM is diminishing in favor of next-generation networks, it still plays a role in the last mile, which is the connection between an Internet service provider and the home user.

Geographic Scale

A network can be characterized by its physical capacity or its organizational purpose. Use of the network, including user authorization and access rights, differ accordingly.

Nanoscale Network

A nanoscale communication network has key components implemented at the nanoscale including message carriers and leverages physical principles that differ from macroscale communication mechanisms. Nanoscale communication extends communication to very small sensors and actuators such as those found in biological systems and also tends to operate in environments that would be too harsh for classical communication.

Personal Area Network

A personal area network (PAN) is a computer network used for communication among computer and different information technological devices close to one person. Some examples of devices that are used in a PAN are personal computers, printers, fax machines, telephones, PDAs, scanners, and even video game consoles. A PAN may include wired and wireless devices. The reach of a PAN typically extends to 10 meters. A wired PAN is usually constructed with USB and FireWire connections while technologies such as Bluetooth and infrared communication typically form a wireless PAN.

Local Area Network

A local area network (LAN) is a network that connects computers and devices in a limited geographical area such as a home, school, office building, or closely positioned group of buildings. Each computer or device on the network is a node. Wired LANs are most likely based on Ethernet technology. Newer standards such as ITU-T G.hn also provide a way to create a wired LAN using existing wiring, such as coaxial cables, telephone lines, and power lines.

The defining characteristics of a LAN, in contrast to a wide area network (WAN), include higher data transfer rates, limited geographic range, and lack of reliance on leased lines to provide connectivity. Current Ethernet or other IEEE 802.3 LAN technologies operate at data transfer rates up to 100 Gbit/s, standarized by IEEE in 2010. Currently, 400 Gbit/s Ethernet is being developed.

A LAN can be Connected to a WAN Using a Router.

Home area Network

A home area network (HAN) is a residential LAN used for communication between digital devices typically deployed in the home, usually a small number of personal computers and accessories, such as printers and mobile computing devices. An important function is the sharing of Internet access, often a broadband service through a cable TV or digital subscriber line (DSL) provider.

Storage Area Network

A storage area network (SAN) is a dedicated network that provides access to consolidated, block level data storage. SANs are primarily used to make storage devices, such as disk arrays, tape libraries, and optical jukeboxes, accessible to servers so that the devices appear like locally attached devices to the operating system. A SAN typically has its own network of storage devices that are generally not accessible through the local area network by other devices. The cost and complexity of SANs dropped in the early 2000s to levels allowing wider adoption across both enterprise and small to medium-sized business environments.

Campus Area Network

A campus area network (CAN) is made up of an interconnection of LANs within a limited geographical area. The networking equipment (switches, routers) and transmission media (optical fiber, copper plant, Cat5 cabling, etc.) are almost entirely owned by the campus tenant / owner (an enterprise, university, government, etc.).

For example, a university campus network is likely to link a variety of campus buildings to connect academic colleges or departments, the library, and student residence halls.

Backbone Network

A backbone network is part of a computer network infrastructure that provides a path for the exchange of information between different LANs or sub-networks. A backbone can tie together diverse networks within the same building, across different buildings, or over a wide area.

For example, a large company might implement a backbone network to connect departments that are located around the world. The equipment that ties together the departmental networks constitutes the network backbone. When designing a network backbone, network performance and network congestion are critical factors to take into account. Normally, the backbone network's capacity is greater than that of the individual networks connected to it.

Another example of a backbone network is the Internet backbone, which is the set of wide area networks (WANs) and core routers that tie together all networks connected to the Internet.

Metropolitan Area Network

A Metropolitan area network (MAN) is a large computer network that usually spans a city or a large campus.

Wide Area Network

A wide area network (WAN) is a computer network that covers a large geographic area such as a city, country, or spans even intercontinental distances. A WAN uses a communications channel that combines many types of media such as telephone lines, cables, and air waves. A WAN often makes use of transmission facilities provided by common carriers, such as telephone companies. WAN technologies generally function at the lower three layers of the OSI reference model: the physical layer, the data link layer, and the network layer.

Enterprise Private Network

An enterprise private network is a network that a single organization builds to interconnect its office locations (e.g., production sites, head offices, remote offices, shops) so they can share computer resources.

Virtual Private Network

A virtual private network (VPN) is an overlay network in which some of the links between nodes are carried by open connections or virtual circuits in some larger network (e.g., the Internet) instead of by physical wires. The data link layer protocols of the virtual network are said to be tunneled through the larger network when this is the case. One common application is secure communications through the public Internet, but a VPN need not have explicit security features, such as authentication or content encryption. VPNs, for example, can be used to separate the traffic of different user communities over an underlying network with strong security features.

VPN may have best-effort performance, or may have a defined service level agreement (SLA) between the VPN customer and the VPN service provider. Generally, a VPN has a topology more complex than point-to-point.

Global Area Network

A global area network (GAN) is a network used for supporting mobile across an arbitrary number of wireless LANs, satellite coverage areas, etc. The key challenge in mobile communications is handing off user communications from one local coverage area to the next. In IEEE Project 802, this involves a succession of terrestrial wireless LANs.

Organizational Scope

Networks are typically managed by the organizations that own them. Private enterprise networks may use a combination of intranets and extranets. They may also provide network access to the Internet, which has no single owner and permits virtually unlimited global connectivity.

Intranet

An intranet is a set of networks that are under the control of a single administrative entity. The intranet uses the IP protocol and IP-based tools such as web browsers and file transfer applications. The administrative entity limits use of the intranet to its authorized users. Most commonly, an intranet is the internal LAN of an organization. A large intranet typically has at least one web server to provide users with organizational information. An intranet is also anything behind the router on a local area network.

Extranet

An extranet is a network that is also under the administrative control of a single organization, but supports a limited connection to a specific external network. For example, an organization may provide access to some aspects of its intranet to share data with its business partners or customers.

These other entities are not necessarily trusted from a security standpoint. Network connection to an extranet is often, but not always, implemented via WAN technology.

Internetwork

An internetwork is the connection of multiple computer networks via a common routing technology using routers.

Internet

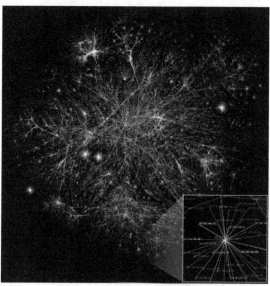

Partial map of the Internet based on the January 15, 2005 data found on opte.org. Each line is drawn between two nodes, representing two IP addresses. The length of the lines are indicative of the delay between those two nodes. This graph represents less than 30% of the Class C networks reachable.

The Internet is the largest example of an internetwork. It is a global system of interconnected governmental, academic, corporate, public, and private computer networks. It is based on the networking technologies of the Internet Protocol Suite. It is the successor of the Advanced Research Projects Agency Network (ARPANET) developed by DARPA of the United States Department of Defense. The Internet is also the communications backbone underlying the World Wide Web (WWW).

Participants in the Internet use a diverse array of methods of several hundred documented, and often standardized, protocols compatible with the Internet Protocol Suite and an addressing system (IP addresses) administered by the Internet Assigned Numbers Authority and address registries. Service providers and large enterprises exchange information about the reachability of their address spaces through the Border Gateway Protocol (BGP), forming a redundant worldwide mesh of transmission paths.

Darknet

A Darknet is an overlay network, typically running on the internet, that is only accessible through specialized software. A darknet is an anonymizing network where connections are made only between trusted peers — sometimes called "friends" (F2F) — using non-standard protocols and ports.

Darknets are distinct from other distributed peer-to-peer networks as sharing is anonymous (that is, IP addresses are not publicly shared), and therefore users can communicate with little fear of governmental or corporate interference.

Routing

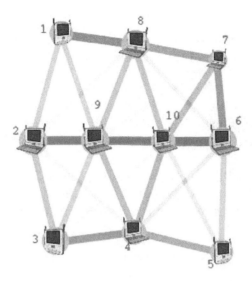

Routing calculates good paths through a network for information to take. For example, from node 1 to node 6 the best routes are likely to be 1-8-7-6 or 1-8-10-6, as this has the thickest routes.

Routing is the process of selecting network paths to carry network traffic. Routing is performed for many kinds of networks, including circuit switching networks and packet switched networks.

In packet switched networks, routing directs packet forwarding (the transit of logically addressed network packets from their source toward their ultimate destination) through intermediate nodes. Intermediate nodes are typically network hardware devices such as routers, bridges, gateways, firewalls, or switches. General-purpose computers can also forward packets and perform routing, though they are not specialized hardware and may suffer from limited performance. The routing process usually directs forwarding on the basis of routing tables, which maintain a record of the routes to various network destinations. Thus, constructing routing tables, which are held in the router's memory, is very important for efficient routing.

There are usually multiple routes that can be taken, and to choose between them, different elements can be considered to decide which routes get installed into the routing table, such as (sorted by priority):

1. *Prefix-Length*: where longer subnet masks are preferred (independent if it is within a routing protocol or over different routing protocol)

2. *Metric*: where a lower metric/cost is preferred (only valid within one and the same routing protocol)

3. *Administrative distance*: where a lower distance is preferred (only valid between different routing protocols)

Most routing algorithms use only one network path at a time. Multipath routing techniques enable the use of multiple alternative paths.

Routing, in a more narrow sense of the term, is often contrasted with bridging in its assumption that network addresses are structured and that similar addresses imply proximity within the network. Structured addresses allow a single routing table entry to represent the route to a group of devices. In large networks, structured addressing (routing, in the narrow sense) outperforms unstructured addressing (bridging). Routing has become the dominant form of addressing on the Internet. Bridging is still widely used within localized environments.

Network Service

Network services are applications hosted by servers on a computer network, to provide some functionality for members or users of the network, or to help the network itself to operate.

The World Wide Web, E-mail, printing and network file sharing are examples of well-known network services. Network services such as DNS (Domain Name System) give names for IP and MAC addresses (people remember names like "nm.lan" better than numbers like "210.121.67.18"), and DHCP to ensure that the equipment on the network has a valid IP address.

Services are usually based on a service protocol that defines the format and sequencing of messages between clients and servers of that network service.

Network Performance

Quality of Service

Depending on the installation requirements, network performance is usually measured by the quality of service of a telecommunications product. The parameters that affect this typically can include throughput, jitter, bit error rate and latency.

The following list gives examples of network performance measures for a circuit-switched network and one type of packet-switched network, viz. ATM:

- Circuit-switched networks: In circuit switched networks, network performance is synonymous with the grade of service. The number of rejected calls is a measure of how well the network is performing under heavy traffic loads. Other types of performance measures can include the level of noise and echo.

- ATM: In an Asynchronous Transfer Mode (ATM) network, performance can be measured by line rate, quality of service (QoS), data throughput, connect time, stability, technology, modulation technique and modem enhancements.

There are many ways to measure the performance of a network, as each network is different in nature and design. Performance can also be modelled instead of measured. For example, state transition diagrams are often used to model queuing performance in a circuit-switched network. The network planner uses these diagrams to analyze how the network performs in each state, ensuring that the network is optimally designed.

Network Congestion

Network congestion occurs when a link or node is carrying so much data that its quality of service deteriorates. Typical effects include queueing delay, packet loss or the blocking of new connections. A consequence of these latter two is that incremental increases in offered load lead either only to small increase in network throughput, or to an actual reduction in network throughput.

Network protocols that use aggressive retransmissions to compensate for packet loss tend to keep systems in a state of network congestion—even after the initial load is reduced to a level that would not normally induce network congestion. Thus, networks using these protocols can exhibit two stable states under the same level of load. The stable state with low throughput is known as *congestive collapse*.

Modern networks use congestion control and congestion avoidance techniques to try to avoid congestion collapse. These include: exponential backoff in protocols such as 802.11's CSMA/CA and the original Ethernet, window reduction in TCP, and fair queueing in devices such as routers. Another method to avoid the negative effects of network congestion is implementing priority schemes, so that some packets are transmitted with higher priority than others. Priority schemes do not solve network congestion by themselves, but they help to alleviate the effects of congestion for some services. An example of this is 802.1p. A third method to avoid network congestion is the explicit allocation of network resources to specific flows. One example of this is the use of Contention-Free Transmission Opportunities (CFTXOPs) in the ITU-T G.hn standard, which provides high-speed (up to 1 Gbit/s) Local area networking over existing home wires (power lines, phone lines and coaxial cables).

For the Internet RFC 2914 addresses the subject of congestion control in detail.

Network Resilience

Network resilience is "the ability to provide and maintain an acceptable level of service in the face of faults and challenges to normal operation."

Security

Network security

Network security consists of provisions and policies adopted by the network administrator to prevent and monitor unauthorized access, misuse, modification, or denial of the computer network and its network-accessible resources. Network security is the authorization of access to data in a network, which is controlled by the network administrator. Users are assigned an ID and password that allows them access to information and programs within their authority. Network security is used on a variety of computer networks, both public and private, to secure daily transactions and communications among businesses, government agencies and individuals.

Network Surveillance

Network surveillance is the monitoring of data being transferred over computer networks such as the Internet. The monitoring is often done surreptitiously and may be done by or at the behest of governments, by corporations, criminal organizations, or individuals. It may or may not be legal and may or may not require authorization from a court or other independent agency.

Computer and network surveillance programs are widespread today, and almost all Internet traffic is or could potentially be monitored for clues to illegal activity.

Surveillance is very useful to governments and law enforcement to maintain social control, recognize and monitor threats, and prevent/investigate criminal activity. With the advent of programs such as the Total Information Awareness program, technologies such as high speed surveillance computers and biometrics software, and laws such as the Communications Assistance For Law Enforcement Act, governments now possess an unprecedented ability to monitor the activities of citizens.

However, many civil rights and privacy groups—such as Reporters Without Borders, the Electronic Frontier Foundation, and the American Civil Liberties Union—have expressed concern that increasing surveillance of citizens may lead to a mass surveillance society, with limited political and personal freedoms. Fears such as this have led to numerous lawsuits such as *Hepting v. AT&T*. The hacktivist group Anonymous has hacked into government websites in protest of what it considers "draconian surveillance".

End to end Encryption

End-to-end encryption (E2EE) is a digital communications paradigm of uninterrupted protection of data traveling between two communicating parties. It involves the originating party encrypting data so only the intended recipient can decrypt it, with no dependency on third parties. End-to-end encryption prevents intermediaries, such as Internet providers or application service providers, from discovering or tampering with communications. End-to-end encryption generally protects both confidentiality and integrity.

Examples of end-to-end encryption include PGP for email, OTR for instant messaging, ZRTP for telephony, and TETRA for radio.

Typical server-based communications systems do not include end-to-end encryption. These systems can only guarantee protection of communications between clients and servers, not between the communicating parties themselves. Examples of non-E2EE systems are Google Talk, Yahoo Messenger, Facebook, and Dropbox. Some such systems, for example LavaBit and SecretInk, have even described themselves as offering "end-to-end" encryption when they do not. Some systems that normally offer end-to-end encryption have turned out to contain a back door that subverts negotiation of the encryption key between the communicating parties, for example Skype or Hushmail.

The end-to-end encryption paradigm does not directly address risks at the communications endpoints themselves, such as the technical exploitation of clients, poor quality random number generators, or key escrow. E2EE also does not address traffic analysis, which relates to things such as the identities of the end points and the times and quantities of messages that are sent.

Views of Networks

Users and network administrators typically have different views of their networks. Users can share printers and some servers from a workgroup, which usually means they are in the same geographic location and are on the same LAN, whereas a Network Administrator is responsible to keep that network up and running. A community of interest has less of a connection of being in a local area, and should be thought of as a set of arbitrarily located users who share a set of servers, and possibly also communicate via peer-to-peer technologies.

Network administrators can see networks from both physical and logical perspectives. The physical perspective involves geographic locations, physical cabling, and the network elements (e.g., routers, bridges and application layer gateways) that interconnect via the transmission media. Logical networks, called, in the TCP/IP architecture, subnets, map onto one or more transmission media. For example, a common practice in a campus of buildings is to make a set of LAN cables in each building appear to be a common subnet, using virtual LAN (VLAN) technology.

Both users and administrators are aware, to varying extents, of the trust and scope characteristics of a network. Again using TCP/IP architectural terminology, an intranet is a community of interest under private administration usually by an enterprise, and is only accessible by authorized users (e.g. employees). Intranets do not have to be connected to the Internet, but generally have a limited connection. An extranet is an extension of an intranet that allows secure communications to users outside of the intranet (e.g. business partners, customers).

Unofficially, the Internet is the set of users, enterprises, and content providers that are interconnected by Internet Service Providers (ISP). From an engineering viewpoint, the Internet is the set of subnets, and aggregates of subnets, which share the registered IP address space and exchange information about the reachability of those IP addresses using the Border Gateway Protocol. Typically, the human-readable names of servers are translated to IP addresses, transparently to users, via the directory function of the Domain Name System (DNS).

Over the Internet, there can be business-to-business (B2B), business-to-consumer (B2C) and consumer-to-consumer (C2C) communications. When money or sensitive information is exchanged, the communications are apt to be protected by some form of communications security mechanism. Intranets and extranets can be securely superimposed onto the Internet, without any access by general Internet users and administrators, using secure Virtual Private Network (VPN) technology.

Network topology

Network topology is the arrangement of the various elements (links, nodes, etc.) of a computer network. Essentially, it is the topological structure of a network and may be depicted physically or logically. *Physical topology* is the placement of the various components of a network, including device location and cable installation, while *logical topology* illustrates how data flows within a network, regardless of its physical design. Distances between nodes, physical interconnections, transmission rates, or signal types may differ between two networks, yet their topologies may be identical.

An example is a local area network (LAN). Any given node in the LAN has one or more physical links to other devices in the network; graphically mapping these links results in a geometric shape that can be used to describe the physical topology of the network. Conversely, mapping the data flow between the components determines the logical topology of the network.

Topology

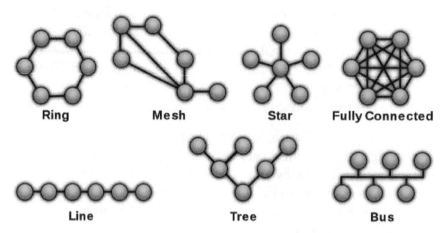

Diagram of different network topologies.

Two basic categories of network topologies exist, physical topologies and logical topologies.

The cabling layout used to link devices is the physical topology of the network. This refers to the layout of cabling, the locations of nodes, and the interconnections between the nodes and the cabling. The physical topology of a network is determined by the capabilities of the network access devices and media, the level of control or fault tolerance desired, and the cost associated with cabling or telecommunications circuits.

In contrast, logical topology is the way that the signals act on the network media, or the way that the data passes through the network from one device to the next without regard to the physical interconnection of the devices. A network's logical topology is not necessarily the same as its physical topology. For example, the original twisted pair Ethernet using repeater hubs was a logical bus topology carried on a physical star topology. Token ring is a logical ring topology, but is wired as a physical star from the media access unit. Logical topologies are often closely associated with media access control methods and protocols. Some networks are able to dynamically change their logical topology through configuration changes to their routers and switches.

Classification

The study of network topology recognizes eight basic topologies: point-to-point, bus, star, ring or circular, mesh, tree, hybrid, or daisy chain.

Point-to-point

The simplest topology with a dedicated link between two endpoints. Easiest to understand, of the variations of point-to-point topology, is a point-to-point communications channel that appears, to the user, to be permanently associated with the two endpoints. A child's tin can telephone is one example of a *physical dedicated* channel.

Using circuit-switching or packet-switching technologies, a point-to-point circuit can be set up dynamically and dropped when no longer needed. Switched point-to-point topologies are the basic model of conventional telephony.

The value of a permanent point-to-point network is unimpeded communications between the two endpoints. The value of an on-demand point-to-point connection is proportional to the number of potential pairs of subscribers and has been expressed as Metcalfe's Law.

Bus

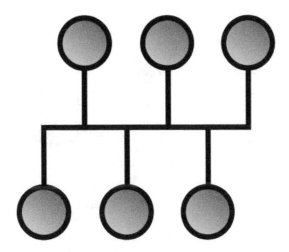

Bus network topology

In local area networks where bus topology is used, each node is connected to a single cable, by the help of interface connectors. This central cable is the backbone of the network and is known as the bus (thus the name). A signal from the source travels in both directions to all machines connected on the bus cable until it finds the intended recipient. If the machine address does not match the intended address for the data, the machine ignores the data. Alternatively, if the data matches the machine address, the data is accepted. Because the bus topology consists of only one wire, it is rather inexpensive to implement when compared to other topologies. However, the low cost of implementing the technology is offset by the high cost of managing the network. Additionally, because only one cable is utilized, it can be the single point of failure.

Linear Bus

The type of network topology in which all of the nodes of the network are connected to a common transmission medium which has exactly two endpoints (this is the 'bus', which is also commonly referred to as the backbone, or trunk) – all data that is transmitted between nodes in the network is transmitted over this common transmission medium and is able to be received by all nodes in the network simultaneously.

Note: When the electrical signal reaches the end of the bus, the signal is reflected back down the line, causing unwanted interference. As a solution, the two endpoints of the bus are normally terminated with a device called a terminator that prevents this reflection.

Distributed Bus

The type of network topology in which all of the nodes of the network are connected to a common transmission medium which has more than two endpoints that are created by adding branches to the main section of the transmission medium – the physical distributed bus topology functions in exactly the same fashion as the physical linear bus topology (i.e., all nodes share a common transmission medium).

Star

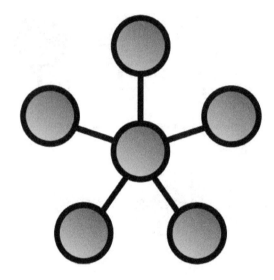

Star network topology

In local area networks with a star topology, each network host is connected to a central hub with a point-to-point connection. So it can be said that every computer is indirectly connected to every other node with the help of the hub. In Star topology, every node (computer workstation or any other peripheral) is connected to a central node called hub, router or switch. The switch is the server and the peripherals are the clients. The network does not necessarily have to resemble a star to be classified as a star network, but all of the nodes on the network must be connected to one central device. All traffic that traverses the network passes through the central hub. The hub acts as a signal repeater. The star topology is considered the easiest topology to design and implement. An advantage of the star topology is the simplicity of adding additional nodes. The primary disadvantage of the star topology is that the hub represents a single point of failure.

Extended star

A type of network topology in which a network that is based upon the physical star topology has one or more repeaters between the central node and the peripheral or 'spoke' nodes, the repeaters being used to extend the maximum transmission distance of the point-to-point links between the central node and the peripheral nodes beyond that which is supported by the transmitter power of the central node or beyond that which is supported by the standard upon which the physical layer of the physical star network is based.

If the repeaters in a network that is based upon the physical extended star topology are replaced with hubs or switches, then a hybrid network topology is created that is referred to as a physical hierarchical star topology, although some texts make no distinction between the two topologies.

Distributed Star

A type of network topology that is composed of individual networks that are based upon the physical star topology connected in a linear fashion – i.e., 'daisy-chained' – with no central or top level connection point (e.g., two or more 'stacked' hubs, along with their associated star connected nodes or 'spokes').

Ring

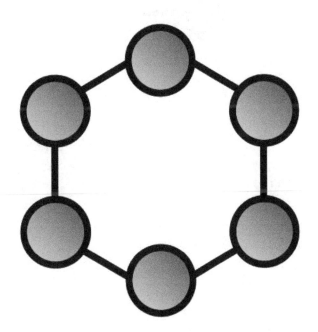

Ring network topology

A ring topology is a bus topology in a closed loop. Data travels around the ring in one direction. When one node sends data to another, the data passes through each intermediate node on the ring until it reaches its destination. The intermediate nodes repeat (retransmit) the data to keep the signal strong. Every node is a peer; there is no hierarchical relationship of clients and servers. If one node is unable to retransmit data, it severs communication between the nodes before and after it in the bus.

Mesh

The value of fully meshed networks is proportional to the exponent of the number of subscribers, assuming that communicating groups of any two endpoints, up to and including all the endpoints, is approximated by Reed's Law.

Fully Connected Network

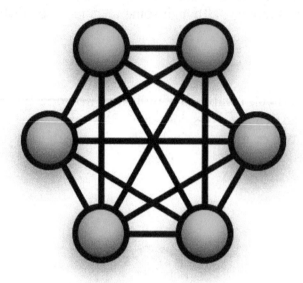

Fully connected mesh topology

In a *fully connected network*, all nodes are interconnected. (In graph theory this is called a complete graph.) The simplest fully connected network is a two-node network. A fully connected network doesn't need to use packet switching or broadcasting. However, since the number of connections grows quadratically with the number of nodes:

$$c = \frac{n(n-1)}{2}.$$

This makes it impractical for large networks.

Partially Connected Network

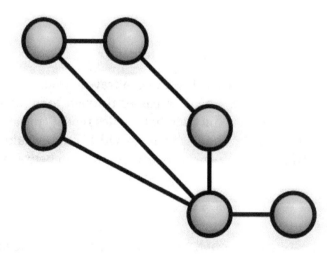

Partially connected mesh topology

In a partially connected network, certain nodes are connected to exactly one other node; but some nodes are connected to two or more other nodes with a point-to-point link. This makes it possible to make use of some of the redundancy of mesh topology that is physically fully connected, without the expense and complexity required for a connection between every node in the network.

Hybrid

Hybrid networks combine two or more topologies in such a way that the resulting network does not exhibit one of the standard topologies (e.g., bus, star, ring, etc.). For example, a tree network (or *star-bus network*) is a hybrid topology in which star networks are interconnected via bus networks. However, a tree network connected to another tree network is still topologically a tree network, not a distinct network type. A hybrid topology is always produced when two different basic network topologies are connected.

A *star-ring* network consists of two or more ring networks connected using a multistation access unit (MAU) as a centralized hub.

Snowflake topology is a star network of star networks.

Two other hybrid network types are *hybrid mesh* and *hierarchical star*.

Daisy Chain

Except for star-based networks, the easiest way to add more computers into a network is by daisy-chaining, or connecting each computer in series to the next. If a message is intended for a computer partway down the line, each system bounces it along in sequence until it reaches the destination. A daisy-chained network can take two basic forms: linear and ring.

- A linear topology puts a two-way link between one computer and the next. However, this was expensive in the early days of computing, since each computer (except for the ones at each end) required two receivers and two transmitters.

- By connecting the computers at each end, a ring topology can be formed. An advantage of the ring is that the number of transmitters and receivers can be cut in half, since a message will eventually loop all of the way around. When a node sends a message, the message is processed by each computer in the ring. If the ring breaks at a particular link then the transmission can be sent via the reverse path thereby ensuring that all nodes are always connected in the case of a single failure.

Centralization

The star topology reduces the probability of a network failure by connecting all of the peripheral nodes (computers, etc.) to a central node. When the physical star topology is applied to a logical bus network such as Ethernet, this central node (traditionally a hub) rebroadcasts all transmissions received from any peripheral node to all peripheral nodes on the network, sometimes including the originating node. All peripheral nodes may thus communicate with all others by transmitting to, and receiving from, the central node only. The failure of a transmission line linking any peripheral node to the central node will result in the isolation of that peripheral node from all others, but the remaining peripheral nodes will be unaffected. However, the disadvantage is that the failure of the central node will cause the failure of all of the peripheral nodes.

If the central node is *passive*, the originating node must be able to tolerate the reception of an echo of its own transmission, delayed by the two-way round trip transmission time (i.e. to and from the central node) plus any delay generated in the central node. An *active* star network has an active central node that usually has the means to prevent echo-related problems.

A tree topology (a.k.a. hierarchical topology) can be viewed as a collection of star networks arranged in a hierarchy. This tree has individual peripheral nodes (e.g. leaves) which are required to transmit to and receive from one other node only and are not required to act as repeaters or regenerators. Unlike the star network, the functionality of the central node may be distributed.

As in the conventional star network, individual nodes may thus still be isolated from the network by a single-point failure of a transmission path to the node. If a link connecting a leaf fails, that leaf is isolated; if a connection to a non-leaf node fails, an entire section of the network becomes isolated from the rest.

To alleviate the amount of network traffic that comes from broadcasting all signals to all nodes, more advanced central nodes were developed that are able to keep track of the identities of the nodes that are connected to the network. These network switches will "learn" the layout of the network by "listening" on each port during normal data transmission, examining the data packets and recording the address/identifier of each connected node and which port it is connected to in a lookup table held in memory. This lookup table then allows future transmissions to be forwarded to the intended destination only.

Decentralization

In a mesh topology (i.e., a partially connected mesh topology), there are at least two nodes with two or more paths between them to provide redundant paths to be used in case the link providing one of the paths fails. This decentralization is often used to compensate for the single-point-failure disadvantage that is present when using a single device as a central node (e.g., in star and tree networks). A special kind of mesh, limiting the number of hops between two nodes, is a hypercube. The number of arbitrary fork in mesh networks makes them more difficult to design and implement, but their decentralized nature makes them very useful. In 2012 the IEEE published the Shortest path bridging protocol to ease configuration tasks and allows all paths to be active which increases bandwidth and redundancy between all devices.

This is similar in some ways to a grid network, where a linear or ring topology is used to connect systems in multiple directions. A multidimensional ring has a toroidal topology, for instance.

A fully connected network, complete topology, or full mesh topology is a network topology in which there is a direct link between all pairs of nodes. In a fully connected network with n nodes, there are $n(n-1)/2$ direct links. Networks designed with this topology are usually very expensive to set up, but provide a high degree of reliability due to the multiple paths for data that are provided by the large number of redundant links between nodes. This topology is mostly seen in military applications.

Network packet

A network packet is a formatted unit of data carried by a packet-switched network. Computer communications links that do not support packets, such as traditional point-to-point telecommunications links, simply transmit data as a bit stream. When data is formatted into packets, packet switching is possible and the bandwidth of the communication medium can be better shared among users than with circuit switching.

A packet consists of control information and user data, which is also known as the payload. Control information provides data for delivering the payload, for example: source and destination network addresses, error detection codes, and sequencing information. Typically, control information is found in packet headers and trailers.

Terminology

In the seven-layer OSI model of computer networking, *packet* strictly refers to a data unit at layer 3, the Network Layer. The correct term for a data unit at Layer 2, the Data Link Layer, is a *frame*, and at Layer 4, the Transport Layer, the correct term is a *segment* or *datagram*. For the case of TCP/IP communication over Ethernet, a TCP segment is carried in one or more IP packets, which are each carried in one or more Ethernet frames.

Packet Framing

Different communications protocols use different conventions for distinguishing between the elements and for formatting the data. For example, in Point-to-Point Protocol, the packet is formatted in 8-bit bytes, and special characters are used to delimit the different elements. Other protocols like Ethernet, establish the start of the header and data elements by their location relative to the start of the packet. Some protocols format the information at a bit level instead of a byte level.

A good analogy is to consider a packet to be like a letter: the header is like the envelope, and the data area is whatever the person puts inside the envelope.

A network design can achieve two major results by using packets: *error detection* and *multiple host addressing*. A packet has the following components.

Addresses

The routing of network packets requires two network addresses, the source address of the sending host, and the destination address of the receiving host.

Error Detection and Correction

Error detection and correction is performed at various layers in the protocol stack. Network packets may contain a checksum, parity bits or cyclic redundancy checks to detect errors that occur during transmission.

At the transmitter, the calculation is performed before the packet is sent. When received at the destination, the checksum is recalculated, and compared with the one in the packet. If discrepancies are found, the packet may be corrected or discarded. Any packet loss is dealt with by the network protocol.

In some cases modifications of the network packet may be necessary while routing, in which cases checksums are recalculated.

Hop counts

Under fault conditions packets can end up traversing a closed circuit. If nothing was done, eventually the number of packets circulating would build up until the network was congested to the point of failure. A time to live is a field that is decreased by one each time a packet goes through a network node. If the field reaches zero, routing has failed, and the packet is discarded.

Ethernet packets have no time-to-live field and so are subject to broadcast radiation in the presence of a switch loop.

Packet length

There may be a field to identify the overall packet length. In some protocols, the length is implied by the duration of transmission.

Class/priority

Some networks implement quality of service which can prioritize some types of packets above others. This field indicates which packet queue should be used; a high priority queue is emptied more quickly than lower priority queues at points in the network where congestion is occurring.

Payload

In general, payload is the data that is carried on behalf of an application. It is usually of variable length, up to a maximum that is set by the network protocol and sometimes the equipment on the route. Some networks can break a larger packet into smaller packets when necessary.

Example: IP Packets

IP packets are composed of a header and payload. The IPv4 packet header consists of:

00	01	02	03	04	05	06	07	08	09	10	11	12	13	14	15	16	17	18	19	20	21	22	23	24	25	26	27	28	29	30	31	(bit position)
Version				IHL				QoS								Length																
ID																0	DF	MF	Fragment Offset													
TTL								Protocol								Checksum																
Source IP																																
Destination IP																																

4 bits that contain the *version*, that specifies if it's an IPv4 or IPv6 packet,

1. 4 bits that contain the *Internet Header Length*, which is the length of the header in multiples of 4 bytes (e.g., 5 means 20 bytes).

2. 8 bits that contain the *Type of Service*, also referred to as Quality of Service (QoS), which describes what priority the packet should have,

3. 16 bits that contain the *length* of the packet in bytes,

4. 16 bits that contain an *identification tag* to help reconstruct the packet from several fragments,

5. 3 bits. The first contains a zero, followed by a flag that says whether the packet is allowed to be *fragmented* or not (DF: Don't fragment), and a flag to state whether more fragments of a packet follow (MF: More Fragments)

6. 13 bits that contain the *fragment offset*, a field to identify position of fragment within original packet

7. 8 bits that contain the *Time to live* (TTL), which is the number of hops (router, computer or device along a network) the packet is allowed to pass before it dies (for example, a packet with a TTL of 16 will be allowed to go across 16 routers to get to its destination before it is discarded),

8. 8 bits that contain the *protocol* (TCP, UDP, ICMP, etc.)

9. 16 bits that contain the *Header Checksum,* a number used in error detection,

10. 32 bits that contain the *source IP address,*

11. 32 bits that contain the *destination address.*

After those 160 bits, optional flags can be added of varied length, which can change based on the protocol used, then the data that packet carries is added. An IP packet has no trailer. However, an IP packet is often carried as the payload inside an Ethernet frame, which has its own header and trailer.

Many networks do not provide guarantees of delivery, nonduplication of packets, or in-order delivery of packets, e.g., the UDP protocol of the Internet. However, it is possible to layer a transport protocol on top of the packet service that can provide such protection; TCP and UDP are the best examples of layer 4, the Transport Layer, of the seven layered OSI model.

Example: the NASA Deep Space Network

The Consultative Committee for Space Data Systems (CCSDS) packet telemetry standard defines the protocol used for the transmission of spacecraft instrument data over the deep-space channel. Under this standard, an image or other data sent from a spacecraft instrument is transmitted using one or more packets.

CCSDS Packet Definition

A packet is a block of data with length that can vary between successive packets, ranging from 7 to 65,542 bytes, including the packet header.

- Packetized data is transmitted via frames, which are fixed-length data blocks. The size of a frame, including frame header and control information, can range up to 2048 bytes.

- Packet sizes are fixed during the development phase.

Because packet lengths are variable but frame lengths are fixed, packet boundaries usually do not coincide with frame boundaries.

Telecom Processing Notes

Data in a frame is typically protected from channel errors by error-correcting codes.

- Even when the channel errors exceed the correction capability of the error-correcting code, the presence of errors is nearly always detected by the error-correcting code or by a separate error-detecting code.

- Frames for which uncorrectable errors are detected are marked as undecodable and typically are deleted.

Handling Data Loss

Deleted undecodable whole frames are the principal type of data loss that affects compressed data sets. In general, there would be little to gain from attempting to use compressed data from a frame marked as undecodable.

- When errors are present in a frame, the bits of the subband pixels are already decoded before the first bit error will remain intact, but all subsequent decoded bits in the segment usually will be completely corrupted; a single bit error is often just as disruptive as many bit errors.

- Furthermore, compressed data usually are protected by powerful, long-blocklength error-correcting codes, which are the types of codes most likely to yield substantial fractions of bit errors throughout those frames that are undecodable.

Thus, frames with detected errors would be essentially unusable even if they were not deleted by the frame processor.

This data loss can be compensated for with the following mechanisms.

- If an erroneous frame escapes detection, the decompressor will blindly use the frame data as if they were reliable, whereas in the case of detected erroneous frames, the decompressor can base its reconstruction on incomplete, but not misleading, data.

- However, it is extremely rare for an erroneous frame to go undetected.

- For frames coded by the CCSDS Reed–Solomon code, fewer than 1 in 40,000 erroneous frames can escape detection.

- All frames not employing the Reed–Solomon code use a cyclic redundancy check (CRC) error-detecting code, which has an undetected frame-error rate of less than 1 in 32,000.

Example: Radio and TV Broadcasting

MPEG Packetized Stream

Packetized Elementary Stream (PES) is a specification defined by the MPEG communication protocol that allows an elementary stream to be divided into packets. The elementary stream is packetized by encapsulating sequential data bytes from the elementary stream inside PES packet headers.

A typical method of transmitting elementary stream data from a video or audio encoder is to first create PES packets from the elementary stream data and then to encapsulate these PES packets inside an MPEG transport stream (TS) packets or an MPEG program stream (PS). The TS packets can then be multiplexed and transmitted using broadcasting techniques, such as those used in an ATSC and DVB.

PES Packet Header

Name	Size	Description
Packet start code prefix	3 bytes	0x000001
Stream id	1 byte	Examples: Audio streams (0xC0-0xDF), Video streams (0xE0-0xEF)
		Note: The above 4 bytes is called the 32-bit start code.
PES Packet length	2 bytes	Can be zero as in not specified for video streams in MPEG transport streams
Optional PES header	variable length	
Stuffing bytes	variable length	
Data		In the case of private streams the first byte of the payload is the sub-stream number.

Optional PES header

Name	Number of Bits	Description
Marker bits	2	10 binary or 0x2 hex
Scrambling control	2	00 implies not scrambled
Priority	1	
Data alignment indicator	1	1 indicates that the PES packet header is immediately followed by the video start code or audio syncword
Copyright	1	1 implies copyrighted
Original or Copy	1	1 implies original
PTS DTS indicator	2	11 = both present, 10 = only PTS

Name	Number of Bits	Description
ESCR flag	1	
ES rate flag	1	
DSM trick mode flag	1	
Additional copy info flag	1	
CRC flag	1	
extension flag	1	
PES header length	8	gives the length of the remainder of the PES header
Optional fields	variable length	presence is determined by flag bits above
Stuffing Bytes	variable length	0xff

NICAM

In order to provide mono "compatibility", the NICAM signal is transmitted on a subcarrier along-side the sound carrier. This means that the FM or AM regular mono sound carrier is left alone for reception by monaural receivers.

A NICAM-based stereo-TV infrastructure can transmit a stereo TV programme as well as the mono "compatibility" sound at the same time, or can transmit two or three entirely different sound streams. This latter mode could be used to transmit audio in different languages, in a similar manner to that used for in-flight movies on international flights. In this mode, the user can select which soundtrack to listen to when watching the content by operating a "sound-select" control on the receiver.

NICAM offers the following possibilities. The mode is auto-selected by the inclusion of a 3-bit type field in the data-stream

- One digital stereo sound channel.

- Two completely different digital mono sound channels.

- One digital mono sound channel and a 352 kbit/s data channel.

- One 704 kbit/s data channel.

The four other options could be implemented at a later date. Only the first two of the ones listed are known to be in general use however.

NICAM packet transmission

The NICAM packet (except for the header) is scrambled with a nine-bit pseudo-random bit-generator before transmission.

- The topology of this pseudo-random generator yields a bitstream with a repetition period of 511 bits.

- The pseudo-random generator's polynomial is: $x^9 + x^4 + 1$.

- The pseudo-random generator is initialized with: 111111111.

Making the NICAM bitstream look more like white noise is important because this reduces signal patterning on adjacent TV channels.

- The NICAM header is not subject to scrambling. This is necessary so as to aid in locking on to the NICAM data stream and resynchronisation of the data stream at the receiver.

- At the start of each NICAM packet the pseudo-random bit generator's shift-register is reset to all-ones.

References

- Simmonds, A; Sandilands, P; van Ekert, L (2004). "An Ontology for Network Security Attack". Lecture Notes in Computer Science. Lecture Notes in Computer Science 3285: 317–323. doi:10.1007/978-3-540-30176-9_41. ISBN 978-3-540-23659-7.

- Sosinsky, Barrie A. (2009). "Network Basics". Networking Bible. Indianapolis: Wiley Publishing. p. 16. ISBN 978-0-470-43131-3. OCLC 359673774. Retrieved 2016-03-26.

- Bradley, Ray. Understanding Computer Science (for Advanced Level): The Study Guide. Cheltenham: Nelson Thornes. p. 244. ISBN 978-0-7487-6147-0. OCLC 47869750. Retrieved 2016-03-26.

- Peter Ashwood-Smith (24 February 2011). "Shortest Path Bridging IEEE 802.1aq Overview" (PDF). Huawei. Retrieved 11 May 2012.

- Jim Duffy (11 May 2012). "Largest Illinois healthcare system uproots Cisco to build $40M private cloud". PC Advisor. Retrieved 11 May 2012.

- D. Fedyk, Ed.,; P. Ashwood-Smith, Ed.,; D. Allan, A. Bragg,; P. Unbehagen (April 2012). "IS-IS Extensions Supporting IEEE 802.1aq". IETF. Retrieved 12 May 2012.

- A. Hooke (September 2000), Interplanetary Internet (PDF), Third Annual International Symposium on Advanced Radio Technologies, archived from the original (PDF) on 2012-01-13, retrieved 2011-11-12

- For an interesting write-up of the technologies involved, including the deep stacking of communications protocols used. Martin, Thomas. "Design Principles for DSL-Based Access Solutions" (PDF). Retrieved 18 June 2011.

- Wood, Jessica (2010). "The Darknet: A Digital Copyright Revolution" (PDF). Richmond Journal of Law and Technology 16 (4). Retrieved 25 October 2011.

History of Software Engineering

The history of computers has also been a history of software. Software that is produced has to keep up with mechanical developments such as computers, tablets and android phones as well as to cultural products such as the cyberculture and social networking. This chapter discusses the methods of software engineering in a critical manner providing key analysis to the subject matter.

History of Software Engineering

From its beginnings in the 1960s, writing software has evolved into a profession concerned with how best to maximize the quality of software and of how to create it. Quality can refer to how maintainable software is, to its stability, speed, usability, testability, readability, size, cost, security, and number of flaws or "bugs", as well as to less measurable qualities like elegance, conciseness, and customer satisfaction, among many other attributes. How best to create high quality software is a separate and controversial problem covering software design principles, so-called "best practices" for writing code, as well as broader management issues such as optimal team size, process, how best to deliver software on time and as quickly as possible, work-place "culture", hiring practices, and so forth. All this falls under the broad rubric of software engineering.

Overview

The evolution of software engineering is notable in a number of areas:

- Emergence as a profession: By the early 1980s, software engineering professionalism, to stand beside computer science and traditional engineering.

- Role of women: In the 1940s, 1950s, and 1960s, men often filled the more prestigious and better paying hardware engineering roles, but often delegated the writing of software to women. Legends such as Grace Hopper and Jamie Fenton, as well as many other unsung women, filled many computer programming jobs during the first several decades of software engineering. Today, fewer women work in software engineering than in other professions, a situation whose cause is not clearly identified. It is often attributed to sexual discrimination, cyberculture, or different educational choices made by women. Many academic and professional organizations consider this situation unbalanced and are trying hard to solve it.

- Processes: Processes have become a big part of software engineering and are hailed for their potential to improve software and sharply criticized for their potential to constrict programmers.

- Cost of hardware: The relative cost of software versus hardware has changed substantially over the last 50 years. When mainframes were expensive and required large support staffs, the few organizations buying them also had the resources to fund large, expensive custom software engineering projects. Computers are now much more numerous and much more powerful, which has several effects on software. The larger market can support large projects to create commercial off the shelf software, as done by companies such as Microsoft. The cheap machines allow each programmer to have a terminal capable of fairly rapid compilation. The programs in question can use techniques such as garbage collection, which make them easier and faster for the programmer to write. On the other hand, many fewer organizations are interested in employing programmers for large custom software projects, instead using commercial off the shelf software as much as possible.

The Pioneering Era

The most important development was that new computers were coming out almost every year or two, rendering existing ones obsolete. Software people had to rewrite all their programs to run on these new machines. Programmers did not have computers on their desks and had to go to the "machine room". Jobs were run by signing up for machine time or by operational staff. Jobs were run by putting punched cards for input into the machine's card reader and waiting for results to come back on the printer.

The field was so new that the idea of management by schedule was non-existent. Making predictions of a project's completion date was almost impossible. Computer hardware was application-specific. Scientific and business tasks needed different machines. Due to the need to frequently translate old software to meet the needs of new machines, high-order languages like FORTRAN, COBOL, and ALGOL were developed. Hardware vendors gave away systems software for free as hardware could not be sold without software. A few companies sold the service of building custom software but no software companies were selling packaged software.

The notion of reuse flourished. As software was free, user organizations commonly gave it away. Groups like IBM's scientific user group SHARE offered catalogs of reusable components. Academia did not yet teach the principles of computer science. Modular programming and data abstraction were already being used in programming.

1945 to 1965: The origins

Putative origins for the term *software engineering* include a 1965 letter from ACM president Anthony Oettinger, use by J.P. Eckert during a conference in 1965 or 1966, lectures by Douglas T. Ross at MIT in the 1950s, or use by Margaret Hamilton while working on the Apollo guidance software.

The NATO Science Committee sponsored two conferences on software engineering in 1968 (Garmisch, Germany) and 1969, which gave the field its initial boost. Many believe these conferences marked the official start of the profession of *software engineering*.

1965 to 1985: The software Crisis

Software engineering was spurred by the so-called *software crisis* of the 1960s, 1970s, and 1980s, which identified many of the problems of software development. Many projects ran over budget and schedule. Some projects caused property damage. A few projects caused loss of life. The software crisis was originally defined in terms of productivity, but evolved to emphasize quality. Some used the term *software crisis* to refer to their inability to hire enough qualified programmers.

- Cost and Budget Overruns: The OS/360 operating system was a classic example. This decade-long project from the 1960s eventually produced one of the most complex software systems at the time. OS/360 was one of the first large (1000 programmers) software projects. Fred Brooks claims in *The Mythical Man Month* that he made a multimillion-dollar mistake of not developing a coherent architecture before starting development.

- Property Damage: Software defects can cause property damage. Poor software security allows hackers to steal identities, costing time, money, and reputations.

- Life and Death: Software defects can kill. Some embedded systems used in radiotherapy machines failed so catastrophically that they administered lethal doses of radiation to patients. The most famous of these failures is the *Therac-25* incident.

Peter G. Neumann has kept a contemporary list of software problems and disasters. The software crisis has been fading from view, because it is psychologically extremely difficult to remain in crisis mode for a protracted period (more than 20 years). Nevertheless, software – especially real-time embedded software – remains risky and is pervasive, and it is crucial not to give in to complacency. Over the last 10–15 years Michael A. Jackson has written extensively about the nature of software engineering, has identified the main source of its difficulties as lack of specialization, and has suggested that his problem frames provide the basis for a "normal practice" of software engineering, a prerequisite if software engineering is to become an engineering science.

1985 to 1989: "No Silver Bullet"

For decades, solving the software crisis was paramount to researchers and companies producing software tools. The cost of owning and maintaining software in the 1980s was twice as expensive as developing the software. • During the 1990s, the cost of ownership and maintenance increased by 30% over the 1980s. • In 1995, statistics showed that half of surveyed development projects were operational, but were not considered successful. • The average software project overshoots its schedule by half. • Three-quarters of all large software products delivered to the customer are failures that are either not used at all, or do not meet the customer's requirements.

Software Projects

Seemingly, every new technology and practice from the 1970s through the 1990s was trumpeted as a *silver bullet* to solve the software crisis. Tools, discipline, formal methods, process, and professionalism were touted as silver bullets:

- Tools: Especially emphasized were tools: structured programming, object-oriented programming, CASE tools such as ICL's CADES CASE system, Ada, documentation, and standards were touted as silver bullets.

- Discipline: Some pundits argued that the software crisis was due to the lack of discipline of programmers.

- Formal methods: Some believed that if formal engineering methodologies would be applied to software development, then production of software would become as predictable an industry as other branches of engineering. They advocated proving all programs correct.

- Process: Many advocated the use of defined processes and methodologies like the Capability Maturity Model.

- Professionalism: This led to work on a code of ethics, licenses, and professionalism.

In 1986, Fred Brooks published his *No Silver Bullet* article, arguing that no individual technology or practice would ever make a 10-fold improvement in productivity within 10 years.

Debate about silver bullets raged over the following decade. Advocates for Ada, components, and processes continued arguing for years that their favorite technology would be a silver bullet. Skeptics disagreed. Eventually, almost everyone accepted that no silver bullet would ever be found. Yet, claims about *silver bullets* pop up now and again, even today.

Some interpret *no silver bullet* to mean that software engineering failed. However, with further reading, Brooks goes on to say: "We will surely make substantial progress over the next 40 years; an order of magnitude over 40 years is hardly magical ..."

The search for a single key to success never worked. All known technologies and practices have only made incremental improvements to productivity and quality. Yet, there are no silver bullets for any other profession, either. Others interpret *no silver bullet* as proof that software engineering has finally matured and recognized that projects succeed due to hard work.

However, it could also be said that there are, in fact, a range of *silver bullets* today, including lightweight methodologies, spreadsheet calculators, customized browsers, in-site search engines, database report generators, integrated design-test coding-editors with memory/differences/undo, and specialty shops that generate niche software, such as information web sites, at a fraction of the cost of totally customized web site development. Nevertheless, the field of software engineering appears too complex and diverse for a single "silver bullet" to improve most issues, and each issue accounts for only a small portion of all software problems.

1990 to 1999: Prominence of the Internet

The rise of the Internet led to very rapid growth in the demand for international information display/e-mail systems on the World Wide Web. Programmers were required to handle illustrations, maps, photographs, and other images, plus simple animation, at a rate never before seen, with few well-known methods to optimize image display/storage (such as the use of thumbnail images).

The growth of browser usage, running on the HTML language, changed the way in which information-display and retrieval was organized. The widespread network connections led to the growth and prevention of international computer viruses on MS Windows computers, and the vast proliferation of spam e-mail became a major design issue in e-mail systems, flooding communication channels and requiring semi-automated pre-screening. Keyword-search systems evolved into web-based search engines, and many software systems had to be re-designed, for international searching, depending on search engine optimization (SEO) techniques. Human natural-language translation systems were needed to attempt to translate the information flow in multiple foreign languages, with many software systems being designed for multi-language usage, based on design concepts from human translators. Typical computer-user bases went from hundreds, or thousands of users, to, often, many-millions of international users.

2000 to Present: Lightweight Methodologies

With the expanding demand for software in many smaller organizations, the need for inexpensive software solutions led to the growth of simpler, faster methodologies that developed running software, from requirements to deployment, quicker & easier. The use of rapid-prototyping evolved to entire *lightweight methodologies*, such as Extreme Programming (XP), which attempted to simplify many areas of software engineering, including requirements gathering and reliability testing for the growing, vast number of small software systems. Very large software systems still used heavily-documented methodologies, with many volumes in the documentation set; however, smaller systems had a simpler, faster alternative approach to managing the development and maintenance of software calculations and algorithms, information storage/retrieval and display.

Current Trends in Software Engineering

Software engineering is a young discipline, and is still developing. The directions in which software engineering is developing include:

Aspects

Aspects help software engineers deal with quality attributes by providing tools to add or remove boilerplate code from many areas in the source code. Aspects describe how all objects or functions should behave in particular circumstances. For example, aspects can add debugging, logging, or locking control into all objects of particular types. Researchers are currently working to understand how to use aspects to design general-purpose code. Related concepts include generative programming and templates.

Agile

Agile software development guides software development projects that evolve rapidly with changing expectations and competitive markets. Proponents of this method believe that heavy, document-driven processes (like TickIT, CMM and ISO 9000) are fading in importance. Some people believe that companies and agencies export many of the jobs that can be guided by heavy-weight processes. Related concepts include extreme programming, scrum, and lean software development.

Experimental

Experimental software engineering is a branch of software engineering interested in devising experiments on software, in collecting data from the experiments, and in devising laws and theories from this data. Proponents of this method advocate that the nature of software is such that we can advance the knowledge on software through experiments only.

Software Product Lines

Software product lines, aka product family engineering, is a systematic way to produce *families* of software systems, instead of creating a succession of completely individual products. This method emphasizes extensive, systematic, formal code reuse, to try to industrialize the software development process.

The Future of Software Engineering conference (FOSE), held at ICSE 2000, documented the state of the art of SE in 2000 and listed many problems to be solved over the next decade. The FOSE tracks at the ICSE 2000 and the ICSE 2007 conferences also help identify the state of the art in software engineering.

Software Engineering Today

The profession is trying to define its boundary and content. The Software Engineering Body of Knowledge SWEBOK has been tabled as an ISO standard during 2006 (ISO/IEC TR 19759).

In 2006, *Money Magazine* and *Salary.com* rated software engineering as the best job in America in terms of growth, pay, stress levels, flexibility in hours and working environment, creativity, and how easy it is to enter and advance in the field.

Prominent Figures in the History of Software Engineering

- Charles Bachman (born 1924) is particularly known for his work in the area of databases.

- Laszlo Belady (born 1928) the editor-in-chief of the IEEE Transactions on Software Engineering in the 1980s

- Fred Brooks (born 1931) best known for managing the development of OS/360.

- Peter Chen, known for the development of entity-relationship modeling.

- Edsger Dijkstra (1930–2002) developed the framework for proper programming.

- David Parnas (born 1941) developed the concept of information hiding in modular programming.

- Michael A. Jackson (born 1936) software engineering methodologist responsible for JSP method of program design; JSD method of system development (with John Cameron); and Problem Frames method for analysing and structuring software development problems.

Permissions

Index

CPSIA information can be obtained
at www.ICGtesting.com
Printed in the USA
LVHW061739050223
738717LV00012B/1721